The Failure of Democracy in Iraq

The Failure of Democracy in Iraq studies democratization in post-2003 Iraq, which has so far failed, due mainly to cultural and religious reasons. There are other factors, such as the legacy of the dictatorial regime, exclusionary policies, the problem of stateness, interference by regional powers, the rentier economy and sectarianism, that have impeded democracy and contributed to its failure, but the employment of religion in politics was the most to blame.

The establishment of stable democratic institutions continues to elude Iraq, 15 years after toppling the dictatorship. The post-2003 Iraq could not completely eradicate the long historical tradition of despotic governance due to deep-seated religious beliefs and tribal values, along with widening societal ethno-sectarian rifts which precluded the negotiation of firm and stable elite settlements and pacts across communal lines. The book examines how the fear in neighbouring countries of a region-wide domino effect of the Iraq democratization process caused them to adopt interventionist policies towards Iraq that helped to stunt the development of democracy. The lack of commitment by the initiator of the democratic process, the United States, undermined the prospects of democratic consolidation. This is compounded by serious mistakes such as de-Ba'athification and the disbanding of the Iraqi army and security apparatuses which caused a security vacuum the US forces were not able to fill.

The Failure of Democracy in Iraq is a key resource for all students and academics interested in democracy, Islam and Middle East Studies.

Hamid Alkifaey is a writer, novelist and journalist. He has published hundreds of articles in English and Arabic over the years. He worked at BBC in London until 2003 when he returned to Iraq to join the Government. He held senior positions in international institutions. He specializes in democratization and writes and lectures on Middle Eastern issues.

Routledge Studies in Middle Eastern Democratization and Government
Edited by: Larbi Sadiki

This series examines new ways of understanding democratization and government in the Middle East. The varied and uneven processes of change, occurring in the Middle Eastern region, can no longer be read and interpreted solely through the prism of Euro-American transitology. Seeking to frame critical parameters in light of these new horizons, this series instigates reinterpretations of democracy and propagates formerly 'subaltern,' narratives of democratization. Reinvigorating discussion on how Arab and Middle Eastern peoples and societies seek good government, Routledge Studies in Middle Eastern Democratization and Government provides tests and contests of old and new assumptions.

For more information about this series, please visit: www.routledge.com/middleeaststudies/series/RSMEDG

The Failure of Democracy in Iraq

Religion, Ideology and Sectarianism

Hamid Alkifaey

Routledge
Taylor & Francis Group

LONDON AND NEW YORK

First published 2019
by Routledge
2 Park Square, Milton Park, Abingdon, Oxon OX14 4RN

and by Routledge
52 Vanderbilt Avenue, New York, NY 10017

Routledge is an imprint of the Taylor & Francis Group, an informa business

© 2019 Hamid Alkifaey

British Library Cataloguing-in-Publication Data
A catalogue record for this book is available from the British Library

Library of Congress Cataloging-in-Publication Data
Names: Alkifaey, Hamid, author.
Title: The failure of democracy in Iraq: religion, ideology and sectarianism / Hamid Alkifaey.
Description: Milton Park, Abingdon, Oxon; New York, NY: Routledge, 2019. | Series: Routledge studies in Middle Eastern democratization and government; 25
Identifiers: LCCN 2018045608 (print) | LCCN 2018049145 (ebook) | ISBN 9780429442155 (master) | ISBN 9780429808203 (Adobe Reader) | ISBN 9780429808197 (Epub) | ISBN 9780429808180 (Mobipocket) | ISBN 9781138337787 | ISBN 9781138337787(hardback) | ISBN 9780429442155(ebook)
Subjects: LCSH: Democratization–Iraq–History–21st century. | Democracy–Iraq–History–21st century. | Iraq–Politics and government–2003– | Islam and politics–Iraq. | Religion and politics–Iraq. | Iraq–Foreign relations–1991– | Iraq–Foreign relations–United States. | United States–Foreign relations–Iraq.
Classification: LCC JQ1849.A91 (ebook) | LCC JQ1849.A91 A45 2019 (print) | DDC 320.9567–dc23
LC record available at https://lccn.loc.gov/2018045608

ISBN: 978-1-138-33778-7 (hbk)
ISBN: 978-0-429-44215-5 (ebk)

Typeset in Times New Roman
by Wearset Ltd, Boldon, Tyne and Wear

This book is dedicated to Akeel Abbas, an Iraqi intellectual who combines intellect with modesty and courage with scruples. May he continue to carry the torch of reason for future generations.

HA

Contents

1 Introduction

Democracy has been spreading across the world, but it has escaped the Arab world for some reason. When the Americans invaded Iraq in March 2003, and toppled the dictatorship of Saddam Hussein, they initiated a process of democratization with many parties participating in it. Yet this democratization process has faltered with the same religious groups clinging to power since 2005. There has been much malpractice, corruption, use of religious symbols and vote-rigging and there have been, false accusations that led to imprisonment and even assassinations, with many 'elected politicians' fleeing the country.

When US forces removed Saddam Hussein's dictatorship, which had committed heinous crimes against humanity, many observers believed the lessons of dictatorship had been learned by Iraqis and that they would never allow such a regime to emerge ever again. They would cling to democracy and reject any other form of rule. Americans firmly believed that Iraqis would be grateful to them for removing the dictatorship. Many Iraqi politicians had similar persuasions. Even Islamists thought they had lost the chance to establish an Islamic state and their discourse became highly conciliatory.

After it toppled Saddam Hussein, the US had created an organization called the Organization of Human Relief and Assistance (ORHA) headed by a retired US general, Jay Garner, to manage Iraq temporarily and prevent any humanitarian crisis from breaking beyond control and oversee the transition to Iraqi civilian rule within three months.[1] But soon after the end of the war in May 2003, the US administration changed its mind, for some mysterious reasons, and appointed a 'Civilian Administrator' who headed what was called 'The Coalition Provisional Authority' (CPA) to replace ORHA, but they didn't specify a duration for it. CPA administered Iraq for over a year with the aim of laying the basis for democracy.[2] This was a reversal of its earlier policy of handing over power to an Iraqi interim government to be formed from a 65-member committee formed by the Iraqi Opposition Conference in London, held at the end of 2002 and sponsored by the Bush administration.

The civilian administrator, Paul Bremer, after consultations with Iraqi political leaders, decided to appoint a 25-member Governing Council (GC) in July 2003 with the aim of handing power to Iraqis in due course.[3] It was officially declared in the presence of UN envoy Sergio de Mello. UN General

Secretary, Kofi Annan, called the establishment of the GC 'an important first step towards a full restoration of sovereignty'.[4] The GC was intended to represent all political, religious, ethnic and regional trends, but it couldn't in the absence of elections legitimize its existence. It remained connected, perhaps unwittingly, to CPA throughout its term of office. Many important political forces remained outside the GC, such as the Sadrist Trend (ST), several Sunni groups, and the Ba'ath Party (BP) or its successors.[5] This is hardly a good start for democracy when major political forces are intentionally excluded. There were suggestions to expand the GC representation to include all groups as a prelude to elections, but Iraqi political groups represented in GC, together with the UN and US, decided to form an interim government to oversee elections for the national assembly and permanent constitution, as demanded by Shia religious leader, Ayatullah Sistani, who insisted on elections to the national assembly.[6] This was the first and clearest sign of interference by the religious authority in politics in recent Iraqi history, which paved the way for more of the same in the coming years as we shall see throughout the book. Such interference has enabled religious parties to seize power in 2005 and keep it till the present day.

The Governing Council served for just under a year as the country's unelected legislature. It appointed a government that worked alongside the CPA. It received UN recognition through the UN Security Council resolutions 1483, 1500 and 1511.[7] It also took Iraq's seat at the UN. Many countries, beginning with Iran, recognized it as the representative of the Iraqi state. Real power, however, remained with the American CPA. GC tried hard to assert its authority. It entered into battles with the CPA, which tried, with marked success, to bypass it. Bremer didn't implement many GC resolutions and sometimes imposed his will on the GC as happened in the 15th of November Agreement.[8]

Another organization that played an important role then was the Iraqi Reconstruction and Development Council (IRDC). IRDC was made up of Iraqi exiles who managed different Iraqi institutions but it reported to CPA.[9] The core of IRDC was an organization in exile called the Iraqi Forum for Democracy (IFD),[10] which aimed to promote liberal democracy in Iraq.[11]

Working closely with CPA, the GC managed to write and adopt the Transitional Administrative Law (TAL)[12] that called for elections on the 30th of January 2005 to elect a national assembly tasked with writing a permanent constitution, getting it approved through a popular referendum on the 15th of October 2005, and then calling for another election based on the new constitution on 15th December 2005. The aim was to put Iraq on the road to legitimate democratic politics as the UN statement of 22 July 2003 called for.[13]

The UN was involved in the process in order to give it an international legality, but the bombing of its Baghdad headquarters in August 2003, resulting in the death of 22 of its staff, including UN envoy Sergio de Mello, led to distancing the UN from the political process after it closed its bureau in Baghdad. After the formation of the GC, the UN was side-lined by Paul Bremer who rejected all UN proposals to give more power to Iraqis. This US attitude angered the UN envoy, Mr de Mello, and made him feel bitter as he thought he was used to legit-imize the GC and then dropped.[14]

Elections were held according to the plan set out in the TAL; a 275-member national assembly was elected which subsequently wrote the permanent consti-tution that was approved by a popular referendum, despite objections to some of its articles by various groups.[15] However, most people in the provinces populated by Sunni Arabs rejected the constitution.[16] This trend revealed a sectarian-based political divide in the country at that earlier stage. This divide would prove later in the process that it's a major impediment to democracy.

Elections were held again in 2005, 2010, 2014 and 2018 in line with the constitution, parliaments were elected and coalition governments were formed. The US regularly said the elections were largely free and fair with 'no evidence of widespread or serious fraud'.[17] The UN came back to the process and was involved in the preparation and observation of all elections since 2005 after both GC and CPA called upon it to provide assistance.[18] Since 2005, Iraq saw three elected prime ministers; one, Noori Al-Maliki, was elected twice (although his second term was questionable).

It was a momentous period in Iraq's history when new political forces emerged. The Islamist parties, previously in opposition to the regime of Saddam Hussein, joined forces and formed the United Iraqi Alliance (UIA). They were also joined by the secular Iraqi National Congress (INC), led by Ahmed Chalabi, regarded by many as the architect of the 'New Iraq' because of his perceived influence over the Americans.[19] The largely Islamist UIA won the first elections on the 30th of January 2005.

Interim PM, Ayad Allawi, who had American and British support,[20] did not do so well. He got only 40 seats in the National Assembly.[21] This number shrank to 25 seats in the following parliament.[22] Since UIA became the 'biggest bloc' with 140 seats,[23] it was officially asked to nominate the PM. In April 2005, PM Allawi handed over the premiership to PM-elect, Ibrahim Al-Jaafari of the Islamic Da'awa Party (IDP), who was chosen by UIA through an internal vote.[24]

Elections and fatwas

The second elections produced a parliament and government also dominated by Islamist Shia parties, mainly because Iraqis voted on sectarian and ethnic lines. The Shia overwhelmingly voted for UIA, which was originally formed by a com-mittee of six appointed by the Ayatullah Sistani.[25] Voters followed the advice of their religious leaders. This was widely reported at the time and documented by official statements, media reports and books.[26] Sheikh Ja'afar Al-Ibrahimi, a popular Shia preacher, acknowledged in a sermon in the city of Samawa that he engaged in publicizing UIA and introducing its members to people who didn't know them, even though he himself didn't know them either, but he did that on behalf of the religious establishment in Najaf. 'It's Najaf that has gotten them into power', he declared.[27] This is a clear acknowledgement by a well-known cleric that clerics widely interfered in Iraqi elections in favour of Islamist parties.

People thought there was a fatwa in favour of UIA. The author was a candidate in both the first and second elections and he reported it to the press.[28] People were told participation in the election had religious sanctity and voting for lists other than UIA would 'bring down God's wrath'. Even an abstention from voting would 'throw the transgressor in hellfire'.[29] This call was made by one of Sistani's closest aids, Sayyid Ahmed al-Safi, on 22 October 2004. Al-Safi was himself a candidate within UIA, then Member of the National Assembly. UIA was regarded by Ayatullah Sistani as an 'electoral vehicle for the Shia and should continue in any post-election government as a unified grouping that would govern the country'.[30]

In many areas of the south, people didn't know the candidates, nor had they even seen their photos or election posters, yet they voted for any candidate standing with the UIA because they were told these were the wishes of Ayatullah Sistani. UIA election posters featured huge photos of Sistani together with the list's numbers (169 and 555) emblazoned on them.[31]

The religious leadership maintained publicly that it didn't recommend any list, but four of Sistani's official representatives were candidates on the UIA ticket.[32] This was used in the UIA election campaign to argue that this list was the one Sistani favoured. Sheikh Najih Al-Abboodi, Ayatullah Sistani's representative, said in a statement published by Al-khaleej newspaper and still appears on Sistani's website, that the religious leader supports UIA list stating its number, 169, for more clarity to his followers.[33] In a statement issued by the office of the 'Scientific Seminary in Najaf', the schools under Sistani's guidance, published by some newspapers and websites, the position was clear: 'Ayatullah Sistani supports UIA'.[34] The list swept the country and the four of Sistani's representatives were elected to the assembly, including Ahmed As-Safi, whose sermons were broadcast live every Friday by many television stations.

The Sunni Arabs boycotted the first Iraqi elections, protesting the American invasion, which changed the power dynamics in Iraq and treated them as a minority.[35] Only one Sunni party, the Iraqi Islamic Party-IIP, decided to participate, although it demanded a delay in the elections to get organized, arguing a delay would enable it to compete with the more organized Shia and Kurdish parties. No delay was granted as the interim constitution, TAL, fixed election and referendum dates.[36]

However, Sunnis participated massively in the second elections held on 15 December 2005, represented by two blocs. An Islamic-leaning list, the Accordance Front-AF, dominated by IIP, and a secular pan-Arab bloc, the National Dialogue Front-NDF which drew its support from the former regime's loyalists. Together, they got 55 seats (AF – 44, NDF – 11), while the Shia UIA bloc got 128 seats.[37] The Kurds participated in full force in both elections and got 58 seats (53 for Kurdish Alliance-KA and five for Kurdish Islamic Union-KIU).[38]

Democracy or shura?

Politicians and electorate have been talking all along about democracy and the democratic experience, but it looked like every group had its own version of democracy, which may not necessarily accord with real democracy. Islamists for example talked of 'democratic mechanisms' as opposed to democracy.[39] Some compared democracy to 'shura,'[40] which simply means consulting 'knowledge-able' people.[41] The political process might have looked democratic, but when it's closely examined, one would have doubts in view of the basic principles laid down in textbooks or applied in established democracies.

In real democracies, people choose their representatives free of pressures after a free and transparent election campaign. Religion and politics are separated; candidates must not use religious symbols or places of worship for political pur-poses. This is not exactly what has happened in Iraq over the last four general elections and three local elections. All the above criteria for democracy have been violated, including the use of religious symbols and places of worship, which is against Iraqi law and election regulations.[42]

UIA splintered into two lists prior to the elections of 7 March 2010, 'State of Law' (SoL), led by PM Noori Al-Maliki, got 89 seats, and the National Iraqi Coalition (NIC), which brought together the Reform Trend (RT), Sadrists Trend (ST), Supreme Islamic Iraqi Council (SIIC), and the Fadhila Islamic Party-IFP, got 70 seats.[43] The list also included Ahmed Chalabi's INC, who won only one seat. Chalabi was unable to win when he ran alone in December 2005 and could only win a seat in his birth place of Kadhimiyya when he joined a religious list.

Sunni electorates were also subjected to campaigns that made them scared of the Shia alliance, and they voted for the tribal-religious list, Accordance Front. They fast developed a feeling of victimhood vis-à-vis the Shia.[44]

The Kurds have their own fears of an Arab rule as well as ambition for a Kurdish state; thus, the electorate voted for the two main parties: the Kurdistan Democratic Party-KDP, led by Masud Barzani, and the Patriotic Union of Kurdistan-PUK, led by Jalal Talabani and Islamist Group.

PUK splintered into two parties prior to the elections of 2010.[45] The new party, Goran (Change), led by Nawshirwan Mustafa, got eight seats in the Baghdad par-liament and 25 seats in the Kurdish parliament.[46] It increased its seats to nine in Baghdad in the following national elections.[47] Goran MP, Aram Sheikh Muhammed, became deputy parliamentary speaker in Baghdad, while another Goran member, Yusuf Muhammed, became the speaker of the Kurdish Parliament in Erbil. KRG President, Masud Barzani, banned Muhammed from entering Irbil to perform his job in October 2015.[48] According to KRG law, Muhammed would have succeeded Barzani in the presidency of KRG after his term expired. Kurdish politics have become family-based, where the Talabani and Barzani families are dominant. Talabani's youngest son, Qubad, has been groomed to succeed his father as a leader of the PUK.[49] He has become deputy PM in the Kurdistan Regional Government headed by Barzani's nephew and son-in-law, Nichervan.

Voters' motivation

What motivated Iraqi voters was not political programmes, which hardly existed, nor a desire for change, since most of them didn't have an idea what sort of change was ahead. Rather, it was religious, sectarian and ethnic passions and fears of the other fuelled by sectarian politicians and their partisan media. There were other pressures put on people to elect certain individuals or parties. These included tribal, familial and regional loyalties, in addition to international pressures. Religious pressures, be they personal or collective, were the most influential in deciding how voters voted in the Arab west, middle and south. In the Kurdish north, the main motives were, and still are, ethnic and irredentist. Fear of the other was the main factor in people's voting decisions.[50]

The constitution was also flawed in many ways, according to experts.[51] It impedes democracy, says Faleh Abdul-Jabbar, director of the Beirut-based Institute for Strategic Studies. One obvious example he points to is Article 2. Clause (A) bars enacting laws that 'contravene the established provisions of Islam'.[52] This was demanded by Islamist parties to block any legislation that loosens their grip on power. Dia Shakarchi, former Islamist MP, charges that Islamists attempted 'to add as much as they could of religious and sectarian colour to the constitution'.[53] Clause (B), which bars enacting laws that 'contradict the principles of democracy' is not a deterrent as some secularists thought.[54] Clause (A) is stronger than Clause (B) since the former refers to a defined religious text, while the latter is a vague floating idea that has no well-defined reference point.[55]

Islamists in parliament used Article (2A) to introduce Sharia with regards to personal status law and the ban of alcohol. Clause (B) did not deter them as there is no text to refer to.[56] In addition, no one can dispute what prominent clerics say because their opinions are obligatory on all believers.[57] On the other hand, democratic principles are not well defined, nor are they agreed upon among democracy-leaning people, let alone those who are opposed to democracy.[58] Unlike Islamic principles, they are not sacred, so no one will enforce them outside the law. They can vary from one country or culture to another. Islamists always argue that each country has its own version of democracy and 'we can have our version too'. Human rights conventions are not obligatory either. Countries can opt out if they wish, so they cannot be made obligatory in Iraq. Article (2) may be contradictory, but Clause (A) gives more weight to clerics to interpret the religious text and when they form the majority, they will prevail.[59]

Although there are many schools within Islam and religious texts can be interpreted in many ways, the fact remains that there are fixed Islamic principles agreed upon among Muslims, Sunni and Shia alike, since they are clearly defined in the Qura'an and Sunnah. Among these are the controversial penal code, the prohibition of alcohol, fighting the 'infidels' and non-believers in Islam, negative attitude towards women and inheritance law. These codes pose a problem for modern democracy and political thought and contravene human rights conventions. Individuals may opt to apply some of these laws voluntarily, but a democratic state must not adopt laws that clearly violate human rights conventions or the principles of democracy. The penal code violates human rights conventions since it permits the amputation of hands for thieves, while inheritance law discriminates against women.

Akeel Abbas rightly argues that

> Democracy and religion belong to diametrically opposed orders of reality. The former is based on debate and questioning that leads to following the opinion of the majority, while protecting the rights of minorities, whereas the latter is based on holy texts that accept no debate or questioning and pay no attention to the opinions of the majority or minority.[60]

Religious symbols were widely used in Iraqi elections and politics in general. PM Al-Ja'afari, for instance, distributed a prayer book, with a photograph showing him praying, emblazoned on it. Many candidates were giving political speeches in mosques and religious centres.[61] Preachers were telling people 'if they did not vote they would be punished by God and go to hell and the list endorsed by the religious authority was UIA, number 169'.[62]

The Independent High Election Commission (IHEC) was too weak to do anything about such violations.[63] According to its first president, Hussein Al-Hindawi, when IHEC fell under the control of parties, this 'distanced the democratic process from propriety and integrity. Members of the former and current IHEC were candidates of political blocs and they represented the interests of their blocs when taking decisions'.[64]

Secularists were too frightened to object to any violation and when they protested, IHEC rejected their complaints. The most prominent Iraqi secular leader, Ayad Allawi, protested to IHEC that UIA had violated the law, but his complaint was rejected.[65] Allawi was portrayed in a hostile poster as looking like Saddam Hussein with a military uniform, marked (Ba'athist).

After years of 'democratization', democracy has not taken root in Iraq. On the contrary, democratic principles are being violated and the country is increasingly heading towards a religious state. Some democratically elected leaders have left the process or fled the country fearing for their freedom or lives after having been accused of terrorism. Former Vice President, Tarik Al-Hashimi, fled to Turkey in 2011, and former finance minister, Rafi Al-Isawi, fled to Jordan in 2012. US mediation efforts to facilitate their return to Iraq to repair the political process haven't succeeded.[66] MP Muhammed Al-Dayni fled Iraq after being accused of planning an explosion in parliament and MP Abdul-Nassir Al-Janabi fled to Jordan in 2007 after the PM accused him in a parliamentary questioning session of kidnapping 150 people.[67]

Others have been implicated in high-level corruption that made it impossible for them to stay in politics, such as former defence minister Hazim Ash-Sha'alan[68] and former electricity minister Ayham As-Samerraei, who received a prison sentence although he managed to escape from a high-security prison in the fortified Green Zone, allegedly with the help of Americans.[69] Some politicians resigned in silent protest at the political process itself such as Ja'afar As-Sadr.[70]

These events show there is a serious problem with Iraqi democracy. If those officials were innocent and were framed with these crimes, it's a huge problem. If they did actually commit these crimes, it's even more serious. In both cases, democratically elected officials break the law in such a flagrant way when they should be upholding it and setting examples for others. It means Iraq lacks nation-builders and inspiring leaders with the stature of the Spanish transitional leader, Adolfo Suarez, who led the Spanish transition to democracy successfully. Political scientist, Kanan Makiya, describes the new leaders as 'small men with no vision. They treated Iraq as booty'.[71] Iraq lacks visionary leaders with a firm commitment to building a true modern democracy. Writer and former minister Ali Allawi says there is no national leader: 'They are only Sunni, Shia and Kurdish politicians, a smattering of self-styled liberals and secularists, each determined to push their particular agenda forward'.[72]

For the first ten years of democratization, there was no law to organize and regulate political parties. The law was passed in 2015 and took effect in 2018.[73] The democratic process runs through agreements among the leaders of political blocs and these agreements are subject to other factors such as having an armed wing or a strong foreign backer. It served the established political parties well not to have a law for political parties in place because it would restrict their activities, especially funding. MP Alia Nassif charges that some politicians use public money to fund their election campaigns and 'there are mafias run by political parties'.[74] Corruption among politicians and government officials is common and this constitutes a problem for democracy.

Some parties are strong because they have militias to protect their activities and personnel and perhaps impose their policies. Militias were formed or came to Iraq from neighbouring countries after the regime's fall in 2003, but they have mushroomed after the fall of Musil in 2014 when the Shia spiritual leader, Ayatullah Sistani, issued a fatwa of jihad against ISIS, after which militia leaders have gained a lot of political weight in the country.[75] With so many armed militias connected to political parties, Iraqi democracy is in real danger.

In 2010, Iraqia list, led by Ayad Allawi, was the biggest bloc in parliament. But the incumbent PM, Noori Al-Maliki, rejected the outcome, requesting a recount of votes, claiming there was vote-rigging in favour of his opponents, although he, not his opponents, was in government. When the recount didn't change the results, he went to the Federal Court and obtained a ruling allowing the formation of parliamentary lists after elections, basically changing the meaning of an electoral win to his favour.[76] Many doubted the soundness of the ruling. Experts warned that this ruling could create a potential for 'endless negotiations after every election', which means that elections results cannot indicate who should form the government.[77] After nine months of wrangling, Allawi gave up his right to form the government, paving the way for Al-Maliki's second term. That government didn't achieve much because of its own failures and the fierce opposition it faced since many people believed that democratic rules were violated.

In August 2014, Al-Maliki increased his parliamentary seats but was forced to relinquish the premiership after Ayatullah Sistani intervened.[78] He advised the Shia National Alliance to choose a new leader after Al-Maliki looked divisive. Although his replacement by Haider Al-Abadi caused a rift within SoL, it eased sectarian and political tensions threatening to tear the country apart.[79] In 2018 elections, Al-Malik and Al-Abadi formed their separate competing lists, although still claiming to belong to one party.

Aims of the book

Doubts began to surface about the viability of Iraqi democracy since people's primary allegiance has been to the pre-modern affiliations of religion, sect and tribe, not to ideas. These affiliations dictated voting decisions. Worse still, there was the fear of the other spread by politicians eager to be elected at any cost. I began to feel those who were elected to office may not actually represent the real interests of the people because they came to political prominence by availing themselves of fortuitous and expedient circumstances; in other words, through a process that violates the basic tenets of democracy in the name of democracy!

This was happening under the eyes of the American sponsors who made it possible for all these mainly undemocratic forces to reach power through a process that may not be fully democratic. Even the current modicum of democracy may not be maintained for long since those in power are not prepared to relinquish it under any circumstances. The only power that was able to make a prime minister leave office, was not that of the ballot box, but the clout of the religious leader.

This book sought to find answers for many questions, the most important of which is whether this current state of affairs can develop into a true democracy. Can pluralism actually exist when most of the parties are religious and undemocratic, ready to unite to exclude others? What are the conditions that are necessary to help a true democracy develop in Iraq over time? Iraqi parties in general deepened social and religious rifts, polarizing society so sharply to the point of triggering a civil war. What kind of parties does Iraq need to make democracy a viable option?

Political parties are essential for any democracy, and their ideological differences are vital to energize democratic debates since these differences represent different socio-political orientations in society. But this has not been the case in Iraq, reflecting a common trend in many developing countries. Haggard and Kaufman (1995) don't place parties in developing countries on the same left-right dimension as is the case in the party system in advanced industrial countries. The authors define political polarization 'by the ideological distance between parties'.[80] Hussein Al-Hindawi contends there are no ideological differences between Islamist parties; they are one group.[81] In other words, there are no genuine legitimate differences among religious parties in Iraq, failing to reflect modern socio-political orientations in the Iraqi society, opting instead for pre-modern allegiances and fears.

Democracy assumes freedom. Personal, associational or political, freedom is an integral part of democracy, guaranteed under democratic systems.[82] Under the Iraqi Islamists, it's restricted. Armed masked men keep raiding nightclubs and professional clubs, such as that of the Literary Union, and terrorize people, beat them up and break furniture frequently. The last time the Literary Union, a famous association for Iraqi literary writers and poets, was attacked was in 2015.[83] Women are no longer free and most of them have to dress in hijab to avoid harassment. Ms Hana'a Edward, head of Al-Amal Charity says 'Iraqi women suffer marginalization and all kinds of violence, including forced marriages, divorces and harassment, as well as restrictions on their liberty, their education, their choice of clothing, and their social life'.[84]

Al-Fadheela Islamic Party sought to enact Sharia law on personal status and got it approved by the Council of Ministers.[85] Some personal freedoms are non-existent such as changing one's faith from Islam to another. Under a democratic rule, freedoms are guaranteed by the government. Although many Islamic scholars support democracy, most Islamist parties are critical of democracy, believing only in its mechanisms as a way to hold power.[86]

Democracy is not just about elections. It's about electing those who can protect people's rights and freedoms. They may fail in their endeavour to serve the people but they abide by democracy's basic tenets. A democratic system doesn't necessarily perform better than a non-democratic one. In fact, democratization coincided with acute economic crisis in Eastern Europe and Latin America, except in Czechoslovakia and Chile.[87]

In an environment where religion and tradition play a central role in shaping people's minds and decisions, is there a place for real democracy? Can democracy work in a society where a high percentage is uneducated or even illiterate?[88] Finally, can democracy actually survive without secularism that can protect it from religious domination and extremism?

There has been a noticeable shift recently in people's thinking, but it has not been electorally reflected. There are new political movements that have the word 'civic' in their names, and this indicates they are secular. Among these is 'the Civic Democratic Alliance' (CDA) that entered the process in the 2014 election. It got thousands of votes nation-wide, but its share in Baghdad was only three seats, because the electoral system worked in favour of established parties.[89] Some of its candidates got thousands of votes but failed to win seats in parliament, while candidates with fewer votes who belonged to big lists were 'elected'.[90] In 2018, there was a list called 'Tamadun' or Modernity, led by Faik Sheikh Ali who was a CDA MP. It gained two seats. CDA only got one seat in Baghdad this time. Another party called 'Civil Party' was led by Hamad Almusawi, but this party is associated with SoL. It's an apparent attempt to attract secular votes for SoL. The party got one seat.

In the 2010 elections, many politicians moved away from the Sunni AF to the secular 'Iraqiyya'. But they soon left Iraqiyya, forming another sect-based group, the Union of Iraqi Forces (UIF). Ayad Allawi has maintained his political base, albeit his parliamentary seats shrank from 40 in 2005 to 21 in 2014 and 2018.[91]

A movement toward secularism is happening but slowly. Still, religious blocs have tried to appeal to voters nationally, but religious rhetoric remains strong.[92] They have adopted patriotic or civic names for their lists, abandoning their old religious names.

Mahmoud Al-Mashhadni, a Sunni Islamist and former speaker of parliament, predicted that Islamist parties will 'change their names; they will carry modern names and formulate political programs, thus they will overcome their failure'.[93] Whether this perceived trend towards civic politics is permanent, or even real, is questionable. Dia Shakarchi, former Islamist MP for IDP, moved away from political Islam in 2006 but he didn't win as a secular politician. Sharwan Al-Waeli left IDP-IO and formed an independent list in the 2014 election. He, too, didn't win.

Islamist parties may have changed their tactics and rhetoric, but not necessarily their ideologies. The electorate may have changed their perception of Islamist politicians. But they are still voting for them due to the absence of credible alternatives. Iraqi Islamists have been in power since early 2005 and they made sure that the electoral arrangements, enshrined in the election law and IHEC, do not make room for secular or small parties to challenge their dominance through the ballot box. Democratic institutions must be 'fair': they must give all the relevant political forces a 'chance to win'; they must be 'effective': They must make even 'losing under democracy more attractive'.[94]

Election turnout has been falling, from 78 per cent in 2005 elections, to 63 per cent in 2010 to 52 per cent in 2014.[95] In 2018, it was 44.5 per cent. Is it apathy or disillusionment with Islamists? I have been following events in Iraq closely for over three decades.[96] I rushed to Iraq in 2003 to participate in building new institutions in pursuit of a truly democratic Iraq.[97] But with so many hurdles in the way of democracy, I thought the best contribution I could make to democracy is to conduct a serious study on democratization to find out the real reasons why democracy has faltered despite all the available opportunities, the most important of which was international support.

If democracy is 'not the "default mode" of humanity, but a rare occurrence proceeding from specific and unique historical sequences' using the words of John Dunn, can this 'rare occurrence' succeed in Iraq?[98] I have undertaken to find out whether democracy can co-exist with theocracy, tribalism, militarism, illiteracy and closed cultures. The findings are listed at the end of the book.

Islamist MP Sami Al-Askari contends tribal values 'don't accord with the spirit of democracy and personal freedom'. He also warns that 'religious despotism' is the worst and most dangerous of all types of despotisms that humanity has ever witnessed over all times because 'it simultaneously dominates the brains and bodies'.[99]

I am arguing that the democratic process has fared poorly in Iraq, especially with the threat posed by armed groups and secret militias within the political process itself, both of which undermine the rule of law necessary to protect any democratic experience. One report by the US War College estimates the number of Shia militias in Iraq to be over 50.[100] I have supported my argument with evidence from political theories, religious texts and political realities of Iraq. Democratization can succeed in Iraq if the impediments are removed, but this requires leaders strong enough to tackle the real problems impeding progress. Many countries have managed to overcome their problems by taking tough decisions. This has to happen in Iraq.

Notes

1 Larry Diamond, *Squandered Victory*, Henry Holt & Company (2005) pp. 30–36
2 CPA regulation to rule Iraq was issued on 16/6/2003 on the basis of UN Resolution 1483: www.iraqcoalition.org/regulations/
3 More on Governing Council members on: www.globalsecurity.org/military/world/iraq/igc.htm
4 UN statement on 22/7/2003: www.un.org/sg/STATEMENTS/index.asp?nid=424
5 Hamid Alkifaey, 'Iraqi Governing Council: pros and cons', Alsharq Alawsat, 26/7/2004: https://goo.gl/z8LgXh
6 Paul Bremer, *My Year in Iraq*, Simon & Schuster (2006) p. 242. Also Diamond (2005) op. cit. p. 44
7 UN Resolutions 1483, 1500 and 1511. Texts can be accessed from the following links: www.un.org/en/ga/search/view_doc.asp?symbol=S/RES/1483(2003)   www.un.org/en/ga/search/view_doc.asp?symbol=S/RES/1500(2003)   www.un.org/en/ga/search/view_doc.asp?symbol=S/RES/1511(2003)
8 Diamond (2005) op. cit. p. 51. Also, the writer was present at the meeting the agreement was presented to the Governing Council on 15 November 2003 in the house of Kurdish leader, Jalal Talabani.
9 Bremer (2006) op. cit. p. 32
10 The author was a member of both IFD and IRDC and spokesman of GC
11 Ali Allawi, *The Occupation of Iraq*, Yale University Press (2007) pp. 99–100
12 Text of the TAL can be accessed from: https://goo.gl/7UApFd
13 UN statement (22/7/2003) op. cit.
14 Diamond (2005) op. cit. pp. 55–60
15 US State Department archives: http://2001–2009.state.gov/p/nea/rls/rpt/60857.htm
16 Patrick Cockburn and Kim Sengupta, 'Sunni voters fail to block Iraq's new constitution', *Independent* (25/10/ 2005): https://goo.gl/Vaj3hk
17 BBC, 27/3/2010: http://news.bbc.co.uk/1/hi/world/middle_east/8590417.stm
18 UN, Iraq factsheet; www.un.org/News/dh/infocus/iraq/iraq-elect-fact-sht.pdf
19 BBC report/Iraqi National Congress List, 20/1/2006: https://goo.gl/m12DcL; also Aram Reston, *The Man Who Pushed America to War*, Nations Books (2008) p. xi
20 Antony Shadid, NY Times, 4/2/2011: https://goo.gl/hKTdFS
21 Inter Parliamentary Union: www.ipu.org/parline-e/reports/arc/2151_05.htm
22 Ibid. and BBC, Iraqi National List, 20/1/2006: https://goo.gl/625E7S
23 Inter Parliamentary Union: www.ipu.org/parline-e/reports/arc/2151_05.htm
24 Al-Jazeera, 7/4/2005: www.aljazeera.com/archive/2005/04/200849145149814789.html
25 Allawi (2007) p. 343
26 Ibid., p. 342. Also, interview with Farid Ayar
27 Video text; for a translation, see Appendix in this volume: www.youtube.com/watch?v=eDSDc_L8ZF8
28 Bloomberg's full text:

> In the January vote 'the religious parties issued a fatwa,' or religious edict, calling on Shiites to back the United Iraqi Alliance, Hamid al-Kifai, head of the Movement for Democratic Society, an independent secular party, said in a December 1 telephone interview from Baghdad. 'There isn't one this time, and so we have a better chance of succeeding'.
>
> Accessed on 1 November 2014: www.bloomberg.com/apps/news?p id=newsarchive&sid=a9VYgcHobTcA&refer=us

29 Allawi (2007) op. cit. p. 342
30 Ibid., p. 343
31 Appendices 5, 6 and 7

32 Among them were Ali As-Safi and Ahmed As-Safi as verified by Sistani's website. (Arabic): www.sistani.org/arabic/in-news/973/
33 Najih Al-Abboodi-Sistani.org: https://goo.gl/srcjAC
34 Statement of the 'Scientific Seminary', Elaph, 19/1/2005: https://goo.gl/d9UvzL
35 Jeffrey White and Brooke Neuman, Washington Institute, 13/12/2005: https://goo.gl/lWw55S
36 Article 2(B-2) TAL Refworld: www.refworld.org/docid/45263d612.html
37 Inter Parliamentary Union: www.ipu.org/parline-e/reports/arc/2151bis_05.htm
38 Ibid.
39 Interviews with Islamist politicians Sami Al-Askari, Walid Al-Hilli and Adil Abdur-Rahim respectively
40 Interview with Walid Al-Hilli
41 Interview with Akeel Abbas
42 Interviews with Sharwan Al-Waeli and Farid Ayar
43 Seat distribution of 2010 parliament: https://goo.gl/IgvS1q
44 Fanar Hadad, Hudson Institute, 4/8/2014: https://goo.gl/EVs1kw
45 The Majalla, The Leading Arab Magazine, 16/6/2010: https://goo.gl/nZnKPU
46 IWPR, August 2009: https://goo.gl/NVRPUH
47 Assyrian International News Agency: www.aina.org/news/20140520151010.htm
48 Ekurd Daily, 24/5/2016: http://ekurd.net/barzani-kdp-coup-iraqi-kurdistan-2016-05-24
49 Michael Rubin, Ekurd Daily, 19/12/2012: http://ekurd.net/mismas/articles/misc2012/12/state6722.htm
50 Fred Kaplan, Slate, 15/12/2005: https://goo.gl/3zQqHu
51 Interview with Faleh Abdul-Jabbar
52 Iraqi constitution (English): www.constituteproject.org/constitution/Iraq_2005.pdf?lang=en
53 Interview with Dia Shakarchi
54 Iraqi Constitution, op. cit.
55 Interview with Akeel Abbas
56 Interview with Maysoon Aldamluji
57 Interview with Dia Shakarchi. Also, see chapter 6 (taqleed)
58 Interview with Akeel Abbas
59 Ibid.
60 Ibid.
61 Mark Kerry, *Tigers of the Tigris*, Dog Ear (2008) p. 130
62 Victoria Fontan, *Voices from Post Saddam Iraq*, Greenwood Publishing Group (2009) p. 140: https://goo.gl/Z8eYgj
63 Interview with Sharwan Al-Waeli
64 Interview with Sami Al-Askari
65 Usamah Mahdi, 'Al-Sistani supports the Shia List', Elaph, 19/1/2005: https://goo.gl/HcAuxb
66 Adnan Hussein, Rudaw, 12/2/2015 www.rudaw.net/english/middleeast/iraq/120220151
67 Mark Santora, 'Iraq leader and Sunni officials in clash on security', *New York Times*, 26/1/2007: www.nytimes.com/2007/01/26/world/middleeast/26iraq.html
68 AFP, Alarabiya, 1/2/2012: https://english.alarabiya.net/articles/2012/02/01/191870.html
69 Michael Howard, 'Americans helped Iraqi ex-minister escape jail', *Guardian*, 20/12/2016: www.informationliberation.com/?id=18907
70 Lebanon wire report, 19/2/2011: www.lebanonwire.com/1102MLN/11021918AP.asp
71 Interview with Kanan Makiya
72 Allawi (2007) op. cit. p. 460
73 Niqash, 20/9/2015, published on ICSSI website: www.iraqicivilsociety.org/archives/4648

74 Adel Fakhir, Rudaw, 1/3/2014: http://rudaw.net/english/middleeast/iraq/01032014
75 Norman Cigar, 'Iraq's Shia warlords and their militias', US Army War College Press, June 2015, pp. 3–15, published on: www.strategicstudiesinstitute.army.mil/pdffiles/PUB1272.pdf
76 David Ghanim, *Iraq's Dysfunctional Democracy*, Praeger, Oxford (2011) p. 122: https://goo.gl/UUCefK
77 Kenneth Pollack, *A Government for Baghdad*, Brookings Institute 27/7/2010: https://goo.gl/7nehTs
78 Wa'el Hashim, Sistani.org, 18/8/2014: www.sistani.org/arabic/in-news/24950/
79 Reuters, 'Iraqi parliament approves new government headed by Haider al-Abadi', 8/9/2014: https://goo.gl/NVQ8P1
80 Stephen Haggard and Robert Kaufman, *The Political Economy of Democratic Transitions*, Princeton University Press (1995) p. 167
81 Interview
82 Robert Dahl, *On Democracy*, Yale University Press (1999) pp. 45–58
83 Salah Nasrawi, Al-Ahram Weekly, 24/1/2015: https://goo.gl/vBds0Z
84 Salam Faraj, Agence France-Presse, 9/3/2012: https://goo.gl/A6dz4t
85 Mushreq Abbas, 'Iraqi justice minister presses Shiite personal status law', Al-Monitor 3/3/2014: https://goo.gl/EhWYom
86 Interviews with Sami Al-Askari, Walid Al-Hilli and Adil Abdur-Raheem Muhammed
87 Adam Przeworski, *Democracy and the Market*, Cambridge University Press (1991) p. 140
88 Larry Diamond estimates the percentage of illiterate people in Iraq to be 40 per cent, [Diamond (2005) p. 21]
89 Election Guide, Republic of Iraq, footnote 2: www.electionguide.org/elections/id/2425/
90 Mithal Al-Aloosi, CDA's number of seats is unfair, 20/5/2014: https://goo.gl/YQCP5I
91 Inter Parliamentary Union, op. cit: www.ipu.org/parline-e/reports/2151.htm
92 Ali Mamouri, 'Will secular parties gain upper hand in Iraq?' Monitor-2/5/2016: https://goo.gl/I4bJIy
93 Umaymah Al-Omar, 'Mashhadani: "I was not forced to resign" ', Naqash-20/2/2009: www.niqash.org/en/articles/politics/2391/
94 Przeworski (1991) op. cit. p. 33
95 Election Guide, op. cit. www.electionguide.org/elections/id/2425/
96 Hamid Alkifaey, *Independent*, 19/9/2002: https://goo.gl/hwclfs
97 Hamid Alkifaey, Breaking the silence, *Guardian*, 14/7/2003: https://goo.gl/qZG3Rh
98 Sami Zubaida, Open Democracy, 18/11/2005: https://goo.gl/Y2RrnL
99 Interview with Sami Al-Askari
100 Norman Cigar, US Army War College Press, February 2015, p. 14: https://goo.gl/sKGmao

2 Methodology

Why case study?

I have chosen the method of 'case study' for my research on democratization in Iraq for several reasons, easiness not among them, since using case studies for research purposes remains one of the most challenging of all social science endeavours.[1] The method is used by many researchers, academics and institutions alike in order to 'contribute to our knowledge of individual, group, organizational, social, political, and related phenomena'.[2] Case study research is used in all fields of life, and it has been a common strategy in philosophy, sociology, political science and social work.[3]

It arises out of a desire to understand complex social phenomena and allows the investigator to retain the holistic and meaningful characteristics of real-life events.[4] Since the issue I am studying has many 'why' and 'how' questions, and since it's a contemporary phenomenon, and because I, the investigator, have no control over events, case study was the preferred strategy to conduct my research.[5]

Information was gathered from many sources, such as social, political and economic theories, and experiences of other countries that democratized in the second half of the twentieth century. Other sources included interviews with experts and current and past Iraqi politicians, both secular and Islamist, in government and opposition. It also compares democratic practices as they are developing in Iraq with the basic principles of democracy, as it exists in established democracies.

In social sciences, it's essential to use a methodological framework to investigate a phenomenon such as democratization. Methods vary between qualitative and quantitative research. Some researchers mix between them to achieve their targets. The two may be different, but they can be used to complement each other.

I have decided to regard democracy in Iraq as a 'dichotomous' variable, not a continuous one, due to the nature of the change in 2003, which was very sudden, and also the repressive nature of the regime that preceded democratization.[6] No civil, political or economic societies existed in Iraq under Saddam, no independent think tanks or study centres whose information the researcher can trust. That's why I needed to test every piece of information for accuracy.

I embarked on trying to find out whether the Iraqi democratic experiment has faltered. If yes, why has it, and what are the reasons or circumstances that led to its failure. The way ahead was to look at documentary evidence and conduct interviews.

I needed to know if certain historical events have actually influenced current ones. Some historical events are distant and there are no living people to ask about them. So, when dealing with the 'dead past', I needed to consult memoirs and books by former politicians or academics, newspapers and journal articles. At one point, I wanted to interview a living minister from the monarchy era, Abdul-Kareem Al-Uzri. He was in his nineties, but his family said he was not in a position to be interviewed. Instead they gave me his book, which proved to be useful.[7]

Interviews

Qualitative research emphasizes the need for primary or naturally occurring data, and interviews and documents are major sources. Jennifer Mason argues that interviews are among 'the most commonly recognized forms of qualitative research'.[8] It has a strong claim to being probably 'the most widely used method in qualitative research'.[9] For Catherine Dawson, there are three types of interviews: 'unstructured, semi-structured and structured'.[10]

In this study, most interviews were in-depth because it would be much easier to analyse and interpret the discourse of interviewees' answers. In-depth interviews focus on open-ended questions, which provide opportunities for both the interviewer and interviewee to discuss certain topics in detail. Different people make different observations regarding the same event while some notice things that others don't. I have conducted 50 interviews; some were face-to-face conversations, while others were via email.

I have interviewed people whom I thought were relevant to the process of democratization. They were senior politicians, experts, clerics, writers or informed observers.

Literature review is a means to an end. Researchers and investigators review previous research in order to develop sharper and more insightful questions about the topic. This is what I have done throughout this research. As I read more literature on the subject, I needed to conduct more interviews and ask different and better-targeted questions.

I have only taken relevant points. Answers that have no basis or defy established facts are not accepted and interviewees are challenged about them until they provide evidence; otherwise, their replies won't be used in the research.

Although this study is about Iraq, the same findings can be generalized to other countries where circumstances are similar. I have found many similarities between the regimes of Ceausescu and Saddam. It's worth mentioning the Romanian democratization was the least consolidated among eastern Europeans.[11] There is a lesson here for Iraq. There are also similarities with Spain regarding irredentist movements and extremist groups hostile to democracy, such as Fuerza Nueva, which Spain dealt with through inclusion and democracy by letting the people decide its fate.

There is also a lesson in the failed parliamentary democracy established by Britain in 1921. It's relevant to the current democratic process, which came about through similar circumstances. I went through the recent history of Iraq, exploring the interaction of sectarian politics, and also the background of Islamic doctrines of Islamist parties, in order to put their policies in context.[12]

Although I was an insider, I made sure I had taken all the relevant information and views to my research, checking their accuracy and authenticity in the process. Because there is a need for 'time boundaries to define the beginning and end of the case', I confined my research to the period 2003–2014.[13]

However, I have looked beyond those dates since I needed to go back to explore sectarian practices and irredentist tendencies since the establishment of the Iraqi state, examining in the process the characteristics of the regime of Saddam Hussein. I also explored the policies of Islamist parties regarding freedom and their treatment of women and how they acted after consolidating their power.

The Iraqi Shia are conscious of the fact they lost out in 1921, because of the intransigence of their leaders then. Current leaders are determined this time round not to repeat that mistake. Therefore, I needed to study these events whenever they happened and include them within the design of my research.

The study design embodies democratic and liberal theories, common institutions of democracy, economic, civil and political societies, which are necessary for democracy, the role of religion in politics, especially political Islam and the religious basis it stands on. As the research developed, more impediments to democratization in Iraq emerged. Many of these difficulties are similar to what other countries have encountered, so there are parallels.

I've avoided giving myself the role of 'theoretician'.[14] I didn't think it's useful to elaborate on democratic theory beyond stating the basics. I have reviewed several works, which are relevant to the study of democratization and referred to them throughout the book. They have enriched the information I have gathered through fieldwork and elite interviews.

I've developed my own theoretical framework, using the information I collected from various sources, which I've referred to throughout.

Because the 'Arab Spring' brought demands for democracy in Arab countries, the Iraqi case could prove to be a sample of what might happen in the region if democratization is to take place there. In fact, when one listens to discussions in Arab countries such as Tunisia, Libya, Egypt, Yemen and Syria, discussants always refer to Iraq. In both Tunisia and Libya, a law similar to 'de-Ba'athification', called 'political isolation', was adopted. It was dropped in Tunisia[15] but kept in Libya. Tunisian Islamist leader, Rached El-Ghannouchi, said his party voted against political exclusion because of what happened in Iraq.[16]

I benefited from being a participant in the Iraqi political process, as a spokesman for the Governing Council, and as leader of the Movement for Democratic Society, which participated in the first two elections. I knew most politicians, officials, journalists, writers and observers.

As a researcher, I was looking for the truth. I needed credible and new information and was never trapped in any ideology or preconceived ideas, so I had a clear inquiring mind when I collected data.[17]

As Yin stated, very few case studies end up as they started.[18] You might start looking for one thing, but you end up finding another. I was not surprised to find new information. As the research progressed, new questions presented themselves, which prompted me to go back to searching for information and conducting new interviews.

An investigator is like a detective. He arrives after the crime has occurred and has to make inferences about what has actually happened.[19] In my case I was 'at the scene of the crime if not a culprit'!

Throughout the research, I made sure that my interviewees came from different backgrounds – politically, ethnically, culturally and educationally. This was important in order to have a full and accurate picture of the whole situation. I also had experts on economics, oil, sociology, elections, Kurdish issues, law, religion and the constitution.

Selecting the candidates for the research was not easy, although I had a wide range of choices, but this complicated, rather than simplified, my task. I chose those who had played important roles, knew what had happened and had relatively informed and unbiased opinions.

Reports have to be checked for accuracy since inaccuracy is not so uncommon. Relying on information provided by the media or even think tanks is not always wise. One report by US Army War College quoted Iraqi VP Ayad Allawi as saying there were 250,000 volunteers in the Popular Mobilization Unit (PMU) or Hashd.[20] The source was the Al-Siyasa newspaper. When I checked the source in Arabic, I found out the newspaper had never quoted Allawi, but an unknown person in his party![21] If an organization such as the US Army War College could make such an inaccuracy, media outlets could do it easily.

Even foreign media could not distinguish accurate from inaccurate information. On 17 July 2004, an Australian television report and the Herald newspaper claimed interim PM Ayad Allawi executed insurgents personally just days after he took office and the Interior Minister 'congratulated' him![22] This was not believable even in an Iraqi context that's rife with rumours; there is a tendency to exaggerate or even make up stories and portray opinions as facts.

With such an environment of widespread rumours, claims and counterclaims, there was a need for a focused and knowledgeable investigator attentive to details and committed to producing accurate information and sound evidence.

I chose a structure that builds up the argument so that at conclusion, I would have gone through all the collected data and evidence. As Yin describes:

> The sequence of chapters will follow some theory building logic which will depend on the specific topic and theory but each chapter should reveal a new part of the theoretical argument made. If structured well, the entire sequence can produce a compelling argument. It's relevant to both explanatory and exploratory case studies.[23]

In consulting political memoirs, both written and recorded, I have found that politician-authors, in Iraq and the larger Arab world, aspire not only to record facts and provide personal accounts but also to vindicate their political positions and stances during their political careers. This may not be peculiar to Iraq, but admissions of error or guilt and self-critical writings are still rare.

I felt there was a need to interview sociologists who could analyse the cultural and psychological status of Iraqi society and what they think is needed for democratization to succeed and what should be implemented for this purpose.

The prominent sociologist, Ibrahim Al-Haidari, is also an expert on German issues since he lived and studied in Germany and translated important works of German writers such as Habermas. I wanted to know whether the process of de-Ba'athification was comparable with de-nazification. This has helped me understand that de-Ba'athification was not necessary in Iraq and there was no need to emulate the German experience as circumstances, culture and geopolitics were totally different.

I have come to the conclusion that the false spirit of 'political religiosity' prevalent in Iraqi politics will deepen sectarian identities and undermine Iraq's national identity; an important factor for democratic consolidation. Religiosity is 'not a condition for integrity or efficiency' as Sharwan Al-Waeli told me.

Although interviews provided important information, I didn't rely on them alone. Any new evidence has to be corroborated by information available in textbooks and evidence from the experience of other countries as well as my own observations and ethnographic evidence I arrived at via interviews. Any information not supported by clear evidence was not accepted.

Notes

1 Robert Yin, *Case Study Research. Design and Methods*, Sage, London (2003) p. 1
2 Ibid., p. 1
3 J.F. Gilgum (1994) 'A case for case studies in social work research', *Social Work*, 39, pp. 371–380 [Yin. (2003) op. cit. p. 1]
4 Yin. (2003) op. cit. p. 2
5 Ibid., p. 1
6 Samuel Huntington, *Third Wave*, University of Oklahoma Press (1991) p. 11
7 Abdul-Kareem Al-Uzri, *The Problem of Governance in Iraq*, self-published (1991) (Arabic)
8 Jennifer Mason, *Qualitative Researching*, Sage (2002) p. 39
9 Jane Ritchie and Jane Lewis, *Qualitative Research Practice: A Guide for Social Science Students and Researcher*, Sage, London (2003) p. 36
10 Catherine Dawson, *Introduction to Research Methods: A Practical Guide for Anyone Undertaking a Research Project*, How To Books, Oxford. (2002) p. 27
11 Juan Linz and Alfred Stepan, *Problems of Democratic Transition and Consolidation*, Johns Hopkins University Press (1996) p. 364
12 Yin (2003) op. cit. p. 13
13 Ibid. p. 26
14 Ibid. p. 29
15 Amal Musa, Al-Sharq Al-Awsat, 12/5/2014: https://goo.gl/2ULOLf
16 USIP, 28/10/2015: www.youtube.com/watch?v=oh5iONtbUv8

17 Yin (2003) op. cit. p. 59
18 Ibid. p. 60
19 Ibid. p. 61
20 Norman Cidar, US Army War College (June 2015) op. cit. p. 7 (the quoted source is in footnote 10, p. 71): www.strategicstudiesinstitute.army.mil/pdffiles/PUB1272.pdf
21 Al-siyasa Newspaper, 4/1/2015: https://goo.gl/BzoU71
22 *Sunday Morning Herald*, 17/7/2004. www.smh.com.au/articles/2004/07/16/10896945 68757.html
23 Yin (2003) op. cit. p. 154

3   Liberty and democracy

Liberty

Liberty is one of the important bases for democracy. The work of John Stuart Mill in this regard is emphasized here because he set out the basic tenets of modern liberalism, building on the work of his father, James Mill, and the philosopher, Jeremy Bentham, to explore the building of a modern liberal democratic state. This is something to which parts of Iraq aspire and others clearly do not. Mill is famous in the Arab world and highly regarded by intellectuals and learned individuals in Iraq. Although his ideas were expressed in the early nineteenth century, they are still as relevant in the early twenty-first century for the purpose of this book. Indeed, they supply something of a benchmark against which Iraq may be measured.

Mill defines liberty as the protection against the tyranny of political rulers, where he puts the rulers in 'a necessarily antagonistic position to the people they ruled'.[1] He expressed liberty in terms of the limitation of the power of the rulers. 'The aim of the patriots was to set limits to the power which the ruler should be suffered to exercise over the community and this limitation is what they called liberty'.[2] Limiting the ruler's power is done in two ways. First via 'a recognition of certain immunities called political liberties or rights'. If the ruler infringed on these rights, specific resistance or general rebellion was held to be justifiable. Second, through 'the establishment of constitutional checks' by consent of the community or those who represent its interests.[3]

The implication here runs against a dominant view that the interests of the rulers are 'habitually opposed to those of the people'. But under democracy, the dynamic has changed. The rulers should now be 'identified with the people and their interests and will should be the interests and will of the people'.[4] This is so because rulers are now elected by the people to represent the popular will rather than imposed through coercion.

Mill defines 'the will of the people' as meaning 'the will of the most numerous of the most active part of the people; the majority or those who succeeded in making themselves accepted as the majority'. This majority may desire to 'oppress a part of their number' which necessitates precautions against this trend to prevent the abuse of majoritarian power.[5] This is what Mill calls 'the tyranny of the majority'; something he regarded as an 'evil' which society needs to guard against.[6]

One of the least understood tenets of democracy in Iraq is the nature of rights in a democratic system. The dominant understanding, promoted by the political class, emphasizes group rights rather than individual rights. In this context, groups are understood as primordial and fixed identities into whose membership all Iraqis have to belong in order to be represented and 'enjoy' their rights as part of the group.

Women, for example, are treated as a group, not individuals. Muslims are also treated as a group with no variations among them. Politicians always talk about Muslim or Shia majority, dismissing individuality altogether. The Islamic Fadheela Party (IFP), sought in 2014 to legislate for a Shia personal status law whereby nine-year-old girls would be eligible to marry.[7] The bill was passed by the council of ministers and it could become law if parliament approved it, something that didn't happen. On 24 October 2016, parliament passed a law to ban alcohol in the whole of Iraq on the basis of the 'Muslims majority'.[8] Mahmoud Al-Hassan, the head of the parliamentary legal committee, announced after the adoption of the law that 'anyone who objects to this law is indirectly objecting to God's law and he will be prosecuted'.[9] Islamist rule is basically the tyranny of the majority.

Tolerance with 'tacit reserves'

Liberty, as a socio-political right in any functioning democracy, is often challenged by religious beliefs asserting absolutist, universalist messages. This challenge commonly translates into intolerance toward non-religious lifestyles or ideas. Mill correctly argues that intolerance about the things that people care about is 'so natural' to mankind and thus, religious freedom has hardly existed anywhere. He argues that tolerance in the minds of religious persons always comes with 'tacit reserves' even in the most tolerant of countries.[10]

Intolerance is widespread in Iraqi religious society, with some zealots taking the law into their hands at times of weak state control.[11] What fuels this religious zeal is the moralist, truth-possessing nature of both political Islam and mainstream religious beliefs in Iraq, both Sunni and Shia. The public expressions of those beliefs are also partially contradictory because of the Shia-Sunni doctrinal differences, something that causes violence and discord among people. Indeed, the emergence of Sunni and Shia doctrines in Islam is associated with the disputes dating back 1400 years, and any expression of such beliefs invokes those old differences between the two sects. This is not conducive to public peace or order.

One example of those differences is the Husseini rituals, commemorating the tragic death of Hussein, the third Shia Imam, in Karbala in 680. Although these rituals have been part of the Iraqi culture for a long time, practiced by Shia, but also accepted by Sunnis, they come to acquire a divisive political meaning post-2003, away from the agreed-upon, communal socio-religious meaning of sorrow and solidarity in the past. In the new Iraq, these rituals point to the political dominance of the Shia as previously oppressed majority (by the Sunni minority) who come now to assert their 'rightful control' over the state and the society.

One manifestation of this control is the official mainstreaming of these rituals as a sign of Iraqism whereby the state officially promotes them, expecting its Sunni citizens to do the same. This removes these rituals from the realm of society and faith, as they have been historically, bringing them into that of politics and the state in post-2003 Iraq. This problematic approach has sown division and distrust among Iraqis based on their sectarian affiliation. Any criticism of these politicized rituals nowadays is seen as a criticism of Shiaism as a religious creed, a deliberate offense to the entire group of Shia, and an encroachment on the liberty of a group.

In the founding literature on democracy the state or society is only warranted to interfere with individuals' liberty when there is a need for self-protection. This is the position that Mill asserts 'the only purpose for which power can be rightfully exercised over any member of the civilized community against his will is to prevent harm to others'.[12] Additionally, the individual is 'sovereign' over himself, his own body and mind except those who are 'in a waste to require being taken care of by others (who) must be protected against their own actions as well as against external injury'.[13] Constraining the individual by the interest of others entails other benefits to society, as it will entice him/her to do other services to society which he/she can benefit from such as contributing to a common good like defence or any other common interest of society.

Human liberty must consist of liberty of consciousness in all its manifestations (liberty of thought and feeling and absolute freedom of opinion and sentiment on all subjects). As for the liberty of expressing and publishing opinion, it falls under another principle since it's connected to others, but it's no less important than the freedom of thought. It also consists of liberty of taste and pursuit, planning our life to suit our own character, doing what we like without impediment from others provided we are not causing any harm to them.

Then comes the collective freedoms which include the freedom to unite for any purpose not involving harm to others and the persons uniting are of full age and not forced or deceived. These liberties are so important to society that 'no society, in which these liberties are not, on the whole, respected, is free … and none is completely free in which they do not exist absolute and unqualified'. Mill continues stating that 'the only freedom which deserves the name is that of pursuing our own good in our own way, so long as we do not attempt to deprive others of theirs, or impede their efforts to obtain it'.[14] 'Mankind are greater gainers by suffering each other to live as seems good to themselves, than by compelling each other as seems good to the rest', Mill contends.

Unfortunately, many Muslim believers disagree with this principle. They believe it's their heavenly duty to stop others from doing what they consider 'vice' under the principle of 'Promotion of virtue and Prevention of Vice'. In some Muslim countries, there is religious police whose duty is to compel people to behave in a certain way.[15]

Sharia law limits individuals' freedoms in many ways. This unitary and truth-possessing mentality fuels the desire to interfere with people's personal lives in order to 'correct' them by making them virtuous, standard practices in Saudi

Arabia and Iran. These practices are now on the rise in Iraq after 2003. Although there are no laws to support this interference in Iraq, unlike the cases of Iran and Saudi Arabia where this interference is mandated by law, the emerging religious piety among many Iraqis made such interferences culturally acceptable, if not tacitly encouraged by Islamist parties at the helm of power. This only highlights the importance of separating the state from religion in the troubled nascent Iraqi democracy.

Mill interprets the separation of religion and politics as 'placing the direction of men's consciences in other hands than those which controlled their worldly affairs'.[16] It's in the nature of human beings, according to Mill, to impose their opinions on others, and there is no difference between rulers and ordinary people in this tendency.[17]

Since Islamists came to power, women have been under increasing pressure to wear the Islamic head scarf (hijab) and there are hardly any women not wearing it outside Baghdad. Even in Baghdad, the number of women who are not wearing hijab is decreasing. Some ministries which are managed by Islamists have issued guidelines for women on how to dress.[18] Signs have been placed in road junctions and on front walls of institutions to tell women to wear hijab. Some signs have even asked Christian women to wear hijab![19]

Freedom of expression

Not many doubt the importance of the freedom of the press to expose corruption and prevent despotism. In fact, Mill rules out the need to defend 'the liberty of the press' since it's one of the essential 'securities' against tyranny and corruption.[20] Any government that attempts to control the expression of opinion 'will make itself the organ of general intolerance of the public'.[21]

However, this may be the case in Western countries, but not in Iraq, where the freedom of the press is in constant danger. It is still threatened due to the existence of armed groups as well as the lack of belief in democracy among ruling parties.

Mill regards the freedom of expression as sacrosanct:

> If all mankind minus one were of one opinion, and only one person were of the contrary opinion, mankind would be no more justified in silencing that one person, than he, if he had the power, would be justified in silencing mankind.[22]

Silencing the expression of an opinion is 'robbing the human race, posterity as well as the existing generation, those who dissent from the opinion more than those who hold it' because

> if the opinion is right, they are deprived of the opportunity of exchanging error for truth: if wrong, they lose what is almost as great a benefit, the clearer perception and livelier impression of truth produced by its collision with error.[23]

He continues; 'we can never be sure that the opinion we are endeavouring to stifle is a false opinion, and if we were sure, stifling it would be an evil still'.[24] This is because those who try to suppress the opinion have no authority to decide the question for mankind while excluding all others from the means of judging it. By opting to decide the idea was wrong, they are assuming they are infallible.

In theory, Mill argues, we all agree we are fallible. In practice, we do not take the necessary precautions against our fallibility. Absolute princes or rulers are accustomed to unlimited deference. They feel so confident in their opinions on nearly all subjects.[25]

Mill laments those who are comfortable with the belief that they are right even though it was mere accident that made them what they are. They could have embraced other religions or creeds had they been born in different cultures: 'The same causes which made (a person) a churchman in London would have made him a Buddhist or a Confucian in Peking'.[26]

This is a fact that is absent from the thinking of religious people with missionary zeal in general. In Iraq, members of a family who were brought up in Anbar or Tikrit are Sunnis, while their cousins who live in Karbala or Samawa are Shia. Shia tribes in southern Iraq are members of the great Sunni clans and confederations in the Arabian Peninsula.[27] But they follow different religious doctrines due to living under different circumstances.

Mill acknowledges opinions do change over ages and the ones that one age regards as valid, other ages consider absurd. This will go on and our ideas now won't be suitable for future generations. That's why if we do not act on our opinions just because they might be wrong, we will never be able to perform our duties or care for our interests.[28]

Governments and individuals must, therefore, 'form the truest opinion they can, form them carefully and never impose them upon others unless they are quite sure of being right'. But once they are sure, it would be cowardice, not conscientiousness, to shrink from acting on their opinion. He acknowledges that it's difficult to reach an absolute certainty on anything, thus 'men and governments must act to the best of their ability'.[29]

The main point here is that opinions must not be imposed on others unless there is a high degree of certainty about their correctness and this is not always possible. Also, opinions do change over time, and what was correct in the past may not be correct now. But Islamic fundamentalists treat all opinions of imams and caliphs as sacred, and hence you cannot discuss or argue against them, and this is a real problem for modern Muslim states in general and for democracy in particular.

The Shia faithful believe in the principle of infallibility of the Prophet and the Twelve Imams; their sayings and traditions are taken without any discussion or objection because the 'imams are infallible'.[30] Devout Shia travel to holy places on foot, instead of using cars or other modern means of transport.[31] This causes disruption across the country, from road closures, government and other business stoppages, to the loss of many work days several times every year. They visit shrines on foot because they are emulating imams and other revered leaders and pious persons who did it in the past. They are also following a religious principle which says, 'the greater the hardship, the greater the reward'![32] This means the more hardship they endure during their pilgrimage, the more reward they will get in Heaven.

What is noteworthy here is the widespread promotion of these rituals through religious propaganda in an attempt to make them a norm of Iraq's national life. It's quite dangerous to engage in any kind of public discussion in Iraq where one can criticize the continuous promotion of these rituals. An opinion like this falls outside legitimate difference in Iraq; it can cost a person his or her life. Practically speaking, discussing these rituals in a critical way does not fall within a person's democratic rights.

According to Mill,

> we may, and must, assume our opinions to be true for the guidance of our conduct and it is assuming no more when we forbid bad men to pervert society by the propagation of opinion which we regard as false and pernicious.[33]

Persecution of opinion is deemed harmful to society. Some believe persecution cannot harm the truth since it will serve to promote it. But this is not always the case. In his attempt to refute such a claim, Mill catalogues the number of ideas and people who disappeared due to persecution. 'History teems with instances of truths put down by persecution. If not suppressed forever, it may be thrown back for centuries'.[34] The Reformation broke out at least 20 times and was put down before the triumph of Martin Luther. Mill's conclusion is that persecution has often succeeded, and the survival of the heretics is because they were too strong a party to defeat.

This actually explains why secularism has not succeeded in the Muslim world so far. It's the persecution of all new ideas that lack religious backing. There are many examples of successful persecution of ideas and groups in Islamic history where reform movements were put down or eradicated completely. One such movement was 'Akhwan-al-safa' (the Brothers of Tranquility) which appeared in Basra around the end of the tenth century and remained secret until it disappeared due to persecution.[35] In modern times, many irreligious ideas or groups appeared but didn't last due to persecution.

A Marxist study group by the name of Mutadarisi al-Afkār al-Ḥurrah or 'Free Ideas Contemplators', began publishing a paper called al-Ṣaḥifah but it was quickly closed down by the authorities because it contained attacks on religion. A political party by the name 'Free Non-religious Party' (al-Ḥizb al-Ḥurr al-Lādīnī) also disappeared because it was vociferous in criticizing religion.[36] Communism, which is perceived to be hostile to religion, only prospered at times when religious forces were weak during the 1950s and 1960s.[37]

In the 1960s, Shia religious leader, Ayatullah Muhsin Al-Hakim, issued a fatwa attacking communism and saying it was 'incompatible with Islam'.[38] This fatwa had adversely affected the communists in Iraq, where previously their ideas were embraced by the Shia youth. The Islamic Party (mainly Sunni) also issued a memorandum blaming PM Abdulkarim Qassim for 'sponsoring' communism.[39] 'Islam began to attract lay Shia in great numbers encroaching on communist influence'.[40] When religion was revived after the establishment of Islamist parties, all secular ideas and groups were suppressed or marginalized.

Resuscitating past evils

Mill acknowledges that people with different opinions are not put to death anymore. 'We are not like our fathers who slew the prophets'.[41] Although this maybe the case in some countries in Europe or North America, in various parts of the world, including Iraq, people are still punished by death if they express ideas critical of the prevalent religious beliefs. If they don't get executed, they get assassinated. Many people were assassinated in Iraq simply because they expressed opinions regarded as dangerous by others.[42] This is even worse than executing opponents, since assassination is done secretly and no one knows the reasons or who is behind it. People can only guess. Whereas execution follows a trial during which people come to know the reasons leading to the case, which would serve to highlight the cause. In Sudan, scholar Mahmoud Muhammad Taha was tried and executed in 1985 for demanding an end to Sharia law. Even though his trial lasted only two hours, his name and cause have remained on people's minds.[43] Those assassinated in Iraq, intellectuals and scholars though they were, have been forgotten.

The death penalty still exists in Iraq. Although there have been no overtly political executions since 2003, there is no guarantee that this wouldn't become common in the future when Islamists' power is entrenched and more laws are enacted to criminalize certain practices such as trading in alcohol. Judicial proceedings also lack transparency, and information is sometimes extracted under duress.[44]

Mill warns of attempts to 'resuscitate past evils' which disturb the 'quiet surface of routine'.[45] He warns of the revival of religion and compares it with bigotry in the uncultivated mind that could 'provoke (people) into actively persecuting those whom they have never ceased to think proper objects of persecution'.[46] This, he contends, 'makes this country not a place for mental freedom'.

The revival of religion has proven a huge impediment to democracy and indeed to the progress and stability of the country as a whole, since it caused civil and sectarian wars between different sections of society and increased tension between Sunnis, Shia and Christians, many of whom had to immigrate within the country or abroad. This is in addition to the restrictions imposed on general freedom and civil life in the country, which is discussed in detail in Chapter 7.

Contesting received opinion should be welcomed by any society because those who contest it are doing something that the believers themselves should be doing. Mill even calls upon people to thank those who contest the prevalent opinion, if they really appreciate being sure about their beliefs and views. In fact, he believes that we should 'rejoice that there is someone to do for us what we otherwise ought to do … with much greater labour ourselves'.[47]

Diversity of opinion can only be advantageous for all times, 'until mankind shall have entered a stage of intellectual advancement which at present seems at an incalculable distance'.[48] Opinions do not have to be true or false. Conflicting doctrines could share the truth among them and 'non-conforming opinion is needed to supply the remainder of the truth of which the received doctrine embodies only a part'.[49]

Different arguments are needed for a healthy state of political life, but they must be political arguments which can be debated and criticized, not sacred views that must be accepted as they are as is the case with religious views. Debate is important for political issues, where compromises and adjustments can be made, but you cannot compromise on religious or doctrinal principles or issues. When politics and religion are intermingled, as they are in Iraq now, this is what happens.

According to Mill, there are usually two parties, one of order or stability and another of progress or reform.[50] The two parties will compete 'until one or the other enlarges its grasp as to be the party of stability or progress, knowing and distinguishing what's fit to be preserved from what ought to be swept away'.[51]

Collision of opinions

Mill argues that fair play of all sides to the truth can only exist through diversity of opinion.[52] Through debate people can arrive at the truth. Although an advocate of freedom, Mill doesn't hesitate to announce that 'unlimited use of freedom' would not necessarily put an end to the 'the evils of religious or philosophical sectarianism' because 'men of narrow capacity' will always act as their truth is the only one.[53] Mill describes religious sectarianism as 'evil'.

I argue that sectarianism is deleterious to the interest of any state or society and it has impeded democracy and progress in Iraq while it protected corruption, inefficiency, nepotism and inefficacy. In one instance, the Integrity Commission announced that the head of the Hajj and Umra Commission, a prominent Shia cleric, had committed many legal violations and financial irregularities, including obtaining degrees through irregular means for himself and his two sons whom he appointed in the commission, yet he remained in his position after a short period of suspension. He was protected by the sectarian quota system. The standing of his party (SIIC) was enhanced in the subsequent elections in 2014 and increased its seats by 14.[54] This corruption didn't deter a prominent religious leader from issuing a 'fatwa' in favour of Supreme Islamic Iraqi Council (SIIC) three days before the election.[55]

The tendency of all opinions to become sectarian, Mill contends, is not cured by the freest of discussion. On the contrary this could often heighten and exacerbate it. In spite of this, the collision of opinion still has a salutary effect, 'not on the impassioned partisan, but on the calmer and more disinterested bystander'.[56] Mill recognizes that freedom of opinion and discussion as necessary to the mental well-being of mankind on four grounds; they are:

1   If an opinion is compelled to silence, it may be true, and to deny it, we assume our own infallibility.
2   The silenced opinion may be an error, but it may contain a portion of truth and it's only by collision of adverse opinions that the remainder of the truth has any chance of being supplied.
3   If the received opinion is the whole truth, but if doesn't suffer any vigorous contest, it will be held as a prejudice.
4   The meaning of the doctrine itself will be in danger of being lost or enfeebled and deprived of its vital effect on the character and conduct: the dogma becomes a mere formal profession, inefficacious for good but cumbering the ground and preventing the growth of real heart-felt conviction, from reason or personal experience.[57]

Individuality is linked to freedom of people to express their opinions as they wish. But Mill distinguishes between freedom of action and freedom of thought. But opinions lose their immunity when they are expressed in certain circumstances which may lead to mischief. Mill explains how the same opinion could be received differently under different circumstances. For example, an opinion that

> corn-dealers are starvers of the poor or private property is robbery, ought to be unmolested when circulated in through the press, but may justly incur punishment when delivered orally to an excited mob assembled before the house of a corn-dealer.[58]

Hence, liberty of the individual can be limited when his words may reasonably pose a danger to other people's lives as in the cases of potential incitement to violence or molestation that Mill correctly alludes to. Freedom must be associated with respect for the law of the land, even if the law is not acceptable to certain sections of society.

Lesson for Iraq

The progressively gradual adoption of democratic principles that emphasize peaceful coexistence among European nations was due to their cultural diversity. 'Individuals, classes, nations, have been extremely unlike one another; they have struck out a great variety of paths, each leading to something valuable'.[59] There is a lesson for Iraqis there. Iraq is made up of diverse communities and cultures, but it has suffered over the years from waves of Bedouin immigrants whose despotic, violence-glorifying values came to dominate its diverse society.[60]

The Iraqi state has often been captured by 'distinct groups of Iraqis' who have not been able to 'ensure that the multiple histories of the Iraqi people are subsumed into single narrative of state power'.[61] This inability to accommodate the multiple Iraqi histories into a larger national narrative has translated into the coercive dominance of one history over other histories, henceforth paving the way for conflict, many times violent, between defenders of different histories. As a result the Iraqi state has been characterized by violence.[62] The era of Saddam Hussein was perhaps the most repressive and violent Iraq has ever seen in recent times. His 24 years in power were characterized by 'murder, plunder and terror'.[63]

Wilhelm von Humboldt contends there are two necessary conditions for human development: 'freedom and variety of situations. These render people unlike one another'.[64] Iraq is diverse, not only socially, racially and religiously, but also geographically; therefore, people are bound to be different in their cultures and attitudes. Not only is diversity a given, it is also beneficial and comes as a result of social and economic development where people go through a 'variety of situations'.

Since society affords individuals protection, they owe it a return for this benefit. Part of it is to abide by certain rules and observe a certain code of conduct towards the rest.[65] An individual who doesn't conform to society's norms doesn't have to be punished by law, but by opinion. As soon as a person's conduct begins to negatively affect the legitimate interests of others, society has the jurisdiction to stop him. For example, drinking alcohol in Iraq is not socially approved but has never been legally banned. People who drink know there is a social cost to be incurred. Alcohol has been banned by an act of parliament passed on 22 October 2016. The ban caused a public outcry, but Islamists' position on the ban didn't move an inch.[66]

Alcohol-drinking by others has not affected the lives of the religious since drinking takes place usually in exclusive clubs or in the confines of people's homes. So, it's not the type of activity that causes any inconvenience to society, but rather, it is the ideological difference that the Islamists have with the whole idea of drinking as immoral and anti-religion. There is no public-interest issue involved here, but only a legitimate difference in life-style that has been criminalized by an intolerant political elite. Mill suggests that even when there are types of conduct by the individuals that cause injury to society, 'society can afford to bear for the sake of the greater good of human freedom'.[67] Such conduct must not violate specific duty to the public nor occasion perceptible hurt to any particular person except the individual himself. Society must not interfere with purely personal conduct, since when it does, 'the odds are that it interferes wrongly and in the wrong place'.[68]

On matters of social morality, the majority must not impose a law on the minority on the question of self-conduct because 'this is quite as likely to be wrong as right'.[69] Therefore, moral conduct should be left to individuals to determine and the state must not interfere there, but the laws that Islamists have introduced or wish to, restrict individual liberties and assume negative judgements about certain types of personal conduct to the point of judicial criminalization such as the alcohol ban that was legislated recently by the Iraqi Parliament with an overwhelming support by Islamist MPs.

The individual is not accountable to society for his or her actions insofar as these concern the interests of no other person but him or herself. 'Advice, instruction, persuasion, and avoidance by other people if thought necessary by them for their own good, are the only measures by which society can justifiably express its dislike or disapprobation of his conduct'. If the actions of the individual are 'prejudicial to the interests of others, the individual is accountable and maybe subjected to either social or legal punishments if society is of the opinion that one or the other is requisite for its protection'.[70]

Liberty may be legitimately 'infringed upon' for the prevention of crime or accident through the interference of the police. Although the function of the government in taking precautions against crime before it has been committed is undisputed, this function is 'far more liable to be abused to the prejudice of liberty than the punitory function'.[71]

Public education is another contentious issue. One function of public education in established democracies is to promote and consolidate a common national identity that represents the agreed-upon values among the population. It is one way to help construct citizenship and promote a 'patriotic' affiliation with the land through a certain inclusive and representative understanding of its history. This is about building some consensus about national meaning. In Iraq, public education does exactly the opposite, as it fractures any possibility of consensus in this regard. This is especially so because history is linked to religion, both of which are divisive in Iraq.

The Shia, for example, regard the Umayyads as 'usurpers responsible for the killing of Shia imams' while Sunnis have a favourable view of them.[72] The Shia also believe the first three caliphs had no right to succeed the Prophet and the rightful caliph was Ali, while Sunnis revere them, hold them in high esteem and believe they were the rightful successors.[73] The two sects have recorded Islamic history in two completely different ways, and one of their main differences is how the political leadership was chosen after the Prophet's death. Teaching religion would also be a problem since there are different interpretations and applications of the Qura'an and Sunna.

Therefore, all contentious issues of history and religion need to be avoided, not only in school syllabi, but also in public debate, since they are likely to cause discord and violence. Liberal democracy needs to be the basis for the democratic system in Iraq so that it can be inclusive and unifying. Civil liberties have got to be sacrosanct. As we will see in Chapter 5, the conception of justice has to be 'free standing' and also not in conflict with any major doctrine as per John Rawls' theory. It must be recognized and shared by all the citizens.

Liberalization

Liberalization is the removal, fully or partially, of restrictions on general freedoms accompanied by strengthening the rule of law and the emergence of civil, political and economic societies. This usually precedes democratization, especially in authoritarian regimes, and it usually facilitates the process of democratization and reduces the time required for its consolidation. But it has different effects in different countries. According to Samuel Huntington, liberalization in

Islamic countries 'enhanced the power of social and political movements whose commitment to democracy is questionable'.[74] This has actually happened in Iraq and elections brought Islamist parties to power who treat democracy with contempt and only want to use the 'democratic mechanism' and confuse democracy with shura.

Dictatorships cannot tolerate independent organizations because they fear any collective action, but not all dictatorships are the same. Adam Przeworski states, 'What is threatening to authoritarian regimes is not the breakdown of legitimacy, but the organization of counter hegemony, collective projects for the future'.[75] Political choice becomes available only when there are collective alternatives. Despite this, authoritarian regimes do lessen the restriction at some point, as happened in Spain, Chile and Poland. Such a moment signals the loosening of the power of the authoritarian power bloc and suggests to civil society that there is a room for autonomous organization.

This loosening is of two types: from above and from below. The first one happened in Hungary as a result of division in the leadership. Communist leader, Karoly Grosz, said 'the party was shattered not by its opponents, but – paradoxically – by the leadership'.[76] The other type happened in East Germany. There was no division in the leadership until hundreds of thousands of people occupied the streets of Leipzig. Przeworski sums this up: 'top-down and bottom-up models often compete to explain liberalization'.[77] But he agrees that decisions to liberalize combine elements from both types. Liberalization is a 'result of an interaction between splits in the authoritarian regime and autonomous organization of the civil society'.[78] It's either a popular mobilization signalling to liberalizers in the regime that they have allies among the people that could change the power bloc to their advantage, or visible splits in the power bloc indicate to civil society that there is a space for autonomous organizations. But the logic of liberalization is the same.[79] Przeworski asserts it's 'unstable'. He borrows a term coined by Ilya Ehrenburg, who called it in 1954 a 'thaw' or a 'melting of the iceberg of civil society that overflows the dams of the authoritarian regime'.[80] The first reaction of civil society to the loosening of the repressive apparatus is an outburst of autonomous organizations such as students' associations, trade unions and 'proto-parties'.

After the advent of Gorbachev's Perestroika in 1985, many were encouraged to establish independent organizations, and by 1989, around 60,000 autonomous groups, associations, circles and federations were established 'probing the limits of the political space' as the newspaper Pravda (10/12/1989) called it. The pace of mobilization of civil society varies in different countries 'depending on whether the authoritarian equilibrium rests mainly on lies, fear, or economic prosperity'. 'Once the king is announced naked, the equilibrium is destroyed instantaneously'.[81]

Przeworski explains that 'the crucial factor in breaking individual's isolation is the safety of numbers'.[82] When the Pope visited Poland in 1979, the Poles discovered the strength of the opposition when two million people poured into the streets. In Bulgaria and Romania, first opposition demonstration grew out of organized demonstrations of support for the two regimes. Regimes that are based on 'tacit exchange of material prosperity for passive acquiescence' are vulnerable to economic crises. Przeworski argues the eruption of mass movements, unrest and disorder, constitutes evidence that the policy of liberalization has failed. 'Since liberalization is always intended as a process controlled from above, the emergence of autonomous movements constitutes the proof that liberalization is not, or at least is no longer, a viable project'.[83] In China, student demonstrations forced the liberalizers to retreat and repression increased again. The opposite happened in South Korea where demonstrations strengthened the liberalizers who later became the democratizers.[84]

Finally, liberalizations are either reversed, taking the country back to the old order, or they succeed, in which case they lead to democratization. In Iraq, liberalization measures had taken place at the same time as democratization and this has made it very difficult since there was a political price to pay. Some reforms were not easy to implement such as subsidies for food given through the ration system. The government had to go back on its decision to abolish the ration system in 2012 because there was public outcry. The system is inefficient with wide-spread corruption and distorts private sector activity.[85]

Although Iraq has adopted the free market economic system officially, it's still struggling with the old system where the state is the biggest employer with at least seven million people drawing salaries from the state. Democracy requires a vibrant economy where the private sector plays an important role. This has not yet happened, as we shall see later.

Zeitgeist

As an ancient idea, democracy began in Athens at the 5th century BC; it has become so relevant to our modern world and come to represent a symbol of modernity. Democracy is never overdetermined, but by the 1970s, it became the zeitgeist in most of the world.[86] No one argues against the legitimacy of democracy anymore and people across the world tend to accept the discourse and ideas of democracy. Explicit arguments against democracy as a concept have almost disappeared from public debate in most countries.[87] A UNESCO report noted in 1951 that

> for the first time in the history of the world, no doctrines are advanced as antidemocratic. The accusation of anti-democratic action or attitude is frequently directed against others, but practical politicians and political theorists agree in stressing the democratic element in the institutions they defend and the theories they advocate.[88]

Although the first democratic government was established by the Athenians, its modern usage dates to the revolutionary upheavals in Western societies at the end of the eighteenth century.[89] The first wave of democratizations began after the American and French Revolutions. However, the emergence of democratic institutions is a nineteenth-century phenomenon.[90] Switzerland, France, Great Britain and several other European countries made the transition to democracy before of the turn of the nineteenth century.[91]

The Athenians introduced the concept of a popular government in 507 BC, where the people (*demos*) rule (*kratia*) themselves.[92] But the Roman republics, established in Rome and other cities in ancient Italy, are no less contributors to the current idea of democracy than the Greek city states.[93]

Power to the people

What does democracy mean? It's the ideal of people governing themselves, of giving power to ordinary people to rule themselves rather than being ruled by a tyrant who gives them little or no say in running their affairs.

Democracy, or demokratia, the government of people by the many, poly-archy, rather than the few, oligarchy, or one ruler, monarchy, has become the aspiration of people around the world because it's thought of as a system charac-terized by continuous responsiveness to all its citizens who are considered to be political equals.[94] It may have been first found in Greece, but it could have been invented in other times and places whenever appropriate conditions existed.[95]

But why has this system of popular government been regarded as ideal for countries and nations with different cultures, when it was devised by the Greek noble, Kleisthenes, when he attempted to reform the Athenian constitution over 2500 years ago? It now entails so many things for people aspiring to have a democratic rule. John Dunn puts it eloquently:

> as it travels through time and space, democracy never travels on its own. Increasingly, as the last two centuries have gone by, it has travelled in fine company, alongside freedom, human rights and perhaps now even, at least in pretension, material prosperity.[96]

All reforming political movements in the last 200 years at least claimed to be democratic or sought to establish a 'democratic' system of government. In fact, even communist governments established in the second half of the twentieth century called themselves democratic, when they weren't really. There are no more ideological contestants to democracy as a political system in most of the world, although Juan Linz and Alfred Stepan (1996) make an exception for the 'reinvigorated fundamentalism in Islamic cultural community' that opposes democracy on an ideological basis.[97] This is perhaps why democracy has not prospered in Muslim countries and this is actually what former Iraqi PM, Ayad Allawi, has indicated in this study.[98] Many Iraqi Islamists do not hesitate to declare their rejection of democracy, although they stress their adherence to 'democratic mechanisms'.[99]

Obviously, the democracy designed by Kleisthenes, and established by the Greek leader, Pericles, 2500 years ago, is not the same as the system established when the Americans adopted their constitution in 1776, nor is it the same system the French adopted after their successful revolution in 1789, and it's certainly not what Britain is governed by today nor what Iraqis aspired to establish after 2003. There has been a long process of 'democratization' from ancient Greece and Rome till today. But all these developments have centred around one idea: people's wishes expressed through elections on how to rule themselves.

After this long process, democracy is not only accepted but demanded by political societies across the world. To reject democracy today is to 'write yourself out of politics' sooner or later.[100] Iraqi Islamists for instance have accepted democracy, albeit reluctantly, merely for the fact they know they would otherwise write themselves out of politics. But they have not given up on the hope of establishing an Islamic system that's not fully democratic.

Democracy and elections

With all the talk of democracy being the rule of the people, we still need to define democracy in today's terms. Joseph Schumpeter provides the eighteenth-century classical definition for the democratic method which is 'institutional arrangement for arriving at political decisions which realizes the common good by making the people itself decide issues through the election of individuals who are to assemble in order to carry out its will'.[101] But Schumpeter goes on to criticize this definition as being inaccurate since

> both the will and the good of the people may be, and in many historical examples have been, served just as well or better by governments that cannot be described as democratic according to any accepted usage of the term.[102]

Schumpeter continued to describe in detail the shortcomings of this definition in neglecting how to choose the leadership, incorporate group-wise volitions, or clarify individual freedoms which subsist with democracy. The classical definition makes producing a government a prime function of democracy but there is no clear method of evicting it. While the definition talks about the will of the people, when democracy operates by simple majorities, this is not the will of all the people. The definition also includes electing individuals to produce a government, but for a national government 'this practically amounts to deciding who the leading man should be'.[103] He argues that this is only done in the US democracy.

Schumpeter then reduces democracy to mean 'the people have the opportunity of accepting or refusing the men who rule them', not what was originally intended, which was 'the rule of the people'.[104] But could people choose or refuse their leaders in undemocratic ways? This fact required another criterion to be added to the definition and this is 'through free competition among the would-be leaders for the vote of the electorates'.[105]

Samuel Huntington regards the definition of democracy in terms of elections as minimal. He states that democracy, to some, must have 'sweeping and idealistic connotations'.[106] To them, he argues, 'true democracy' means 'liberté, egalité, fraternité, effective citizen control over policy, responsible government, honesty and openness in politics, informed and rational deliberation, equal participation and power and various other civic values'.[107] Although these are 'good things', as Huntingdon acknowledged, defining democracy in those terms, he argues, 'raises all the problems that come up with the definitions of democracy by source or purpose'. He concludes that 'elections open, free and fair are the essence of democracy, the inescapable sine qua non'.[108]

Requirements for democracy

But how do we define democracy in today's terms? Or can a definition actually sum up everything about democracy? There are necessary political institutions for modern representative democratic governments and these must exist in any democratic country. Robert Dahl describes six political institutions that need to exist for a modern democracy to function.[109] Although different political thinkers have provided different definitions and descriptions, Dahl's description sums up what modern democracy is all about.

1   Elected officials: All decisions and policies in a democratic government have to be taken by officials elected directly by the people, thus modern democratic governments are representative of their people and decisions are taken on people's behalf.
2   Free, fair and frequent elections: Elected officials are chosen in frequent and freely conducted elections in which coercion is comparatively uncommon. So, when a government is elected, it really represents the true wishes of the people. The term of the government must be limited in time so that people can pass their judgements on the performance of their elected representatives after a specific period has passed. If people are happy with them, they will vote for them again so that they continue their good work for the benefit of the country and its people. If not, they will elect others who they think are better placed to serve them and the country at large. Therefore, there is a need for frequent elections in order to keep the rulers in check and punish those who do not do well by replacing them with others.
3   Freedom of expression: Citizens have a right to express themselves without the danger of severe punishment on political matters broadly defined, including criticism of officials, the government, the regime, the socio-economic order and the prevailing ideology. Debating important issues without fear of any repercussions will encourage people to express their views freely and tell the truth about what is happening to them and in the country at large.
4   Access to alternative sources of information: Citizens have a right to seek out alternative and independent sources of information from other citizens, experts, newspapers, magazines, books, telecommunications and the like. Alternative sources of information that are not under the control of the

government and political parties must exist in a democracy, and must be protected by law. This way, the people will have a choice to hear information from all sides and also it will put pressure on government and partisan media to tell the truth or at least be fairer and more reasonable in covering events since they will be competing with other independent media that will be covering events in a fair and transparent way.

5   Associational autonomy: Citizens have the right to form independent organizations and associations in order to achieve their various rights and demands, including those related to the effective operation of democratic institutions. These associations help democratic institutions achieve their goals and help people pursue aims without having to belong to political parties. The organizations also monitor political parties and put a check on their activities.

6   Inclusive citizenship: All citizens are equal before the law and have equal rights and duties. No one should be denied the rights available to other citizens in the land and are necessary for the implementation of the other five political institutions. They include: voting in regular, free and fair elections to elect officials, running for elective office, free expression, forming and participating in independent political parties and organizations, having access to independent sources of information, the rights to civil liberties and opportunities that may be necessary to the effective operation of the political institutions of large-scale democracy.

Why is democracy necessary?

One interesting definition of democracy is a system in which parties 'lose elections', explaining that the presence of a party that wins elections does not define a system as democratic.[110]

Linz (1984) characterizes democracy as a system with temporary government or 'government pro tempore', where conflicts are regularly terminated under established rules. But Coser (1959) contends that conflicts are terminated temporarily, not resolved definitely under democracy because losers do not give up their right to compete again in future elections, and even rules 'can be changed according to rules'.[111]

Participants in a democratic competition have unequal economic, organizational and ideological resources, since some groups have more resources and are better organized than others. Others are superior ideologically or have 'arguments that persuade'.[112] Those with greater resources are better placed to win in a democracy. But the presence of recognized unions and federations of employers is important in a democracy because they act as a 'counterbalance' for strong political parties.[113]

According to Pizzorno (1978) 'protagonists are collectively organized ... have the capacity to formulate collective interests and act strategically to further them'.[114] The nature of democratic institutions imposes a relation of representation on society and individuals do not defend their interests directly; they delegate this responsibility to their representatives (Luxemburg, 1970, p. 202).[115] This also extends to associations and unions which act on behalf of their members. Thus, democratic societies are populated 'not by freely acting individuals but by collective organizations that are capable of coercing whose interests they represent'.[116] But no single force can control outcomes in a democracy although they depend on what participants do, believing it to be in their best interest.

Although it has often been said that dictators are unpredictable, and this is true about Saddam Hussein who invaded two independent states, Iran and Kuwait, within ten years, according to Adam Przeworski, 'uncertainty is inherent in a democracy, although this doesn't mean everything is possible or nothing is predictable ... democracy is neither chaos nor anarchy'.[117] But democracy's unpredictability happens with defined rules that participants are aware of. Actors do know what is possible and what is likely to happen because 'the probability of particular outcomes is determined by institutional framework and the resources that different political forces bring to the competition'. What is not known is 'which particular outcome will occur'.[118] Actors in a democracy can attach probabilities to the consequences of their actions and hence they can calculate what is best for them to do. Thus, democracy constitutes an opportunity for all to pursue their respective interests.

Przeworski asserts that despite the majoritarian foundation of representative democracy, the system generates outcomes that are predominantly a product of negotiations among leaders of political forces, not a universal deliberative process. 'Democratization is an act of subjecting all interests to competition, of institutionalizing uncertainty. The decisive step towards democracy is the devolution of power from a group of people to a set of rules'.[119]

Democracy is a collectively rational exercise if: (1) a unique maximum exists; (2) the democratic process converges towards this maximum, where democracy is superior to all its alternatives, (3) the democratic process is the unique mechanism, that converges towards this maximum – no benevolent dictator could know what is in the general interest.[120]

Rousseau believed that the general interest is given a priori and that the democratic process converges towards it, while Marx argued that no such general interest can be found in societies divided into classes. Arrow (1951) argued that even if such a maximum existed, no process of aggregating individual preferences will reveal it.[121]

Przeworski regards the assumption that preferences are exogenous to the democratic process as unreasonable and he quotes Schumpeter (1950, p. 263) that 'the will of the people is the product, not the motive power of the political process'.[122]

Habermas and Joshua Cohen (1989) think deliberations lead to convergence on a unique maximum. Przeworski doesn't agree and regards their views as 'too strong to be realistic'. He agrees with Manin (1987) who believed that deliberation stops short of convergence on a unique maximum, but it educates preferences and makes them more general.[123] He accepts that not all conflicts can be resolved by deliberation, quoting Schmitt (1988), who argues this is the case since reasons and facts get exhausted at some point while conflicts remain; therefore, democracy generates winners and losers. 'Democratic institutions render an intertemporal character to political conflicts and offer a long time horizon to political actors' allowing them to 'think about the future rather than being concerned exclusively with present outcomes'.[124] But outcomes under democracy 'hold only if they are mutually enforced in self-interest or enforced externally by some third party'.[125] Democracy can minimize arbitrary violence as Przeworski argues.[126]

In Iraq, the US was the guarantor of democracy, but not anymore. Iran has emerged as the most influential power. Since democratic culture is not yet entrenched in Iraq, political, ethnic and sectarian rivalry is very intense. As some groups have militias to impose undemocratic solutions, and the guarantor is no longer interested in performing its previous role, democracy in Iraq could be under threat. Democracy needs unequivocal international support, politically and financially, for a long period for it to survive. A study by Rand Corporation found that nation-building enterprises (democracy in Iraq is one such enterprise) 'have succeeded only with enormous investments of labour, money and time – five years at minimum'.[127]

American expert on democracy, Larry Diamond, who was sent to Iraq by the US administration to help build democracy, wrote in 2003,

> it's possible that Iraq could grow into a democracy, but the task is huge and the odds are long against it.... It will require a prolonged and internationalized engagement with Iraq, costing billions of dollars over a number of years.[128]

Samuel Huntington believes that the obstacles to democracy in the Muslim world are mainly cultural, in Africa they are economic, while in China (at least in 1990) they are political, economic and cultural.[129] This view is largely accurate regarding Iraq as a Muslim country, although impediments to democracy are not limited to culture. There are others such as religion, stateness, rentier economy, armed groups and militias, and a hostile environment among others. Impediments will be discussed in detail in the latter half of this study.

In his evaluation of the Indian democracy, Barrington Moore (1967) argues that the Indian democracy is 'not a mere sham' and India 'belongs to the modern world' politically. He lists six positive features of the Indian democracy: (1) a working parliamentary system since independence; (2) independent judiciary; (3) standard liberal freedoms; (4) free general elections in which the ruling party accepts defeat; (5) civilian control over the military; and (6) a head of state who made very limited use of his formal extensive powers.[130] But Moore lists two important negative factors of the Indian democracy. They are: Asian setting and lack of industrial revolution. He attributes India's 'appalling problems' to these two factors. Iraq shares with India the two negative factors and both apply to it, the Asian setting and having a rentier economy (non-industrial).

The Middle East still has no democracy with the exception of Lebanon which has a limping democratic system that is based on sectarian divide (consociational democracy).[131]

The other two regional democracies, Turkey and Israel, cannot act as a model for Iraqi democratization because they are distrusted by most Iraqis.[132] Iraq had the worst dictatorship in recent times, and now has a democratic system that is weak and under threat from many quarters, including terrorist groups believed to be helped by regional powers, and Islamist politicians whose belief in democracy is questionable.

Currently, large parts of Iraq are controlled by ISIS terrorists, including Iraq's second largest city, Musil. The Kurds in the North keep threatening to declare independence; it is likely that they will 'at the right time'. This clearly means there is a stateness problem since there is a large minority that doesn't believe in the current Iraqi state.[133] The Iraqi state has broken down entirely and rebuilding it is a slow process that requires extensive support from the international community.[134]

Benefits of democracy

So, what are the benefits of democracy and why do prosperous nations living under other regime types want to be democratic? Since I have quoted Dahl for the necessary institutions of democracy, and in order to be consistent, I would like to comment on what he views as ten benefits of democracy:[135]

1   Avoiding tyranny and autocratic rule. The most pressing problem in politics is the development of dictatorships which results in oppression and repression as well as loss of freedom and dignity for citizens. Under Stalin's tyranny, millions of people were imprisoned, tortured of killed for political reasons. Under democracy, people can choose their leaders carefully and keep an eye on their performance. Once they do not fulfil their obligations, people can 'evict' them, using Schumpeter's term. Any non-democratic rule, be it authoritarian, totalitarian, post-totalitarian or sultanistic, will be oppressive in various degrees.
2   Guaranteeing essential rights. One of the basic tenets of democracy is that essential human rights are guaranteed because elected officials cannot violate the law and are constantly checked by the law of the country as well as by opposition parties and free press. Democracy is inherently a system of citizen rights while a non-democratic rule, especially authoritarian, may give certain freedoms, but they are not guaranteed and can be withdrawn at any time as is the case in many benign monarchies, republics or sheikhdoms in various parts of the world.[136]
3   Ensuring general freedom. When there is a law that is made by a representative body, the democratic government will be under duty to respect such a law. Laws produced by a democracy usually guarantee citizen's basic freedoms such as freedom of speech, association, assembly and so on.

4 Self-determination. People can determine how they want to live with no compulsion from individuals who happen to be their rulers. They can choose their constitution and laws and they can change them if and when they so wish.

5 Moral autonomy. Only democratic governments can provide a maximum of opportunity for persons to exercise freedom of self-determination and live under laws of their own choosing.

6 Human development. Democracy fosters human development more fully than any feasible alternative. Although this is controversial, evidence suggests that human development in democratic countries is highly plausible.

7 Protection of essential personal interests. Under a democratic system, legitimate interests are protected by the state.

8 Political equality. Democratic systems treat citizens equally. However, this needs to be regularly checked by civil society in order to make sure equality is realized. In certain cultures, such as the Iraqi one, preferential treatments are given to friends and relatives of high officials.[137] This has continued under democracy and siblings of holders of high posts are appointed in senior positions without any challenge from civil society or the law. Ministers look up to their leaders, rather than the public, for instruction. They brought their party followers and relatives to their ministries with no fear of breaking the law.[138]

9 Conducive to Prosperity. Countries with democratic governments, with regular checks and balances in place, tend to be more prosperous than non-democratic countries. Although this may be accurate in theory, in practice, it's not always the case as some democracies remain poor such as India, and non-democratic governments have delivered economic prosperity, while others served people better.[139]

There is no evidence that democratic governments perform better than non-democratic. In fact some studies have indicated that democratic governments perform less well.[140] The Spanish economy deteriorated sharply during the transition while unemployment under Franco (in 1970) was around 3 per cent. It went up to 20 per cent, in the 1980s. Economic growth was over 7 per cent from 1960–1975, it went down to 1.7 per cent between 1975–85.[141] Huntington points out that governments produced by elections can be 'inefficient, corrupt, short-sighted, irresponsible, dominated by special interests and incapable of adopting policies by the public good'.[142]

Prosperity under democracy in Iraq has not materialized and the Iraqi economy is weaker than ever due to falling oil prices, wide-spread corruption and extra military spending to fight terrorist groups.[143] As a sign of the wide-spread corruption in the country, one Iraqi politician admitted, in a rare moment of truth, that 'everyone is corrupt, including me'.[144]

10 Conducive to Peace. Modern representative democracies do not fight wars with one another. No war has been fought in recent history between two democratic countries. Many regard this as one of the most important attributes of democracy.

The final idea of 'democratic peace' was first formulated by Immanuel Kant and Thomas Paine. Bruce Russet wrote a book on this in the 1990s.[145] In recent times there has been no war between two democratic nations. From the nineteenth century down to 1990, democracies didn't fight other democracies, with trivial exceptions.[146] But Jack Snyder (2000) argues that democratization is a double-edged sword that can provide impetuses for heightening nationalist violence, conflict and aggression.[147]

While acknowledging that established democracies often have peaceful inter-actions in their foreign policies toward each other, Snyder demonstrates that the early phases of democratic transitions are often fraught with the potential for conflict, 'which not only raises the costs of transition but may also redirect popular political participation into a lengthy antidemocratic detour'.[148] But even Snyder acknowledges that mature democracies have not fought wars against each other.

John Stuart Mill also argues 'unlimited use of freedom' would not necessarily put an end to the 'the evils of religious or philosophical sectarianism' because 'men of narrow capacity' will always act as if their truth is the only one.[149] He also acknowledged that the tendency of all opinions to become sectarian is not cured by the freest discussion. On the contrary, he argues this could often heighten and exacerbate it.

There are two opposing points of view about democracy: static and dynamic. From a static point of view, democratic institutions must be 'fair': they must give all the relevant political forces a chance to win. From a dynamic point of view, they must be effective: They must make even losing under democracy more attractive.[150] One of the dilemmas for the Left that Adam Przeworski (1991) highlights is that 'even procedurally perfect democracy may remain an oligarchy: the rule of the rich over the poor', while the traditional dilemma for the Right is 'democracy may turn out to be the rule of the many, who are poor, over the few rich'.[151]

A glimpse at the personalities ruling Iraq today reveals that they are a few families who inherit political positions or dominance. Leaders of political parties or blocs, presidents, ministers and prime ministers are sons or siblings of past political leaders or their associates and followers. The Barzani, Talabani, Hakeem and Sadr families bequeath leadership positions in a systematic manner and appoint their associates and their heirs to leadership positions. In the 2014 elections, five of PM Noori Al-Maliki's family were candidates, including his two sons-in-law and two nephews, who were elected.[152]

As we will see in the next chapter, the establishment of democracy requires a state, without which there can be no secure democracy.[153] When there is a lack of identification with the state by large groups or individuals in the territory, fundamental and often unsolvable problems are at hands for democracy. Iraqi Kurds didn't think of themselves as Iraqis and prefer to have their own inde-pendent state.[154]

Notes

1   John Stuart Mill, *On Liberty*, Dover, New York. (2002) p. 1
2   Ibid., p. 2
3   Ibid.
4   Ibid.
5   Ibid., p. 3
6   Ibid., p. 4
7   Mushreq Abbas, 'Iraqi justice minister presses Shiite personal status law', Al-Monitor, 3/3/2014: https://goo.gl/iLQcUf
8   BBC, 'Iraq alcohol: Parliament imposes ban in a surprise move', 23/10/2016: www.bbc.co.uk/news/world-middle-east-37743180
9   Mahmoud Al-Hassan, Video (Arabic): www.youtube.com/watch?v=1m5S-M8GLqU
10 Mill (2002) op. cit. p. 7
11 Interview with Sami Al-Askari. See also: Patrick Cockburn, *Muqtada Al-Sadr: The Shia Revival and the Struggle for Iraq*, Simon & Schuster (2008) p. 173
12 Mill (2002) op. cit. p. 8
13 Ibid.
14 Ibid., p. 10
15 Nabil Mouline, *The Clerics of Islam*, Yale University Press (2014) pp. 147 and 203–234
16 Mill (2002) op. cit. p. 11
17 Ibid., pp. 11–12
18 Adnan AbuZeed, 'To veil or not to veil: Iraqi women face scrutiny over their choices', Al-Monitor, 24/8/2015: https://goo.gl/bpwlIc
19 Christian Dogma, 'In pictures: Posters call upon Christian women to wear hijab', 14/12/2015: https://goo.gl/snI9DF
20 Ibid., p. 13
21 Ibid., p. 14
22 Ibid.
23 Ibid.
24 Ibid.
25 Ibid., p. 15
26 Ibid.
27 Judith Yaphe (Eisenstadt and Mathewson (2003) op. cit. p. 39)
28 Mill, (2002) op. cit. p. 16
29 Ibid.
30 Mohammed Hussein Al-Ansari, *Infallibility in Shia School of Thought*, Alansari Foundation & Al-Mahdi Media, Sydney (no date) p. 29: https://goo.gl/lyp5an
31 Susannah George, 'Millions of Shiite pilgrims flock to Iraqi holy city for annual Arbaeen commemorations', Associated Press, 2/12/2015: https://goo.gl/XXYyF4 See also Najaf-Karbala, Walking Guide for religious justification for performing pilgrimage (ziyarat) on foot: www.najaftokarbala.info/
32 Centre of Fatwa, 'The correct understanding of the phrase "Reward" is as much as hardship', (Arabic) Islam Web, 26/7/2007. (It explains the virtues of travelling on foot): https://goo.gl/UhooBk. Also, see Abu Uwais, 'The greater the hardship, the greater the reward', Tawheed First (English): https://goo.gl/hcXg63
33 Ibid.
34 Ibid., p. 23
35 Omar Farrukh, Ikhwan al-Safa, Islamic Philosophy online, Chapter 15: www.muslimphilosophy.com/hmp/18.htm
36 Johan Franzén, 'Musings on Iraq', 15/7/2014: https://goo.gl/Yfm73l
37 Roger Shanahan, Meria Journal, June 2004: www.rubincenter.org/2004/06/shanahan-2004-06-02/

38 Yitzhaq Nakash, *The Shia of Iraq*, Princeton University Press (1994) p. 135
39 Ibid.
40 Ibid., p. 136
41 Mill (2002) op. cit. p. 7
42 Kamil Shya, Hadi Al-Mahdi among others (see Chapter 7)
43 Mahmoud Muhammad Taha, Biography, Alfikra: www.alfikra.org/index_e.php
44 Radio Free Europe, 'UN slams executions in Iraq', 23/8/2016: www.rferl.org/a
    /iraq-un-slams-executions/27940763.html
45 Mill (2002) op. cit. p. 25
46 Ibid., pp. 25–26
47 Ibid., p. 37
48 Ibid.
49 Ibid., p. 38
50 Ibid., p. 39
51 Ibid.
52 Ibid., p. 40
53 Ibid., p. 43
54 Sumeria News, 'Suspending Al-Mawla is an administrative measure', 17/2/2014
    (Arabic): www.sotaliraq.com/mobile-news.php?id=137001#axzz4Pg0SQPFS See
    also a report by Fadak Network, 'In a face-saving move, the Integrity Commission
    acquits Al-Mawla', 20/3/2014. (Arabic): www.afadak.com/news/17300. Also,
    Altahreer news: http://altahreernews.com/inp/view.asp?ID=17546
55 Video on this link: www.youtube.com/watch?v=hAjA-5oump8
56 Mill (2002) op. cit. p. 43
57 Ibid.
58 Ibid. p. 46
59 Ibid. p. 60
60 Ali Al-Wardi, *A Study in the Nature of Iraqi Society* (Arabic) Saeed Bin Jubair Pub-
    lications, Qum. (2005) p. 11
61 Charles Tripp, *A History of Iraq*, Cambridge University Press (2000) p. 4
62 Ibid. p. 6
63 Diamond (2005) op. cit. p. 20
64 Mill (2002) op. cit. p. 61
65 Ibid., p. 63
66 Associated Press, *Guardian*, 23/10/2016: https://goo.gl/haoGwN
67 Mill (2002) op. cit. p. 69
68 Ibid., p. 70
69 Ibid.
70 Ibid., p. 79
71 Ibid., p. 81
72 Abbas Kelidar, *US Policy in Post-Saddam Iraq: Lessons from the British Experi-
    ence*, edited by Michael Eisenstadt and Eric Mathewson, Washington Institute for
    Near East Policy (2003) p. 30
73 This is one of the main differences between the two sects with numerous sources
    detailing their differences: (John Green, 'People of our every day life') published on
    the following website: https://goo.gl/9UlMwB
74 Huntington (1991) op. cit. p. 309
75 Przeworski (1991) op. cit. pp. 54–55
76 Ibid., p. 56
77 Ibid.
78 Ibid., p. 57
79 Ibid.
80 Ibid., 58
81 Ibid.

82 Ibid., p. 59
83 Ibid., p. 60
84 Ibid.
85 Latif al-Zubaidi, 'Why Iraq's ration card can't be scrapped', Niqash, 15/11/2012: www.niqash.org/en/articles/economy/3156/
86 Linz and Stepan (1996) p. 75
87 Huntington (1991) op. cit. p. 47
88 Richard McKeon, 'Democracy in a world of tensions', [Samuel Huntington (1991) op. cit. p. 47]
89 Huntington (1991) op. cit. p. 6
90 Ibid., p. 16
91 Ibid., p. 17
92 Dahl (1989) op. cit. p. 3
93 David L. Stockton, *The Classical Athenian Democracy*, Oxford University Press (1990); Allen M. Ward, 'How democratic was the Roman Republic?', *New England Classical Journal*, 31/2. (2004) pp. 101–119; Robert Alan Dahl, *Democracy and Its Critics*, Yale University Press (1989) p. 13
94 Dahl (1998) op. cit. p. 9
95 Ibid.
96 John Dunn, *Setting the People Free: The Story of Democracy*, Atlantic Books (2005) p. 24
97 Linz and Stepan (1996) op. cit. p. 75
98 Interview with Ayad Allawi
99 Interviews with Sami Al-Askari, Walid Al-Hilli and Adil Abdur-Raheem respectively
100 Dunn (2005) op. cit. p. 41
101 Joseph Schumpeter, *Capitalism, Socialism and Democracy*, Routledge (2010) p. 225
102 Ibid., p. 242
103 Ibid., pp. 244–245
104 Ibid., p. 253
105 Ibid.
106 Huntington (1991) op. cit. p. 9
107 Ibid.
108 Ibid.
109 Dahl (1998) op. cit. pp. 85–86
110 Przeworski (1991) op. cit. p. 10
111 Ibid., p. 11
112 Ibid.
113 Ibid., p. 27
114 Ibid., p. 11
115 Ibid.
116 Ibid., p. 12
117 Ibid.
118 Ibid., p. 13
119 Ibid., p. 14
120 Ibid., p. 16
121 Ibid.
122 Ibid., p. 17
123 Ibid., p. 18
124 Ibid., p. 19
125 Ibid., pp. 22–24
126 Ibid., p. 16. (footnote 11)
127 James Dobbins, *et al.*, *America's Role in Nation-Building: From Germany to Iraq*, RAND (2003) p. 166

128　Larry Diamond, *Squandered Victory*, Henry Holt (2005) p. 18

129　Huntington (1991) op. cit. p. 315

130　Barrington Moore Jr., *Social Origins of Dictatorship and Democracy*, Beacon Books (1993) p. 314

131　Bilal Saab and Elie Al-Chaer, Brookings, 6/11/2007: https://goo.gl/beUGyE

132　Diamond (2005) op. cit. p. 21

133　Linz and Stepan (1996) op. cit. pp. 16–37

134　Diamond (2005) op. cit. p. 23

135　Dahl (1998) op. cit. pp. 45–58

136　Linz and Stepan (1996) op. cit. pp. 44–45

137　Khuloud Ramzi, 'A family tie too tight: Nepotism runs deep in Iraqi politics', Niqash, 21/7/2011

138　Musings on Iraq, 'How the US ran into party politics', 9/1/2013: https://goo.gl/6vvnDp

139　Schumpeter (2010) op. cit. p. 242

140　Haggard and Kaufman (1995) op. cit. p. 152

141　Linz and Stepan (1996) op. cit. p. 113

142　Huntington (1991) op. cit. p. 10

143　Joseph Sassoon, MEEA's 15th International Conference, Doha, 23–26/3/2016: https://goo.gl/9O59Ob

144　Mishaan Al-Jabouri, *Guardian*, 19/2/2016: https://goo.gl/Vjbejl

145　Bruce Russett, *Grasping the Democratic Peace: Principles for a Post-Cold War World*, Princeton University Press. (1994)

146　Philip Cutright, [quoted by Samuel Huntington. (1991) op. cit. p. 29]

147　Jack Snyder, *From Voting to Violence: Democratization and Nationalist Conflict*, W.W. Norton. (2000)

148　Ibid., p. 20

149　Mill (2002) op. cit. p. 43

150　Przeworski (1991) op. cit. p. 33

151　Ibid., p. 34

152　Harith Al-Qarawee-Al-Monitor-15/5/2014: https://goo.gl/2FiZj2. Also, Ali Muhsin Radhi, Burathnews, 23/4/2014: http://burathanews.com/arabic/news/234959

153　Linz and Stepan (1996) op. cit. p. 19

154　Diamond (2005) op. cit. p. 22

4 Democratization

Introduction

Democratization is the process whereby countries become democratic, and this takes time, depending on several factors related to society's readiness for democracy. Countries go through a period of transition before they become consolidated democracies. But what is a consolidated democracy? Juan Linz and Alfred Stepan (1996) give a very simple but eloquent definition: it's a political situation when democracy becomes the only game in town.[1]

Przeworski (1991) offers similar explanation but he adds 'it's a system in which parties lose elections', explaining that the presence of a party that wins elections does not define a system as democratic.[2] Przeworski regards democracy as consolidated

> when a particular system of institutions becomes the only game in town, when no one can imagine acting outside the democratic institutions, when all losers want to do is to try again within the same institutions under which they have lost.[3]

Philippe Schmitter sees consolidation as

> the transformation of the institutional arrangements and understandings that emerged at the time of the transition into relations of cooperation and competition that are reliably known and regularly practiced and voluntarily accepted by those persons or collectivities ... that participate in democratic governance.[4]

So, democracy becomes established and entrenched within a society when it is 'self-enforcing' and when all the participants feel they find it best for their interests to use the existing system and have hope to get improvement sometime in the future; and when democracy becomes a benefit to all and it's harmful for any political force to try and subvert it. Coleman's (1989) view on this is 'minority doesn't consist of losers and the majority winners. Instead minority members have false beliefs about the general will; members of the majority have true beliefs'.[5] This means that losing and winning under democracy is temporary and those who lose have a hope of winning in the future.

Democracy becomes the only game in town in a territory when:

1   Behaviourally, there is no significant national, social, economic, political or institutional actor spending significant resources attempting to achieve their objectives by creating a nondemocratic regime or turning to violence or foreign intervention to secede from the state.

2   Attitudinally, there is a strong majority of the public that holds the belief that democratic procedures and institutions are the most appropriate way to govern collective life in a society such as theirs and when the support for the anti-system alternatives is quite small or more or less isolated from the pro-democratic forces.

3   Constitutionally, when governmental and nongovernmental forces alike, throughout the territory of the state, become subjected to, and habituated to, the resolution of conflict within the specific laws, procedures and institutions sanctioned by the new democratic process.[6]

State and nation

Democracy is governance system for a state, so the first requirement for the consolidation of this system is the existence of a state. Without a sovereign state there can be no secure democracy.[7] When there is a 'lack of identification with the state that large groups or individuals in the territory want to join a different state or create an independent state, it raises fundamental and often unsolvable problems'.[8] In Iraq there is at least one irredentist tendency represented by a large Kurdish minority which has been demanding self-determination since the creation of the state.

There are now more irredentist tendencies such as Turcoman, Assyrian, Yazidis and even Sunni groups who either demand a separate federal entity or autonomous region.[9]

Although the terms *nation* and *state* are now used interchangeably, there is a distinction between the two. A nation may have a 'nation-state'. According to Max Weber, a nation belongs to the sphere of values, i.e. the expected sentiment of solidarity among some groups. A nation is not necessarily identical with the people of a state or a membership of a given polity.[10]

A nation can be divided in more than one state as was the case in Germany prior to unification in 1990 and perhaps now in Korea which is one nation divided between two states. The Arab nation is divided into 22 states; all are members of the Arab League.[11]

A nation doesn't have officials, and there are no clear rules of membership nor defined rights and duties that can be legitimately enforced. National leaders don't have coercive powers or taxes.

In contrast, a state has resources and coercive powers and controls over its citizens.[12] Some national movements could exercise power, use violence or exact contributions without or before gaining statehood, but this always happens when 'that movement is taking the function of another state, subverting its order so that a state is breaking down in the process.'[13] Sometimes, nationalists have private armies to enforce their aspirations and challenge the authority of a state, which can lose control of some of its territory, but this signals the beginning of a civil war or national liberation struggle which could end in the creation of another state.[14]

The emergence of a state dates back to the fifteenth century, before the emergence of modern ideas about nationalism in the late eighteenth century, and the idea of a nation-state becoming a major force in the second half of the nineteenth century.[15] Most of the nation states that were created in the twentieth century were not actually nation-states. Most of them, such as Czechoslovakia, Poland, Latvia, Lithuania and Estonia, were made up of different ethnicities. The disintegration of empires and redrawing of boundaries between states were not directly the result of nation-building movements.[16] Since very few states are ethnically pure, nationalism can be a counter-democratic force because it's divisive, since it focuses on a primordial identity that is not shared by all the people of the state.

Belgium for example became independent of the Netherland in 1830, but when it was confronted by Flemish nationalism, it created political institutions and practices that made it a democratic multinational state.[17] In some nation-states, national leaders pursue policies that aim to increase 'cultural homogeneity'. They send messages that the state should be 'of and for the nation'.[18] So, the language of the nation becomes the 'official language' and the religion and culture of the dominant nation become privileged if not 'official'.[19] This flies in the face of democratic principles and practices which emphasize inclusive citizenship and equal rights. Under democracy, all citizens identify with one subjective idea of the nation, and the nation is congruent with the state.

Irredenta

Other factors are also important for democratization. If there is a significant irredenta outside the state boundaries, or there are diverse cultures and more than one nation existing, pursuing democratization would be difficult. 'Congruence between polity and demos would facilitate the creation of democratic nation-state'.[20] This congruence is supportive of democratic consolidation because it reduces or even eliminates stateness problems. But in the real world there are a few nondemocratic states that are homogeneous enough to start democratic transition. Polis/demos incongruence creates problems for democratic consolidation unless carefully addressed.[21]

State legitimacy in the eyes of its citizens is important for the consolidation of democracy and when this legitimacy is questioned by one group or more within the state it creates complications for democracy. Further problems arise if a large minority is considered an irredenta by another state and this could jeopardize peace. On the other hand, if nationalist extremists among the majority group, the titular nation as they are called in the former Soviet Union, pursue nationalist policies that alienate other groups, this may push them to turn to neighbouring countries for support and protection. When irredentist policies become dominant, they become a serious strain on democracy in both the external 'homeland' of the minority and the neighbouring nation-building state.[22] It is a problem for democracy in particular since it requires agreements by the citizens of the territory, while a non-democratic regime can suppress irredentist aspirations imposing acquiescence over a large group of people for a long period of time without threatening the coherence of the state.[23]

In Iraq, irredentist aspirations are particularly manifested in the Kurdish large minority whose members feel they do not belong to the state of Iraq but should have a state of their own. This is partly due to the harsh treatment they received from the central government and partly because they have a different racial and cultural identity. They also feel they are part of a larger 'Kurdish nation' that is dispersed over four countries – Iraq, Iran, Turkey and Syria. Kurdish nationalist leaders, such as Masud Barzani, feed into this challenge often by threatening to declare the independence of Kurdistan from Iraq.[24] The American diplomat and writer, Peter Galbraith, had two descriptions for the current Kurdish sense of belonging to Iraq: 'For the older generation, Iraq was a bad memory, while the new generation has no feeling of being Iraqi'.[25]

Sunni Arabs also feel part of the bigger Arab world. According to Abbas Kelidar, a prominent writer and expert on Iraq, the ideology of Arab nationalism, imbued by King Faysal and his Sharifian officers, was seen by Shia and Kurds as a 'means to ensure Sharifian (Sunni) hegemony over the Iraqi political process'. 'Pan-Arabism took for granted that language, religion and historical experience shared by the Arabic-speaking peoples constituted the essential qualities of nationhood'.[26] Kelidar argues that

> the pan-Arabist reading of religion has alienated Shia heartland by emphasizing that the Umayyad dynasty (661–750) as the epitome of Arab genius. The Shia viewed the Umayyads as usurpers responsible for the killing of Shia imams. Hence they strongly objected to the government invocation of the dynasty seeing it as a means of validating the Sunni political hegemony.[27]

Arab emphasis on the nation's political discourse has also alienated the Kurds. Kelidar affirms Arab nationalism has 'ill-served the new Iraq since it failed in its drive to remake Arabs via a process of individual immersion in Arab political culture'.[28] He concludes that the nationalist ideology imposed by the British on Iraqis was 'externally irredentist and internally divisive'.[29]

Judith Yaphe has a slightly different view regarding the divisiveness of Arab nationalism. She states that 'Arab nationalism was particularly strong in the Shia cities of Karbala and Najaf where students and scholars encouraged the teachings of Arab civilization and culture'. She attributes this to the fact that 'southern tribes had a common sense of Arab identity, shared traditions and customs and links to the great clans and confederations that originated in Arabia and spread throughout the region'.[30] The question remains whether these cross-country links between Arabs contribute to irredentist feelings or cause others in different territories to interfere in territories they do not live in, or they can be considered as normal cultural links that exist between all peoples of the world.

As we saw above, the Iraqi state was built on shaky grounds from the beginning since the brand of Arab nationalism brought by the state's founding fathers alienated the non-Arabs who nearly form a fifth of the population and also divided Arabs since they embrace two faiths which have different readings of history. Arab nationalism ideology suited Sunnis, while many Shia disagree with its basic tenets.

Citizens not subjects

Democracy is characterized by citizens not subjects, and a democratic transition often puts the polis/demos at the centre of politics. But the more linguistic, cultural and national diversity, the more difficult politics becomes, because it would be difficult to reach an agreement on the fundamentals of a democracy. Still, democracy can still be consolidated in a multilingual, multicultural and multireligious societies but it needs considerable political crafting of democratic norms, practices and institutions.[31]

Many of the existing states are multi-national, multi-cultural and multilingual, and it is difficult to make them homogeneous (nation-states) and the only democratic possibilities to make them homogeneous are through voluntary assimilation.[32] But there are political elites, especially among minorities who emphasize primordial values and characteristics for emotional and self-interest-related reasons. Those elites didn't exist in preindustrial societies, but they do exist now even in agrarian societies.[33] With so many ethnicities, cultures and languages (around 8000 in the world), and people living in multinational settings, a nation-state will be difficult to achieve by democratic means.[34]

In multinational settings, the chances to consolidate democracy are increased by state policies that grant inclusive and equal citizenship and that give all citizens a common 'roof' of state-mandated and enforced individual rights. Such states have a greater need than other polities to explore a variety of non-majoritarian and non-plebiscitarian formulas.[35] Federalism is an option but only if there are spatial differences between the different groups. In Iraq, the spatial differences between groups are not always well-defined.

Although the Kurds live in the northern/north-eastern region, but there are many of them who live with other Iraqi communities in Kirkuk, Musil, Dyala and Baghdad. The current Kurdish Federal Region encompasses only three provinces which are largely inhabited by Kurds. But it will be difficult to have all the Kurds in one federal region. The same goes for the Sunnis and Turcoman who are dispersed in many provinces although there are areas where they constitute the majority.

Both the state and society might allow a variety of publicly supported institutions such as media and schools in different languages, symbolic recognition of cultural diversity, a variety of legally accepted marriage codes, legal and practical tolerance for parties representing different communities and a whole array of political procedures and devices that Arend Lijphart has described as 'consociational democracy'.[36]

The choice of electoral systems is also important. Proportional representation can facilitate representation of spatially dispersed minorities.[37] But this system, according to which the first election of January 2005 was conducted, was abolished by Islamists when they controlled the National Assembly in 2005. The current system (Iraqi-Modified Saint Lague) allows candidates with a few hundreds of votes to become MPs, while it bars others with thousands of votes. Many complain about its unfairness. Due to this unfairness, there have been calls to change the system recently by the Sadrist Trend and the Civil Democratic Alliance.[38]

Democratic consolidation

It's now established that modern democratic governance is inevitably linked to stateness. Without state there can be no citizenship and without citizenship there can be no democracy.[39] Citizenship can be acquired in three different ways. These are by descent, birth, or naturalization.[40] In all three cases, citizenship is linked to the state, especially in the third type since the state has to grant the citizenship to the individual requesting it.

But the absence of effective institutional structures in the state 'to attach the citizenry to the state' prompts political elites to 'attempt to create loyalty through cultural attachments', such as culture, ethnicity, language and religion.[41] This may have happened in Iraq. Citizens and politicians were influenced by the tide of sectarian media.[42]

After stateness, there are five conditions that must be present for democracy to be consolidated. These are free and lively civil society, autonomous and valued political society, rule of law to ensure that citizens' freedoms and independent associational life are guaranteed, usable state bureaucracy and institutionalized economic society.[43]

Civil society can destroy a non-democratic regime and then generate political alternatives to monitor government and state. A full democratic transition and consolidation must involve political society, which consists of political parties, elections, electoral rules, political leadership, interparty alliances and legislature. Both civil and political societies need to be protected by the rule of law that is embodied in a spirit of constitutionalism, and this requires strong consensus over the constitution and a commitment to 'self-binding' procedures of governance that require exceptional majorities to change as well as a hierarchy of laws interpreted by an independent judicial system and supported by strong legal culture in civil society.

The state also needs a functioning bureaucracy, usable by the democratic government in order to have the capacity to command, regulate and extract. Unfortunately, the last condition was not found in Iraq after the fall of the regime. Ali Allawi affirms

> when the Coalition arrived in Baghdad on 9 April 2003, it found a fractured and brutalized society, presided over by a fearful, heavily armed minority.

The post 9/11 jihadi culture, that was subsequently to plague Iraq, was just beginning to take root. The institutions of the state were moribund; the state exhausted. The ideology that had held Ba'athist rule together had decayed beyond repair.[44]

In other words, the state had to be recreated almost from scratch.

There must also be an institutionalized economic society. Modern democracies neither exist in a pure market economy nor in a command economy. People must have the freedom to conduct business profitably, and at the same time a government that intervenes to remedy market failures. The very working of a modern democracy would lead to the transformation of a market economy into a mixed economy.[45] The Iraqi economy was rentier with 98 per cent of the budget coming from oil revenue.[46]

The consolidation of democracy is closely linked to the consolidation of economic reforms which are necessary for any country undergoing democratization. Democracies are 'unlikely to become institutionalised if broad assumptions underlying the management of the economy lack widespread support or are subject to continuous challenge'.[47] Iraq is a divided society and political and sectarian groups undermine each other. The management of the economy does lack widespread support and is continuously challenged.

Paths to democracy

Different polities may vary in the paths available for transition to democracy, depending on the type of the nondemocratic regime they have been ruled by. There are four types of nondemocratic regimes and two subtypes of democracy, since democracy has 'sufficient value to be retained as one regime'.[48] Still, there are two subtypes of democracy: consociational and majoritarian.

Types of nondemocratic regimes

1 Totalitarian is characterized by the following characteristics: absence of pluralism; official party has de jure and de facto power; party has eliminated almost all pre-totalitarian pluralism; no space for second economy or parallel society; elaborate guiding ideology that articulates a reachable utopia; leaders, individuals and groups derive their sense of mission, legitimation and often specific policies from their commitment to some holistic conception of humanity and society; extensive mobilization into a vast array of regime-created obligatory organizations; emphasis on activism of cadres and militants; efforts at mobilization of enthusiasm, private life is decried; leadership rules with undefined limits; great unpredictability for members; often charismatic leaders; recruitment to top leadership highly dependent on success and commitment in party organization; adherence to utopian ideology; undefined limits and great unpredictability, vulnerability for elites and non-elites alike.

2 Post-totalitarian is characterized by the following characteristics: the regime has almost all the other control mechanisms of the party-state in place,

but there is limited but not responsible social, institutional and economic pluralism; almost no political pluralism because the party still formally has monopoly of power, may have a second economy but state still has the overwhelming presence; most manifestations of pluralism in 'flattened polity' grew out of tolerated state structures of dissident groups consciously formed in opposition to totalitarian regime; opposition creates a second culture or parallel society in mature totalitarianism; guiding ideology still officially exists and is part of the social reality, but weakened commitment to, or faith in, utopia; shift of emphasis from ideology to programmatic consensus that is presumably based on national decision-making; limited debate without too much reference to ideology; progressive loss of interest by leaders and non-leaders involved in organizing mobilization; routine mobilization of population within the state-sponsored organizations to achieve a minimum degree of conformity and compliance; many cadres and militants are mere careerists and opportunists; boredom, withdrawal and ultimately privatization of population's values become an accepted fact; growing emphasis on personal security; checks on top leadership via party structures, procedures and internal democracy; top leaders are seldom charismatic, recruitment to top leadership is restricted to official party, but less dependent on building a career within the party's organization; top leaders can come from party technocrats in state apparatus.

3 Authoritarian is characterized by the following characteristics: limited but not responsible political pluralism; often quite extensive social and economic pluralism, most of which has been in place before the establishment of the regime; often some space for semi opposition; no elaborate ideology but distinctive mentalities, no extensive or intensive political mobilization except at some points in their development; the leader or small group of leaders operates within formally ill-defined but quite predictable norms; effort at cooperation of old elite groups; some autonomy in state careers and in the military.

4 Sultanistic regime is the most bizarre in all of the nondemocratic regimes. It is characterized by the following characteristics: unpredictability; social and economic pluralism doesn't disappear but is subject to unpredictable and despotic intervention; no individual or group in civil society, or political society or the state free from the sultan's exercise of despotic power; no rule of law, no law institutionalization, and high fusion between private and public; high manipulation of symbols; extreme glorification of the ruler; no elaborate or guiding ideology, or even distinctive mentalities outside the despotic personalism; no attempt to justify major initiatives on the basis of ideology; pseudo ideology not believed by subjects or staff; low but occasional and manipulative mobilization of a ceremonial type by clientelistic methods without permanent organization; periodic mobilization of para-state groups who use violence against groups targeted by the sultan; the leadership is highly personalistic and arbitrary; no rational legal constraints; strong dynastic tendency; no autonomy in state careers; leader unencumbered by ideology; compliance with leaders is based on intense fear and personal rewards; staff of the leader are drawn from members of his

family, friends and business associates, or men directly involved in the use of violence to sustain the regime, and staff's position derives from their purely personal submission to the ruler.

What type is Saddam's regime?

It will be inaccurate to assign any of the above types to the regime of Saddam Hussein since it had all the characteristics of totalitarian regime, plus most of the Sultanistic features, from assigning top posts to family members,[49] unpredictability to no one in civil or political societies or the state being free from his exercise of despotic power and so on. In fact, the Ba'ath regime destroyed the remaining civil society institutions when it came to power in 1968 under Ahmed Hassan Al-Bakir and Saddam Hussein, and Iraq became a one-party state.[50] I argue the closest to Saddam's regime was the Ceausescu regime in Romania since there were so many similarities between them. Ceausescu's regime was regarded as Sultanistic by Linz and Stepan (1996).[51]

However, Saddam's regime changed after the defeat in 1991 after his invasion of Kuwait, not because it evolved and was willing to reform, but because it was weakened by wars, sanctions and defections of supporters to the opposition. Even the dictator's sons-in-law defected with his two daughters in 1995.[52] The definition of sultanism as given by Weber, applies to the regime of Saddam Hussein:

> Patrimonialism, in extreme cases, sultanism, tend to arise whenever traditional domination develops an administration and a military force which are purely instruments of the master ... where domination ... operates on the basis of discretion, it will be called sultanism.[53]

Sultanism looks similar to Saddamism:

> Under sultanism, there is no rule of law, no space for semi-opposition, no space for regime moderates who might negotiate with the democratic moderates and no sphere of the economy or civil society that is not subject to the despotic exercise of the sultan's will.[54]

Although a sultanistic ruler has no elaborate ideology, Saddam Hussein claimed to believe in the Ba'ath ideology which embraces Arab unity, freedom and socialism, although there were no instances where he actually applied these principles. He failed to achieve any unity with any Arab country, including Syria, which is governed by a 'Ba'ath' party (BP).

Tahir Al-Ani, a senior member of BP leadership bureau and Saddam loyalist, stated that Saddam was opposed to the unification efforts with Syria which Presidents Ahmed Al-Bakir and Hafidh Al-Assad were pursuing.[55] Freedom hardly existed under his regime, while socialism was in name only, even though there were some attempts during the early years of his rule to implement some socialist principles, such as nationalization and the establishment of farm cooperatives, but they were to placate BP leftist members. It was more 'symbolic politics being conducted at a senior level of the regime, than a policy adopted out of ideological convictions'.[56]

After Saddam assumed the presidency, the party broke away with socialism. 'In the 1980s, the socialist ideology of the [Ba'ath] party accommodated itself to capitalism. Nationalised industries were privatised. Iraqi businessmen trying to take advantage of the country's oil wealth often pursued their ambitions through the party'.[57] Loyalty to Saddam personally became the only criterion by which any Iraqi is judged. As Charles Trip stated, 'Obedience to Saddam Hussain and proximity to him were now to be the criteria for promotion and indeed for political – and sometimes actual – survival'.[58] There is also the element of personal grandeur in Saddam's behaviour that is close to sultanism. During the UN-imposed sanctions on Iraq after its invasion of Kuwait in 1990, which was regarded as 'the most comprehensive and severe ever imposed against one nation',[59] Saddam built 50 palaces across Iraq using money ear-marked for the Iraqi people in the famous Oil-for-Food programme (OFF). General Tommy Franks called it the 'Oil-for-Palaces' programme.[60]

There was also an obvious streak of Machiavellianism in Saddam's turn to religion. Ahmed Hashim notes that

> despite its original allegiance to militant secularism, Saddam's regime began in the early and mid-1990s to promote the re-Islamization of Iraqi society to buttress its legitimacy. Saddam implemented an official policy of religious revival so that the regime could control the rising tide of faith.[61]

Hashim further argues that the regime of economic sanctions imposed on Iraq after Saddam's invasion of Kuwait 'promoted the return to religion among the Iraqi population'. An Iraqi sociologist had told an American journalist in 2001: 'when a society is in crisis like the one we are in, the embargo and all, religion plays a greater part in soothing the psyche of the people and giving the people greater strength to face the crisis'.[62]

Why does regime type matter?

According to several political scientists, 'the characteristics of the previous non-democratic regime have profound implications for the transition paths available and the tasks different countries face when they begin their struggles to develop consolidated democracies'.[63] This is because the structures the previous regime leaves behind can facilitate democratization if the regime was authoritarian, as was the case in Spain in the 1970s, since it would have left reasonably developed civil society, economic society, rule of law and a usable bureaucracy. The only item that needs to be created for the process of democratization to succeed would be a political society. But if the starting point for the transition was a totalitarian regime, the democratic transition could entail crafting, not only political society and economic society, but also every single aspect of democracy at the same time.[64]

As for a sultanistic regime, democracy crafters, as was the case in Haiti, have to begin the construction of civil society, economic society, political society, constitutionalism and rule of law and professional norms of state bureaucracy from a low point.[65] This was the case in Iraq, although there was a kind of political society, thanks to the exiled opposition parties which returned immediately after the fall of the regime, despite the fact that they were not fully aware of the social and political developments inside Iraq. But many Iraqis resented their domination and associated them with foreigners, even though they contributed new ideas and brought in much-needed foreign support.[66] Other sectors such as civil and economic societies, rule of law, and a usable state bureaucracy were next to non-existent.

Democratization and economic development

There is a documented correlation between the level of economic development and democracy. It's well documented that there are 'few democracies at very low levels of socioeconomic development and that most polities at high levels of socioeconomic development are democracies'.[67] Most of the major modern transition attempts take place in countries at medium levels of development. 'Robust economic conditions would appear supportive of any type of regime', but 'there are good theoretical reasons why sustained economic growth could erode a nondemocratic regime ... [but] no theoretical reason why sustained economic growth would erode a democratic regime'.[68] Sustained economic growth and low unemployment always support democratic forces under a dictatorship. When people are better off, they tend to demand more rights. Spain under Franco, Chile under Pinochet, Brazil in the 1970s and South Korea all had some of the world's highest economic growth under dictatorship. This economic success led to demands for democracy.[69] This has contributed to the enhancement of democratic movements in these countries. Non-democratic regimes have a problem when they do well economically and when they do badly. If they do well, it will encourage people to demand more rights. If they do badly, it will erode the basis of their legitimacy.

But 'if a regime is based on the double legitimacy of democratic procedures and socioeconomic efficacy, the chances of fundamental regime alternatives (given the absence of stateness problem) being raised by a group in society is empirically negligible'.[70] No regime is immune to economic downturns, but the effects will be different: 'Severe economic problems affect democratic and non-democratic regimes, especially authoritarian ones, very differently'.[71] There are good theoretical reasons why sharp economic decline will adversely affect the stability of both democratic and nondemocratic regimes, although it will affect the latter substantially more because such regimes always base their legitimacy on their performance.

Economic performance of any regime is important for its survival, but, according to Linz and Stepan, 'it's not changes in the economy but changes in politics that trigger regime erosion – that is the effects of poor economy often have to be mediated by political change'. They go on, 'the question of system blame is crucial for the fate of democracies... A country that is experiencing positive growth, other things being equal, has a better chance to consolidate democracy than a country that is experiencing negative growth'.[72]

But it is the political perceptions of citizens that really matter to the stability of any regime:

> Where the citizens come to believe that the democratic system itself is compounding the economic problem or incapable of defining or implementing a credible strategy of economic reform, the system blame will aggravate the political effect of economic hard times. More importantly, economic crises will tend to lead to democratic breakdown in those cases where powerful groups outside, or – more fatally – inside the government increasingly argue that non-democratic alternatives of rule are the only solution to the economic crisis.[73]

There are powerful groups outside the Iraqi government (Ba'athists) and even inside it who believe in non-democratic alternatives.

The current economic downturn in Iraq is causing a lot of problems for the regime itself as many people have begun to question the efficacy of democracy. Mahdi Al-Hafidh, MP, has called for the declaration of emergency due to terrorist threats and economic difficulties.[74] If reforms are to be successful, the ruler must have personal control over economic decision-making and the ability to recruit a 'cohesive reform team and the political authority to override bureaucratic and political opposition to policy change'.[75] The current PM doesn't have such authority and he is struggling to maintain the cohesiveness of his government which is made up of many rival parties. He is unable to replace the ministers who lost the confidence of parliament. As Haggard and Kaufman argue, 'centralization of authority has been crucial for economic reform in both authoritarian and democratic regimes'.[76] This is not possible under the current consociational arrangement that exists in Iraq whereby all political parties have to share power according to their representation in parliament.

Where the democratic political actors are incapable or unwilling to search for solutions and even compound the problem by such actions as infighting and corruption, key actors will search for alternatives. But alternatives might not be available. As Linz and Stepan write:

> In such circumstances, many of these actors might resign themselves to a poorly performing democracy. Such resignation may not prevent crises, upheavals and attempted local coups, but is not conducive to regime change, but it certainly makes consolidation difficult and can even deconsolidate a democracy.[77]

This means there is a need for continuous action to keep democratization on track. 'Even the easiest and most successful transition was lived as a precarious process constantly requiring innovative political action'.[78] What is keeping the balance now is perhaps the inability of any of the parties to seize power and rule on its own.

The Spanish economy deteriorated sharply during the transition and didn't improve until three years after consolidation in 1982. Spanish unemployment in 1970, under Franco, around 3 per cent, was one of the lowest in Europe. In the mid 1980s, it was 20 per cent, the highest in Europe. Economic growth was over 7 per cent from 1960 to 1975; it went down to 1.7 per cent between 1975 and 1985.[79]

This goes to prove two things. First, democracy doesn't always lead to prosperity; and second, economic downturn under democracy doesn't necessarily lead people to abandon democracy. The rules of democracy 'guarantee opposition groups the right to challenge incumbent rulers and policies and to replace those rulers through competitive elections'.[80] What complicates this problem is the 'uncertainty of the loyalty of groups associated with the old order'.[81] These groups have certainly played a destabilizing role but were not able to derail the process.

Outcomes of democratization

The path to democracy is like a land mine, as Adam Przeworski explains, and 'the final destination depends on the path'.[82] It's fragile in most countries where it has been established, while in others, transitions into democracy were not successful. In other words, transitions don't necessarily lead to consolidated democracy:

> Democracy is consolidated when most conflicts are processed through democratic institutions, when nobody can control the outcomes *ex post* and the results are not predetermined *ex ante*, they matter within predictable limits and they evoke the compliance of the relevant political forces.[83]

Przeworski reveals 'the breakup of an authoritarian regime may be reversed, as was the case in Czechoslovakia in 1968, in Brazil in 1974, and in Poland in 1981, or it may lead to a new dictatorship as in Iran and Romania'. Even when democracy is established, it may not be consolidated, as democratic institutions may generate outcomes that cause some politically important forces to opt for authoritarianism.[84] Przeworski predicts five outcomes:

1   The structure of conflicts is such that no democratic institutions can last and political forces may end up fighting for a new dictatorship. Conflicts over the political role of religion, race, or language are least likely to be solvable by any set of institutions as in Iran.
2   The structure of conflicts is such that no democratic institutions can last and political forces agree to democracy as a transitional solution as in Argentina between 1953 and 1976.

3   The structure of conflicts is such that some democratic institutions will be durable if adopted, but the conflicting political forces fight to establish a dictatorship. This outcome may ensue when political forces have different preferences over institutional framework: unitary versus federalism. This may result in civil war and dictatorship.

4   Political forces agree to an institutional framework that cannot last, although the structure of conflicts is such that some democratic institutions will be durable if adapted.

5   The structure of conflicts is such that some democratic institutions will be durable if adopted and they are.[85]

Prospects

A consolidated democracy is, therefore, one option among at least five. Any of the first four outcomes may apply to Iraq, depending on different readings of the political process. The optimists believe there is hope for Iraqi democratizations to develop and consolidate, while the pessimists believe the only hope is to start from scratch once again, which will be almost impossible as the gains made by some parties are not going to be foregone easily by them.

The Iraqi democratization is neither consolidated nor failed completely. A reversal can happen, as in Czechoslovakia in 1968, in Brazil in 1974, and in Poland in 1981, or it may lead to a new dictatorship as in Iran and Romania, especially with the help of neighbouring countries hostile to democracy for fear of upsetting their internal political setup. But it's clear no single group, political, religious or sectarian, can rule on its own in the foreseeable future. It's also clear that no one country, currently, could really impose its will on all Iraqis. But things could change in the future with Iran being the most influential power in Iraq, with all the Shia groups that it supports or controls.

Ali Allawi describes the emerging political map as combining 'elements of intrigue and corruption'.[86] Regrettably, as Allawi put it, 'plots, as opposed to democracy-building and democratic practice of politics, dominated the political scene, as politicians from various communities engaged in endless bickering over the spoils of power and privilege'. Not many people are working towards consolidating the democratic system at present.

Yes, there has been some progress, but that was due to 'deal-making between political leaders', as Ali Allawi stated. It has failed to produce the national consensus necessary to bridge the widening ethnic and sectarian rifts and consequently create a modern democratic state. The constitution, for example, 'had all the hallmarks of a series of deals by political operatives'.[87] Article 2A could be triggered by Islamists to achieve their goals. At the same time, it's difficult to change the constitution since this requires consensus among the three main components (Shia, Sunni and Kurds). Any constitutional amendment requires the approval of the majority and must not be rejected by two thirds of the electorate in three provinces as per Article 142-Fourth.[88]

Ali Allawi is pessimistic about the prospects of democracy in Iraq. He contends,

> there was no national vision for anything, just a series of deals to push forward a political process, the end state of which was indeterminate. There was also no governing plan. The corroded and corrupt state of Saddam was replaced by the corroded, inefficient, incompetent and corrupt state of the new order.[89]

Despite all the doom and gloom, democratization in Iraq has not completely failed, but it has faltered and it could fail with the militarization of society, the proliferation of militias and spread of corruption. Islamization of society is not going to lead to democracy and unless it slows down, the future for democracy is bleak.

Liberalism, which is the most important basis of democracy, has shrunk in Iraq, and the first victims of this are civil liberties and women. This is manifested in repeated attacks on social clubs and shops selling alcohol. Democracy is not just about elections and changing political leaders, but about freedoms and civil liberties and these must be preserved and protected if democracy is to succeed.

Samuel Huntington predicts 'time is on the side of democracy'. This is true, but it also requires political leaders who believe it's 'the least worse form of government for their societies and for themselves'.[90] This principle perhaps is the one that governs the Iraqi political process currently, but the main political operators have designs for other alternatives, and this could constitute a fatal danger to democracy.

Challenges to democracy

Democracy becomes consolidated when it is 'the only game in town' according to Linz and Stepan. It's not the only game in town in Iraq currently since political parties can have other 'games' to play. Most of them rely on foreign countries for support and the major ones have armed militias and could resort to using arms when they do not get their way in the democratic process. They have not done it so far on a large scale, although they resorted to assassinations against each other's personnel.

They have committed other violations such as using religious symbols, inciting sectarian, regional and ethnic hatred, twisting facts and giving distorted information. The existence of militias has deterred and will always deter the press, the judiciary and the people from investigating, reporting on, or exposing their mistakes and corruption. In a democracy, there is no place for a militia or any kind of compulsion. People must vote according to their conscience.

Democracy is also described as a 'system where parties lose elections'. So far in Iraq, the Shia alliance (UIA), now called (National Alliance), has won all elections since the first one in January 2005. It's true that governments since 2005 have been coalitions, where other parties have participated, but the Shia alliance chose the prime minister and all the ministers, even those fielded by other parties. They also occupied most important positions in the country. Institutional arrangements have not yet been transformed into 'relations of cooperation' between political parties, and democracy is not yet 'self-enforcing'.

There is still a lack of identification with the state since there are still groups and individuals who wish to join or form other states. The Kurds for example have publicly declared their intentions to establish an independent state, while the Sunnis are talking about a federal region or even an independent state. The Christians and the Yazidis have also come to the same conclusion after their areas were occupied by ISIS and found themselves defenceless while other communities, the Kurds, Sunnis and Shia, have defended their areas and left them to their fate. There are political groups and leaders who emphasize primordial identities for emotional and self-interest-related reasons.

Arab and Kurdish nationalisms are still strong and this is not helpful to democratic consolidation, which is enhanced by equal citizenship and the 'common roof' provided by the state for all citizens. The imposition of Shia religious culture on the rest of the country, especially in areas with Shia majority, is not helpful for the development of an Iraqi national identity. Federalism cannot solve the ethnic, religious or sectarian problems, since there are no spatial differences between communities and people have been living together for centuries. Although there are provinces in the north with Kurdish majorities, the Kurds live in large numbers in three other provinces: Nineveh, Kirkuk and Dyala as well as the capital Baghdad.

Rules of democracy guarantee the opposition the right to challenge incumbent rulers and replace them in competitive elections. This didn't happen in 2010 when Ayad Allawi won the elections. The incumbent Islamist PM, Noori Al-Maliki, refused to vacate his position and he got the Federal Court to issue a ruling allowing him to form a coalition after the elections. The idea behind this was that Allawi led a list that was largely Sunni while the leadership of the government should remain in the hands of the sectarian majority group, the Shia, not the political majority led by Allawi which was not entirely Sunni, but cross-sectarian.

Democracy is successful when most conflicts are resolved through democratic institutions, but this is clearly not the case in Iraq with the Shia insisting on leading the government and with the existence of militias and armed groups.

With so many ethnicities, sects and religions, the Iraqi population is certainly not homogeneous, and this requires more efforts from democracy crafters. This is not to say that democracy cannot be consolidated in a multilingual, multicultural and multi-religious society such as the Iraqi one, but it requires considerable political crafting of democratic norms, practices and institutions. This is not happening yet.

In the interim constitution, approved by the Iraqi Governing Council in March 2004, the PR electoral system was chosen, with Iraq being one constituency. This type of PR system promotes a national political agenda and allows spatially dispersed communities to be fairly represented in parliament. The first elections of January 2005 were conducted according to this highly representative system. But it was changed by Islamists in the permanent constitution approved by the Islamist-controlled National Assembly. Elections are now conducted according to Iraqi-Modified Saint Lague system which favours established parties over new ones. This will ensure the continuation of Islamist rule for a long time to come.

Finally, polis/demos incongruence is not helpful to democracy, but it is very clearly present in Iraq. There are at least three obvious polities in the country: Shia, Sunni and Kurdish. Within those polities, there are also secular, Arab and Islamist polities. This incongruence creates problems for democratic consolidation especially when it's not addressed at all. In fact, there are people who are working hard to deepen it in order to craft permanent constituencies for the different polities.

Notes

1 Linz and Stepan (1996) op. cit. p. 5
2 Przeworski (1991) op. cit. p. 10
3 Ibid., p. 26
4 Haggard and Kaufman (1995) op. cit. p. 15
5 Przeworski (1991) op. cit. p. 16
6 Linz and Stepan (1996) op. cit. p. 6
7 Ibid., p. 19, and Diamond (2005) p. 23
8 Linz and Stepan (1996) op. cit. p. 7
9 Perry Chiaramonte, Fox News, 16/2/2017: https://goo.gl/lby2ej
10 Linz and Stepan (1996) op. cit. p. 21
11 Soumaya Ghannoushi, 'The erosion of the Arab State', Aljazeera, 26/9/2005: https://goo.gl/R2m3h5 Also, Future Directions, 'League summit sees Arab nations divided on Syria', 4/4/2012: https://goo.gl/HkznmN
12 Linz and Stepan (1996) op. cit. p. 22
13 Ibid.
14 Ibid.
15 Ibid.
16 Ibid., p. 23
17 Ibid.
18 Ibid., p. 25
19 Ibid.
20 Ibid.
21 Ibid., p. 26
22 Ibid.
23 Ibid., p. 27
24 Guy Taylor, *Washington Times*, 6/5/2015: https://goo.gl/tO4gSc
25 Diamond (2005) op. cit. p. 22
26 Eisenstadt and Mathewson (eds) (2003) op. cit. p. 30
27 Ibid.
28 Ibid.
29 Ibid., p. 36
30 Eisenstadt and Mathewson (2003) op. cit. p. 39
31 Linz and Stepan (1996) op. cit. p. 29
32 Ibid., p. 30
33 Ibid., p. 31
34 Ibid., pp. 31–32

35 Ibid., p. 33
36 Arend Lijphart, *World Politics*, volume 21, issue 2, January 1969, pp. 207–225
37 Linz and Stepan (1996) op. cit. p. 33
38 Omar Sattar, 'Sadrist call to change electoral law could push local elections to 2018', Al-Monitor, 10/10/2016: https://goo.gl/X0ZO7G
39 Linz and Stepan (1996) op. cit. p. 28
40 Ibid.
41 Jack Snyder, *From Voting to Violence: Democratization and Nationalist Conflict*, W.W. Norton. (2000) p. 79
42 Ali Mamouri, 'Iraqi media also characterized by political, sectarian bias', Am-Monitor, 23/2/2009: https://goo.gl/B2FpzO
43 Linz and Stepan (1996) op. cit. pp. 7–15
44 Allawi (2007) op. cit. p. 16
45 Linz and Stepan (1996) op. cit. pp. 7–13
46 David Nummy in Bremer (2007) op. cit. p. 28
47 Haggard and Kaufman (1995) op. cit. p. 16
48 Linz and Stepan (1996) op. cit. p. 40
49 LA Times, 'Hussein names half-brother to high Iraqi post', 14/11/1991: http://articles.latimes.com/1991-11-14/news/mn-1894_1_security-forces. Also, Con Coughlin, *Saddam: The Secret Life*, Pan Books (2007) p. 122
50 Eric Davis, Foreign Policy Research Institute, 'U.S. foreign policy in post-SOFA Iraq', 3/9/2011: www.fpri.org/article/2011/09/u-s-foreign-policy-in-post-sofa-iraq/
51 Linz and Stepan (1996) op. cit. p. 349
52 Yousif Ibrahim, *New York Times*, 10/5/1996: https://goo.gl/D1BX8z
53 Linz and Stepan (1996) op. cit. p. 51
54 Ibid., p. 53
55 Tahir Al-Ani, interview, *Russia Today* (Arabic) 24/7/2016: https://goo.gl/py0FqT
56 Tripp (2007) op. cit. p. 198
57 Tarik Kafala, BBC News-Online, 25/3/2003: https://goo.gl/vbvs1T
58 Tripp (2007) op. cit. p. 215
59 Phebe Marr (quoted by Toby Dodge, *Iraq: From War to New Authoritarianism*, Routledge (2012) p. 25
60 Bremer (2006) op. cit. p. 29
61 Ahmed S Hashim, *Insurgency and Counter-Insurgency in Iraq*, Cornell University Press. (2006) p. 110.
62 Ibid., p. 111
63 Linz and Stepan (1996) op. cit. p. 55
64 Ibid.
65 Ibid., p. 56
66 Phebe Marr, USIP Special Report, March 2006: https://goo.gl/EmkM20
67 Linz and Stepan (1996) op. cit. p. 77
68 Ibid.
69 Ibid., p. 78
70 Ibid., p. 79
71 Ibid.
72 Ibid., p. 80
73 Ibid., p. 81
74 New Sabah newspaper (Arabic) 22/8/2015: www.newsabah.com/wp/newspaper/58576
75 Haggard and Kaufman (1995) op. cit. p. 9
76 Ibid., p. 10
77 Linz and Stepan (1996) op. cit. p. 81
78 Ibid., p. 89
79 Ibid., p. 113

80 Haggard and Kaufman (1995) op. cit. p. 13
81 Ibid., p. 14
82 Przeworski (1991) op. cit. p. 51
83 Ibid.
84 Ibid.
85 Ibid., pp. 52–53
86 Allawi (2007) pp. 348–369
87 Ibid., p. 417
88 Iraqi Constitution: www.iraqinationality.gov.iq/attach/iraqi_constitution.pdf
89 Allawi (2007) op. cit. p. 460
90 Huntington (1991) op. cit. p. 316

5 Religion and politics

Relevance of religion

Religion has become so relevant to our modern world, especially in the Middle East since the advent of the Islamic awakening in the 1970s following the Arab defeat of 1967.[1] Farag Foda, the Egyptian scholar who was murdered by extremists because of his critical views, believed that the defeat of 1967 was not regarded as a defeat for Egypt or the Egyptian leadership, but a condemnation of the way that Egypt had adopted Western culture and civilization. Foda believed this idea gained support because of the fact that Israel is a religious entity. He observed that violent Islamic extremism appeared in all Arab countries in the wake of the 1967 Arab defeat.[2] Islamic fundamentalism triumphed in February 1979 when the Iranian Islamic revolution succeeded in toppling the Shah.

Islam has been a potent force almost everywhere in the world. In Iraq, Islamist parties, be they Sunni or Shia, were voted into parliament in 2005, and they have been leading the government ever since. This chapter explores the thoughts of John Rawls, based on his book *Political Liberalism*,[3] as applied to the idea of incorporating religious believers into political debate and participation. Since it's difficult in a democracy to exclude an important section of society from the political debate, especially in Islamic societies where this section may constitute the majority, it's important to look at ways to incorporate them without compromising either the principles of democracy or the freedom of belief. Since the issue of religion and politics is not exclusive to Muslim societies, which are new to democracy, it's important to find out how democratic societies have dealt with it, and Rawls' ideas provide insight into the issue.

The thoughts of a prominent Muslim scholar, Sheikh Ali Abdur-Razik, regarding the role of Islam in politics, based on his landmark study, *Islam and the Fundamentals of Governance*, are also examined.[4] Many Islamic scholars, Sunni and Shia, just like Razik, believe that the government should be civil since it's a worldly affair and not concerned with the afterlife. The traditional Shia school (the quietest school) approves of this view.[5] A quietist cleric doesn't demand to participate in government nor presumes to exercise control over the state. He can remain aloof from all political matters, but he is not totally apolitical. 'During times of moral decadence, political corruption, serious injustice, or foreign occupation, he can become more active in politics by offering advice, guidance, and even the promotion of sacred law in public life'.[6]

Razik, an Islamic scholar at Al-Azhar Mosque and University, first published his ideas in 1925, but they came to prominence after the rise of Islamic fundamentalism in the Arab world in the 1970s and 80s. It has become more relevant now with popular uprisings going on in some countries of the Middle East, widely referred to as the 'Arab Spring'.[7] I contend that democracy cannot succeed unless it finds a way to reconcile religion with politics. Rawls' thoughts dealt with Christian societies while Razik's thoughts dealt with Muslim societies. A major pillar of democracy is that the government guarantees civil liberties and personal freedoms using the power at its disposal. On the other hand, the politically religious seek to limit civil liberties and personal freedoms. This paradox needs to be resolved for societies to live in peace and harmony and for democracy to succeed. This study explores possible solutions based on Rawls' and Razik's thoughts in their different contexts. Shia scholars such as Hani Fahs, Muhammed Mahdi Shamsuddeen and Muhammed Hussein Fadhlalla have similar thoughts.

The Shia quietist school, which I have referred to in different places of this study, provides the ultimate solution to this paradox by making it a religious duty not to interfere in politics except at times of crisis. This is similar to the position of Ali Abdu-Razik. But Islamist political parties follow the interventionist school politically, even though they may follow the quietist school on religious issues. This may sound contradictory to some, but it's expedient politically for political Islam since they want to show ordinary people, who follow the quietist school, that their position accords with the teachings of this school. It's likely that the next generation of religious leaders may not belong to the quietist school for many reasons that are beyond the scope of this study.

Political liberalism

John Rawls' 'political liberalism' calls for the integration of all sections of society within a democratic system, including religious believers, who are 'not going to go away', so they must be integrated into the political debate. It is important to involve all sections of society in the political debate and preserve the interests of all by finding a common denominator among them.

Rawls proposes a political conception of justice that all citizens, be they religious or not, can recognize as valid and acceptable, and be prepared to adhere to. He proposes a political conception that can deal with fundamental political questions that a democratic society usually faces. This conception includes an agreement on what he calls 'constitutional essentials'.[8] These are of two types: principles and rights.

The first type deals with the political process and structure of the government while the second deals with the rights and freedoms of citizens that the political majorities must respect and not take away from them. They include liberty of conscience, freedom of thought and association and the protection of the rule of law. The conception that Rawls seeks to establish is one that all citizens, of all creeds and persuasions, can publicly recognize as valid so that society's 'main institutions and how they fit together into one system of social cooperation can be assessed in the same way by each citizen, whatever that citizen's social position or more particular interests'. He calls this political conception of justice 'justice as fairness'.[9]

Rawls cites three traits of modern democratic society. They require that justice as fairness to be seen as a political conception.[10] These traits are:

1 Pluralism

Modern society (or Post-reformation) is characterized by the presence of 'reasonable pluralism', which could constitute a 'reasonable comprehensive doctrine'. This means a moral theory that includes

> conceptions of what is of value in human life, and ideals of personal character as well as ideals of friendship and of familial and associational relationships, and much else that is to inform our conduct, and in the limit to our life as a whole.[11]

Rawls suggests that 'reasonable disagreement is an inherent part of modern democratic life' and that is why

> no one comprehensive religion, doctrine or philosophical or moral doctrine is affirmed by all citizens generally and it would be wrong to expect in the foreseeable future one of them or some other reasonable doctrine will ever be affirmed by all or nearly all citizens.[12]

This means that pluralism of thought and creed will be a permanent feature of modern society and pluralism means no prominence to any doctrine, creed or moral philosophy.

2 Objection to oppression

Post-reformation society recognizes that you can only maintain the dominance of one religion or ideology through oppression, namely by the use of massive power by the state. Oppression, by nature, is anti-democratic and anti-modern; therefore, it would be oppressive of the modern state to impose on its citizens any way or ways of living. Since there is reasonable pluralism, oppression won't be allowed by the majority of people, and this oppression-fearing majority won't allow dominance by any religious or philosophical doctrine in society.[13]

3 Quest for justice

For the concept of justice to endure in a post-Reformation society, 'it must be actively supported by all citizens, freely and willingly'.[14] Given the presence of reasonable pluralism, a concept of justice needs to be endorsed by widely different and opposing, though reasonable, comprehensive doctrines, for it to be the basis of justification for a pluralistic constitutional regime.

Modern democratic society is characterized by dissensus and debate, since there is no single doctrine or philosophical or religious ideology that can form the basis of political regulation without oppressing or excluding some sections of society. Therefore, any conception of justice 'that may be shared by citizens as a basis for a reasoned, informed and willing agreement' must be one that can gain the support of an overlapping consensus of reasonable religious, philosophical and moral doctrines in a society regulated by it'.[15]

A conception of justice must be 'free standing'. That is, it must not exclusively refer to any particular doctrine, be it ideological, religious or philosophical.[16] Justice as fairness must be articulated in such a way that all or most members of the democratic society in question feel they can relate to it. Its basic idea must be found in the 'public political culture' of that society.[17] But at the same time, it must not be, wherever possible, in conflict with any reasonable comprehensive doctrine or doctrines so that the followers of these doctrines won't find it conflicting with their beliefs if they adopt such a concept.

To achieve this correlation between the political conception of justice and religious doctrines, the principles of toleration should be applied to the philosophy behind it; in other words, the political conception of justice must avoid any religious, philosophical and moral issues which are in dispute.[18] These issues must be left to the believers to settle among themselves through civil and peaceful means in accordance with the views that they freely affirm.[19] This has to be done through removing religious issues from political agendas.[20] Once they have been removed, they are 'no longer regarded as appropriate subjects for political decision by majority or other plurality voting'.[21] Removing religious questions from the political agenda is 'not because they are unimportant or regarded with indifference, but because we think they are too important and recognise that there is no way to resolve them politically'.[22]

This attempt to integrate religious believers into the political process may run into obstacles especially when all religious questions and issues are left out of the political debate. But what if the religiously devout do not agree to this? Rawls distinguishes between the 'public' basis of justification that forms the public political culture of a democratic society, and the non-public justification which belongs to 'civil society' or 'the background culture'.[23]

It's the public reason, represented by an elected government that can exercise the final coercive power on any section of society because the citizens are regarded as equal by the same public reason and because they all share one political conception, a public one, irrespective of the reasonable comprehensive doctrine they may affirm.[24] While a distinction between believers, or followers of different doctrines, can be made within the civil society, in a democratic society there is no distinction between citizens; they are all equal before the law. The reason is public because it's the reason of citizens or the public. Its nature and content are public (as opposed to private); its subject is the good of the public and matters of fundamental justice.[25]

But public reason has limits.[26] This precludes the expression of certain forms of conviction and argument in public debates, especially when 'discussing constitutional essentials and matters of basic justice'.[27] This limit will not extend to 'personal deliberations and reflections about political questions or to the reasoning about them by members of associations such as churches and universities'. 'Religious, philosophical and moral considerations of many kinds may here play a role'. Limits of public reasons also hold true for citizens as well 'when they are engaged in public advocacy in the public forum and they vote in elections when constitutional essentials and matters of basic justice are at stake'.[28]

Disallowing the employment or the expression of any form of religious arguments and beliefs in public debates is not so rigid. 'Citizens are allowed to present what they regard as the basis for political values rooted in their comprehensive doctrine, provided they do this in ways that strengthen the ideal of public reason itself'.[29] Rawls originally allowed this only in civil society, not political society.

But one can legitimately ask who decides which values strengthen public reason and which ones don't? Is it the citizen him/herself? If yes, how far can this go and when and who will stop him or her if they wanted to employ all their religious values in public debates on the assumption that they 'strengthen' public reason? Religious believers have convictions. They firmly believe in the teachings of their doctrines and they follow them to the letter. How can they be persuaded to follow a different path that may lead them to a different set of values which they may find in conflict with their original beliefs?

Muslim believers, for example, firmly believe it's their religious duty to change others and bring them to their way of thinking and they may not be prepared to compromise on this tenet.

Society types

Rawls divides society into three types, depending on the political circumstances they live under.[30] First, a society that is 'well-ordered and its members recognise a firm overlapping consensus of reasonable doctrines and it's not stirred by deep disputes'. In this society, religious convictions should be excluded from public debates in what is called 'exclusive approach'. Second, a society that is 'nearly well-ordered' but subject to serious disputes with respect to applying one of its principles of justice. An 'inclusive approach' should be adopted, especially regarding allowing the state to support religious schools.[31]

Third, a society that is 'not well-ordered' and where there are 'profound divisions' about constitutional essentials when certain religious arguments were tolerated.[32] In this case the focus should be on whether the religious convictions of the believers truly contravene the ideal of public reason. 'Longer term views must be taken whereby the ideal maybe best achieved in good times by following what at first sight may appear to be an exclusive view, in less good times, to be the inclusive view'.[33]

Allowance is given to the timing and circumstances under which the ideal of excluding religious convictions from political debate is implemented. This 'timeline' for the achievement of the goal, or the permitted circumstantial convenience, softens the impact of excluding religious convictions from political debate. It's a pragmatic way of reaching the original goal of total exclusion of religious convictions form political debate through stages if and when it is difficult to achieve it in one go.

Rawls wants religious issues to be taken out of the political agenda completely.[34] This is because religious issues do not serve the political aim of the majority of the public in a democratic society since they are controversial and should be confined to the civil society which nurtures all sorts of issues and arguments.[35] Religious questions, arguments and convictions should not even form part of the political vocabulary of the religious believer. The employment of religious convictions or arguments can be tolerated in public debate, only if they supported the 'clear conclusion of public reason'.[36]

Islam and governance

Sheikh Ali Abdur-Razik argues that the 'Islamic government' (caliphate) was not stipulated in the Qura'an nor in the Prophet's Tradition (Sunna). He could not find any evidence in the religious texts to support establishing it. He affirms Muhammed was not a ruler as such; he was a prophet like other prophets before him.

Razik acknowledges that people may have regarded some actions of the Prophet as 'governance', but they were part of his duties as a prophet even though they may have looked as governmental but this was because people 'obeyed him and followed his orders and advice because he was a prophet, not because he was their ruler'.[37] 'The position of the message requires an authority that is wider than that of the ruler and even wider than that of the father on his children'.[38]

He argued 'If there was a near-evidence to this effect, the proponents of this idea would not have hesitated to use it, but they have failed to bring a shred of evidence to support their claim'.[39] The Qura'an, according to Razik, didn't call for such a government and all the legitimacy that its proponents claim stems from 'consensuses' or 'logic' or 'necessity'.

Caliphate was a mistake

Razik acknowledges that calling the government after the Prophet 'caliphate' was a mistake and the rulers who came after the Prophet should not have called themselves caliphs (successors) because this was misleading. 'Only prophets can succeed prophets', he avers.

He reveals the caliphs were not absolute rulers at the beginning, but were restricted by the principles and rules laid out in the Qura'an and the Prophet's tradition.[40] People obeyed caliphs because they believed that 'caliphs had the same status as the Prophet who the Muslims hold in the highest regards and also because they were applying Islam which was the dearest thing to Muslims in the whole universe'.[41]

Razik states that Caliphs remained restricted by Islamic legal jurisdiction until the Abbasid Caliph, Haroon Ar-Rasheed, when the caliphate changed and remained in name only 'due to Arab fanaticism'.[42] It became an absolute rule, yet people kept their allegiance to it nevertheless. He calls on those who attached holiness to caliphate to show the evidence and the source of the caliph's authority. 'They neglected this as they did with all things related to the science of politics or anything that resembled caliphate'.[43]

Razik explains the existence of two views regarding the caliph's position. First, the caliph's authority is bestowed on him by God. This view is 'prevalent among most clerics and people. Some caliphs like Mansour claimed he was 'the shadow of God on His earth'.[44]

In addition, scholars and people bestowed this heavenly authority on caliphs. This was widespread, and scholars and poets spoke of such an authority for the caliphs. Scholars, especially those who came after the fifth century of the Islamic calendar, had persistently regarded caliphs as 'above human' and not far from the status of God, Razik charges.

Second, a caliph takes his authority from the nation.[45] Razik quotes a poem recited before the second caliph, Omar, by the Arab poet, Al-Hutay'aa, in which he told him he was actually authorized and appointed by the nation (as opposed to God).[46]

He states that scholars such as Al-Kasani likened the authority of the caliph to that of the judge whose authority is linked to people's approval of him since he works in their interest and is appointed by them.[47] He compared the authority of the caliph to that of European kings, which led to European development. He likened the first school where caliphs drew their authority from God to the doctrine of Thomas Hobbes, while the second school where caliphs drew their authority from the nation to the doctrine of John Locke.[48]

The four caliphs who succeeded the Prophet, Abu-Bakir, Omar, Othman and Ali, were actually rulers who dealt with worldly issues. Razik challenged all those who believe there was a stipulation for an Islamic government in the Qura'an to provide the evidence to support their claims.[49] 'All fair-minded scholars could not find any evidence in the Book, so they turned to other forms of evidence such as consensus, reason and logic.'[50] Razik explains verses of the Qura'an which might be used as evidence, such as verses 59 and 83 of Chapter 4 which call on Muslims to refer any outstanding issues to the Prophet or those in charge of their affairs to sort out. But because these verses are not used by the proponents of caliphate or imamate to support their claim, he decided not to 'spend a long time on them in order to avoid vanity and fighting with a non-foe'.[51] The most these verses say, Razik explains, 'Muslims have other people they should go to regarding their affairs' and this is a lot wider than the specific 'Islamic government'. The Qura'an has dealt with every aspect of religion, and it actually states this clearly, yet it has no specific verse about universal caliphate or imamate. It is a great wonder that the Qura'an, from the first chapter to the last one, has described everything in details regarding this religion, but you cannot find, not even a mention of, caliphate or imamate in it. Hence, there is a space here for an opinion.[52]

After exhausting the Qura'an, Razik turns to the Sunna, and hadeeth, both regarded as legal sources for Islamic jurisprudence. 'It is not just the Qura'an that has neglected caliphate and didn't address it. The Sunna has done the same. It left it and never dealt with it'. This, Razik contends, proves that Islamic scholars could not find any evidence from the tradition to support of their argument; otherwise they would have used it.[53]

Arabs and politics

Razik raised many questions about why the Arabs neglected to learn politics and why they neglected to study Plato's book, the Republic, and Aristotle's book, the Politics, even though both men are highly respected by the Arabs to the point that Aristotle was described as the 'First Teacher'. He laments that Muslims in general have been left 'in total ignorance of the principles of politics and the types of governments in Greece'.[54]

Muslim scholars did not leave the science of politics out of their own accord, it appears. 'It was forced upon them by caliphs and kings', Razik concluded. He asserted it was a direct action by their rulers who felt threatened by any political knowledge by their subjects.

Razik's view of the caliphate is damning:

The Caliphate, throughout its history, was built on defeating the other. Its throne was always erected on the heads of people and has always been laid on their necks and what is called crown has no life except what it takes of human life, has no power except the one it takes of their power, no greatness or dignity except what it steals of their greatness and dignity, just like the night; when it's long, it always comes at the expense of the dawn; its brightness comes from the brightness of the sword and the flame of the wars.[55]

But he reserved a totally different description for Islam. 'It is a religion that, not only has taught its followers brotherhood and equality theoretically', mentored them that 'people are as equal as the teeth of a comb', and told them that the slaves you keep are your brothers in religion, but it also trained them on this practically and showed it to them in reality until they began to feel it. Their prophet didn't leave them till he impressed their hearts with this religion and accustomed them to it and their state was not established before an ordinary citizen calls upon the caliph: 'If you go wrong, we will correct you with our swords'.[56]

He made a clear distinction between the caliphate as a system of government imposed by force, and the religion of Islam which preaches equality and dignity. The first is established and maintained through oppression and comes at the expense of people's power and dignity, while the second is in people's hearts and consciences, enhances their dignity and calls for equality among them.

Razik states that Muslims were taught by their religion to be free while the caliphate imposes on them a ruler who will curtail their freedom and reduces their dignity and power. Razik concludes:

> Muslims are too proud to bow to anyone but God, and they communicate with their God 17 times a day at five specific times with this very belief in mind. Obviously, it is natural for these free people not to submit to one man from among themselves, the type of submission that kings demand of their subjects, unless they are forced to do so by sheer force.[57]

He goes further by asserting that caliphate contravenes the basic principles of Islam.

Religion doesn't need a government

Razik explored other evidence that the proponents of caliphate can come up with to prove their point.[58] One of their arguments is that for Muslims to perform their Islamic rituals and rites, they need a government.[59] Acknowledging the need for government for any civil society, whether it had a religion or not, be it Muslim, Christian, Jewish or else, Razik ponders:

> If the religious scholars meant by the caliphate/imamate the same as what the scholars of politics meant, then they are right that the performance of the religious ritual and rites and interest of the nation do need a caliphate as in 'government' of any type, be it monarchic or republican, despotic, consulta- tive or democratic, absolute or restricted, constitutional, Bolshevik or social- ist.... But if they meant by caliphate the type of government that they know (religious requirement), then their evidence is shorter than their claim. It does not stand.[60]

Razik contends Islam performed better over the years without an Islamic gov- ernment, while it was adversely affected when there was one ruling in its name. He states that performing religious duties did not depend on the government, whatever type it may take. 'In reality, the welfare and worldly interests of Muslims didn't depend on anything like that. We don't need this caliphate for our religion, nor for our worldly welfare'. Razik went further than this by declar- ing that 'the caliphate has been and still is a catastrophe to Islam and Muslims, and a source of harm and corruption'.[61]

In conclusion, Rawls' ideas regarding incorporating the religious within polit- ical debate are relevant to all societies, not just Christian or American societies.

As he stated, modern society is characterized by pluralism, debate and dissensus, and no religious or philosophical doctrine is affirmed by all or nearly all people. If a state is to impose a religion or doctrine on all its citizens, it can only do that by oppression and this is anti-democratic and anti-modern, and there is always an oppression-fearing majority within society which will not let it stand. A conception of justice has to be 'free standing' and recognized by all people of different religions and persuasions, but must not be in conflict with any of the reasonable doctrines in society.

Razik has coherently argued that there is no stipulation in the Qura'an or Sunna for a specific type of government. In fact, he described the 'caliphate' or 'imamate' as catastrophe to Islam and Muslims. The main Shia traditional school, the quietist tradition, believes firmly in the separation of religion and politics. Shia religious leaders, including the current one, Ayatullah Sistani, do not belong to the interventionist school of Ayatullah Khomeini. Islam in general favours a just and fair government and this principle is also affirmed by democracy. Therefore, democratic government can unite the people, achieve justice through a conception of justice that's not in conflict with any reasonable religious or philosophical doctrine, yet it relates to political culture of all or most people at the same time.

Since the creation of the Iraqi state in 1921, the conception of justice has never been 'free standing'. It always appealed to one constituency in the country. There was never a conception of justice that appealed to the common political culture of the country which is so diverse ethnically and religiously. The Iraqi state was established as an Arab and Sunni state. The first appealed to the Arabs who are the majority and the second appealed to the Sunnis (Kurds and Arabs) who are under half of the population. But the Sunni Arab ideology ended up alienating both Shia and Kurds who both form the overwhelming majority of the population. Being Arab, it alienated Kurds, and being Sunni, it alienated Shia. Abbas Kelidar regards it as 'externally irredentist and internally divisive'. All the state symbols were Sunni and Arab. The school syllabi, history and religion books, national holidays and religious holidays were all designed according to the Sunni doctrine.

Shia and Sunni doctrines were founded on two different narratives of history and theology. When the state follows one of them, it basically abolishes the other automatically. In response, the Shia, by and large, boycotted the government and the state institutions altogether and this remained the case for a long time before the mainstream Shia began to participate in political and other state activities. The Kurds took up arms against the state right from the beginning, demanding their own nation state. Their armed resistance never stopped until 2003.

The monarchy was never able to unite the diverse people of Iraq on one shared conception of justice, and when the army coup brought it down, it was largely welcomed by the majority of Iraqis, especially the Kurds and Shia. The republic created by General Qassim had a national Iraqist conception of justice. It was 'free standing' since it was shared by most of the people, but it came into direct conflict with Arab nationalism represented at the time by Col. Nassir of

Egypt. It was subjected to enormous pressures from Arab nationalists in Iraq and the wider Arab world, agitated by Nassir's pan-Arab rhetoric and also from the largely Shia tribal-religious alliance which had lost out under the new regime when it tried to be fair to the poor. Qassim's republic finally fell in 1963 and the Arab nationalists came back to control Iraq once again with their old one-constituency discourse and ideology.

When the Ba'athist took over in 1968, the tone of Arab nationalism was enhanced while the state remained symbolically Sunni Arab. Although it was officially secular, everything in the state relates to Sunni Arabism. The announcement of the beginning of Ramadan, the declaration of the two religious festivals (Eid ul Adha and Eid ul Fitr) as well as the pilgrimage to Mekka (haj) were made by the Baghdad First Judge who was always Sunni. The call to prayer over the state radio and television has always been performed according to the Sunni doctrine. Official school books on history and religion were overtly Sunni with no mention or reference to the opinion of the Shia. This has angered the Shia leaders and caused a crack in the national unity even among the Arabs themselves who embraced both doctrines. Continuous denial of Kurdish rights has alienated the Kurds further and pushed them to fight their most ferocious war against the state during the Ba'ath regime. The Kurdish rebellion weakened the Ba'athist regime and pushed it to make significant territorial concessions to Iran in the 1975 Algiers agreement to persuade the bellicose Shah to stop supporting the Kurdish guerillas in the north.

The conception of justice was not shared by all citizens, because it was not based on a shared political culture and it came in conflict with the Shia doctrine and the Kurdish sense of nationalism and culture. The state's discourse was never convincing nor acceptable to the rest of the population. It sought to overlook all sub-identities and impose an Arab Sunni identity on all the people including non-Arabs such as the Kurds, Turcoman and Assyrians. On top of that, the state had also imposed the Ba'athist ideology and way of thinking on everyone and those who didn't assimilate were persecuted.

When the Islamists came to power in 2005, they continued with the same single-constituency discourse and narrow conception of justice, imposing Shia discourse, beliefs and practices on everyone else. Their conception of justice has been for all Iraqis to accept or at least tolerate the Shia narrative of history, religion and culture. This has caused Sunni resentment and contributed to discord, violence, at times civil war, and instability of the country. When there is a Shia religious occasion, the whole country comes to a standstill, with major roads closed, work suspended and Shia posters and flags littering the streets of major cities, even the ones inhibited by Sunnis and Christians, and loudspeakers broadcast Shia religious messages and chants. This has continued to cause resentment among non-Shia and non-religious who may constitute a large component of the population.

The de-Ba'athification law which was issued by the Americans and enthusiastically applied by the new Shia political class has divided society and caused animosity and discord since it targeted a large section of society and it, not only alienated them, but it turned them against the state. In fact de-Ba'athification was used as a weapon against all Iraqis who lived under Saddam. It was also used selectively against political opponents. Sunnis in particular felt it was designed to marginalize them since most senior Ba'athists were Sunnis. All the rhetoric against Ba'athism that Shia Islamists engaged in was divisive and acrimonious. It alienated a large section of Iraqi society.

The political discourse was not national but Shia, Sunni or Kurdish. This has created at least three polities, in addition to a fourth non-religious one. There are common vocabularies repeated by Shia Islamist leaders which indict all Sunnis. For example, the expression 'incubator environment' (al-bee'ah al-hadhina) refers to the Sunni areas from where terrorists launch their attacks on civilians. This expression in fact embodies a tacit accusation of all Sunnis of being terrorists or terrorist sympathizers. It makes them feel they lack patriotism and it encourages others to insult them and/or mistreat them.

The Iraqi political discourse is full of divisive terms and issues. Iran, Turkey and Saudi Arabia all represent different concepts. If someone attacks Iran, the Shia automatically believe his/her attack is directed at them. Similarly, if Saudi Arabia or Turkey are criticized, Sunnis feel the criticism is done for sectarian reasons. You do find Shia criticizing Iran, and Sunnis Turkey and Saudi Arabia, but these three countries have also become symbols of division, especially Iran.

Over the years, there has never been a conception of justice in Iraq that was 'free standing' or not in conflict with a major doctrine, and this has contributed to the alienation and perception of injustice felt by large sections of the population, as well as to the division of society. In order to have a stable democracy and strong state, a 'free standing' conception of justice must be devised, and this must relate to the shared political culture of most citizens and at the same time it's not in conflict with any major religious or philosophical doctrine. Although the Iraqi society is diverse culturally, ethnically and religiously, but there are common characteristics relating to the country and its shared culture as well as certain Islamic and Christian values that can be promoted. At the same time, certain divisive sectarian or ethnic practices must be jettisoned in order to create this shared conception of justice that is free standing and appeals to all citizens.

It's clear that employing religion in politics is divisive and doesn't lead to enhancing the national identity or unifying the country. Since there is no stipulation in the Qura'an or Sunna for a religious government, according to the theory promoted by Ali Abdu-Razik and has now been recently embraced by the most senior authority in Sunni Islam, Al-Azhar Mosque.[62] And because the Shia traditional school (quietist trend) approves of separation of religion and politics, and this is supported by the views of many prominent and highly respected Shia scholars and religious leaders such as Muhammed Mahdi Shamsudeen, Hani Fahs and Muhammed Hussein Fadhlallah, devout Muslims, be they Sunni or Shia, can live happily and conscientiously under a secular system whereby there is a free-standing conception of justice that appeals to all citizens and is not in conflict with any major doctrine.

In fact, they could make it a religious duty to promote shared values that promote national unity and social coherence. This in turn enhances Iraq's stability and prosperity and maintains the pluralism, debate and dissensus that have become permanent features of modern society.

Major hurdles to democracy

Modern society is characterized by pluralism, quest for justice, rejection of oppression and dissensus. The new political class in Iraq has not recognized these principles and still raises the banner of Shiaism, Sunnism, Arabism and Kurdism among others. The mainstream thinking among the Shia is that their way of life, doctrine and culture must prevail because they are the majority. This does not accord with a 'free standing conception of justice' stated by Rawls.

What is needed is a conception of justice that is recognized and endorsed by all or nearly all citizens. This will achieve justice, remove oppression and at the same time preserve the current pluralism. Democracy is about inclusion of all citizens, regardless of their differences, be they religious, ethnic or regional. Since Shia and Sunni doctrines contrast each other in almost everything, from the religious calendar to jurisprudence and rituals as well as their readings and interpretations of historical events, it's important to formulate a common ground between all citizens that distances society from disputes and division and adopts a political discourse that is recognized by all citizens, yet not in conflict with any reasonable doctrine.

People can still express and practice their religious views and values, but within civil society. The Iraqi society is deeply divided on religious and doctrinal matters and not well-ordered. Therefore, in line with Rawls' theory, certain religious matters can be tolerated, but they must support and strengthen public reason. Any divisive issue must be relegated to civil society. This means that most religious issues should be left out of the public debate. However, religious principles such as fairness, charity, brotherhood and justice can be included in the political debate since they strengthen public reason and all citizens can identify with them.

In the last 20 years or so, Iraq has become a religious society, but since religion is divisive, in Iraq at least, due to its religiously diverse population, only those religious vocabularies that support clear conclusion of public reason should be allowed. This concept needs to be investigated further and consensus among the enlightened and upstanding religious scholars is needed for it to be implemented successfully. However, in a religious society such as the Iraqi one, this would be difficult to implement all at once. A gradual approach is needed. However, for democracy to consolidate there must be serious efforts on the parts of the political class to jettison any divisive matter from the public domain. So far, there has been no such effort. In fact, the opposite is happening where the Shia are trying to impose their doctrine and culture on the rest of the population, while the Sunnis have resorted to violence to defend their culture and religion.

It has been established in the previous pages that Islam doesn't require a religious government. Muhammed was not a ruler to be emulated, but a prophet, and the Shia traditional school, the quietist trend, believes in separation of politics and religion in the era of the 'Major Occultation of the Absent Imam'.[63] Yet, the main political parties currently operating in Iraq are Islamist, which take a different view to the above. They wish to establish a controversial system of religious government that is in conflict with traditional Islamic schools, be they Sunni or Shia, and at the same time anti-democratic by their own admission. They regard the democratic system as anti-Islamic and believe only in 'democratic mechanisms'. This is a big impediment to democracy especially with the spread of traditional religiosity, which was suppressed under Saddam Hussein, as well as illiteracy and political naivety.

If democracy is to succeed in Iraq, there is a need to establish a secular system where only secular parties are allowed to operate and where the national identity is paramount to all other sub-identities. Political Islam can be dealt with in two ways:

1   From an Islamic point of view, it runs counter to traditional the Sunni religious school and Shia quietist trend, both of which believe in the separation of religion and politics.
2   From a modern democratic viewpoint, democracy is accepted as the best governing system across the world and Muslims are no different to the rest of human beings. Islamists, despite their lack of belief in democracy, can operate and have been operating, within the democratic secular system with relative ease. They were able to win elections and govern through democracy. If people reject them at some point, they should try harder to win.

There has been a distortion, probably intentional, of the meaning of secularism in the Muslim world as Hani Fahs made clear.[64] It has been portrayed as anti-religion when it's an impartial system that allows all creeds and thoughts to prosper. If this distortion is dispelled though education and awareness-raising measures, people will choose a secular system that will preserve their religious beliefs and culture and at the same time serve their interests in creating a modern society with advanced political and economic systems.

People's unawareness in politics is also an impediment to democracy, especially when this field has been neglected, on purpose, by rulers for centuries, as Ali Abdur-Razik explained.[65] This will take time and it can be remedied though the spread of independent, free and professional media and social media as well as through the accumulated experience as the democratic process moves on. Therefore, people's electoral choices will remain lacking clarity, regarding which of the parties serves them best, until such time as political awareness is improved.

Islamist parties want to establish a system of government that is similar to the caliphate or imamate which Razik identified as un-Islamic, despotic and detrimental to people's dignity. It's also undemocratic since it cannot legislate laws that run counter to established Islamic teachings as the Iraqi constitution stipulates in Article 2A. This is another impediment to democracy which is all about representing the interests of the people it serves. In sum, certain religious values, which can strengthen public reason and accord with democratic principles, can be allowed, but, unless this is all done in democratic and secular settings, some political groups will resort to religion as a way of climbing to power.

Notes

1 Yvonne Haddad, in Johannes Janssen, *The Dual Nature of Islamic Fundamentalism*, Cornell University Press. (1997) p. 161
2 Farag Foda, in Johannes Janssen. (1997) op. cit. p. 161
3 John Rawls, *Political Liberalism*, Columbia University Press. (1993)
4 Ali Abdur-Razik, *Islam and the Fundamentals of Governance*, Lebanese Book House (1925)
5 Allawi (2007) p. 208
6 Babak Rahimi, 'Ayatollah Sistani and the Democratization of Post-Ba'athist Iraq', USIP, June 2007: www.usip.org/sites/default/files/sr187.pdf
7 More on 'Arab Spring': *Routledge Handbook of the Arab Spring*, ed. Larbi Sadiki, Routledge, London. (2015)
8 Rawls (1993–1996–2005) op. cit. p. 227
9 Ibid., p. 9
10 Ibid.
11 Ibid., p. 13
12 Ibid., p. xvi
13 Ibid., p. 37
14 Ibid., p. 38
15 Ibid., p. 10
16 Ibid., p. 12
17 Ibid., p. 9
18 Ibid., p. 10
19 Ibid., p. 154
20 Ibid., p. 151
21 Ibid., p. 151, footnote 16
22 John Rawls, 'Justice as fairness: Political not metaphysical', *Philosophy & Public Affairs* (1985) p. 230
23 Rawls (2005) op. cit. p. 220
24 Public reason is an idea developed by John Rawls which requires the adoption of a standard by which moral or political rules can be assessed. It also requires people to refrain from advocating or supporting rules that cannot be justified to those on whom they would be imposed. Only rules that can be justified by appeal to suitably shared or public considerations, such as freedom and equality, should be accepted. At the same time, there must be an abstention from appealing to religious arguments, or other controversial views over which reasonable people are assumed to disagree. For more on public reason, see: https://plato.stanford.edu/entries/public-reason/
25 Ibid., p. 213
26 Ibid., p. 153
27 Ibid., pp. 224–225
28 Ibid., p. 215
29 Ibid., p. 247
30 Ibid., p. 248
31 Ibid.
32 Ibid., p. 249
33 Ibid., pp. 251–252
34 Ibid., p. 151
35 Ibid., p. 220

36 Ibid., p. 250
37 Razik (1925) op. cit. p. 31
38 Ibid., p. 31
39 Ibid., p. 7
40 Ibid., p. 4
41 Ibid., p. 3
42 Ibid., p. 4
43 Ibid., p. 4
44 Ibid., p. 4
45 Ibid., p. 6
46 Ibid.
47 Ibid.
48 Ibid.
49 Ibid., p. 7
50 Ibid.
51 Ibid., p. 8
52 Ibid., p. 8
53 Ibid.
54 Ibid., p. 12
55 Razik. op. cit. p. 13
56 Ibid.
57 Ibid.
58 Ibid., p. 16
59 Ibid.
60 Ibid., pp. 16–17
61 Ibid., p. 17
62 As-Safir Newspaper, 'Al-Azhar launches its document on the future of Egypt: No religious state in Islam-21/6/2011: http://assafir.com/Article/241878
63 Jassim Hussain, 'The occultation of the Twelfth Imam: A historical background', Muhammadi Trust (1982). Also, Allawi. (2007) op. cit. p. 210
64 Interview with Hani Fahs
65 Razik (1925) op. cit. p. 12

6 Political Islam and democracy

Introduction

As we saw in the previous chapter, the ideologies of Islamist political parties are based on perceived religious principles. In order to understand their different political approaches and ideologies, it's important to examine the main Islamic principles for both Shia and Sunni Islam. But this book is about democracy, not religion, and therefore, I will limit the discussion to aspects relevant to politics and democratization.

Since Sunni Islamist political parties no longer form the main Sunni political body in Iraq, as most Sunni Islamists have given up on political Islam prior to 2010 elections, I will be focusing on the Shia doctrine and Shia political parties, especially when they have been ruling the country since 2005. Their religious beliefs are no longer a matter for them since they are using them to govern everyone in the country, including those who do not share them.

Historical background

After the death of Prophet Muhammed, the Muslims were divided into two groups on the issue of succession. One group supported Muhammed's cousin and son-in-law, Ali ibn-Abi-Talib, to be his successor, while others decided it was a matter of discretion among Muslims and it was up to them to choose his successor.[1] They gathered at the public house of Beni Sa'eda tribe, and elected Abubakir As-Siddique, Muhammed's father-in-law and long-time friend, as his successor. Although the dispute was settled within six months, when Ali recognized the new caliph, the two sides, who were later called Sunni and Shia, remained divided politically and doctrinally.[2]

There are at least seven recognizable Islamic doctrines or 'schools of jurisprudence,' (Mathahib) followed widely by Muslims, four in Sunni Islam and three in Shia Islam. These seven doctrines are named after their founders: Al-Hanafi, Al-Maliki, Al-Hanbali and Ash-Shafiei (Sunni); Al-Ja'afari, Az-Zaidi and Al-Ismaili (Shia). Since the latter two have few followers in Iraq, if any, I shall only discuss the former.

The Shia doctrine

Shi'ism began as a protest movement directed at the way the succession to the Prophet was conducted by his companions and in opposition to naming Abuba-kir as caliph. Although Abubakir's accession to power was largely accepted by the majority of Muslims, a group of other companions, who were later called 'the Shia' or 'followers', believed that succession should have remained within the Prophet's family, and since Muhammed had no son, his cousin, Ali, who was married to his daughter, Fatima, should have succeeded the Prophet. The Shia in this sense can be described as 'royalists' since they believe authority rests with the family of the Prophet. It was a political dispute, not a religious one.[3] This protest movement developed into a distinct doctrine, led by the descendants of Ali who were the 12 imams revered by the Shia. The development of Shi'ism won't be relevant here and has been discussed elsewhere.[4]

What matters are the beliefs and practices that could impede (or enhance) the application of democracy. Believers are inclined to impose their beliefs and practices on others when in government. All citizens and residents of Iraq are likely to be affected, when these beliefs or practices are regarded as part of public life, although they can remain part of civil society as per Rawls theory. Any political conception of justice must be 'free standing' so that all citizens can recognize it as valid and acceptable and can adhere to it.[5] If those beliefs become public they will impinge on the lives of the non-religious and other religious groups who will 'become more dogmatically biased toward their own sect'.[6] There are at least five religious traits, described below, that distinguish the Shia from Sunnis and these can adversely affect the application of democracy.

Imamate/infallibility[7]

This stipulates that the nation must be governed by infallible imams designated by God.[8] These are the infallible 12 imams, beginning with Ali and ending by the Mahdi, who the Shia believe to be in occultation for the last 1200 years. He is referred to as the Absent Imam (al-gha'eb) or the Expected Messiah (Al-Mahdi Al-Muntadhar).[9]

There are two Shia schools within the Twelvers to deal with the vacuum left by the occultation of the Absent Imam politically. One believes that people should take care of their affairs as they see fit until the imam re-appears, and this school is referred to as the 'quietist' school to which the late prominent Shia spiritual leader, Ayatullah Khoei belonged.[10] Traditionally, most Shia religious leaders belonged to the quietist school, including the current religious leader, Ali Sistani, although some scholars, such as Ali Allawi, have noticed a change in his position in this regard. Allawi believes Sistani now belongs to a new middle school.[11] Prior to 2003 Sistani was thought to believe in the principle of 'separa-tion of mosque and state'.[12] However, after 2003, he believed 'the state was necessary to protect Islam' but this is not the same as demanding direct clerical rule as a precondition to ensuring the Islamic identity of the country'.[13] Although

Sistani's representatives, such as Abdulmahdi Alkarbalaei, do discuss political issues in their Friday sermons, the Ayatullah himself has not commented on any political issue nor received any Iraqi politician since 2010. He has never given an interview to the press nor has he spoken publicly on radio or television.

Some scholars may have changed their positions after the rise of the second school, which believes that Islamic teachings and codes should be applied through the application of Sharia law by an Islamic government supervised by a jurisprudent. The most prominent proponent of this interventionist school is Ayatullah Khomeini who developed the theory of the 'Rule of the Jurisprudent' which is applied in Iran.[14] The idea of infallibility and 'jurist leadership' are questioned by some Shia scholars, such as Abdulla Nuri, who was Iran's minister of interior in the 1990s. Nuri wonders, if the 'Jurist Leader' is unveiled, and the Absent Imam is the one who appoints him, 'how can we interpret what caliph Ali said, "I'm not free of mistakes" … how can we interpret the Quran verses that mean "consult them in affairs", and "their affairs is established through consultation"'.[15]

According to Haider Al-Khoei, grandson of Ayatullah Khoei (who died in 1992), Sistani opposes Khomeini's school since he calls for a civil state.[16] Iraqi Islamists would establish a system similar to the Iranian one, or even stricter in applying Sharia law, and this won't be democratic since it excludes the non-believers in the theory of 'the Rule of the Jurisprudent' from participation in government or elections. An Islamic government would automatically exclude non-Muslims, non-religious or even those who believe faith should remain a private matter, from participation and benefits. Those excluded would be a substantial portion of society in Iraq, where the majority of people are thought to be secular.[17] Democracy stipulates that no one should be excluded.

Emulation (Taqleed)

Taqleed literally means 'emulation' and it refers to the requirement of every believer who is not well versed in religious matters to follow the guidance of a senior cleric, who is carefully picked from a few prominent clerics, as his religious guide.[18] This cleric must have a long record of religious studies and must have declared himself to possess 'the highest knowledge in religion' (marji) with the ability to pass a religious judgement (ijtihad).

During the 'Major Occultation' of the Absent Imam, a believer must follow strictly the guidelines of one of the highly acclaimed religious scholars. These scholars have the rank of 'Deputy of the Absent Imam' and have the same authority as the Imam himself.

What the 'marji' says is obligatory on his followers. If he declares jihad, the faithful must obey without hesitation or they are regarded as sinners if not total infidels. This is where the threat to democracy lies as ordinary Shia develop deep reverence for their religious leaders to the point that they would not question their views, including voting for a specific candidate or list.[19]

Although taqleed is confined to religious matters,[20] ordinary people do not recognize the difference and ask their religious leaders for political guidance.

Many religious leaders do not abide by the boundaries of religion when passing religious judgements. Ayatullah Basheer An-Najafi, a prominent Shia leader, issued a televised guidance/fatwa three days before the 2014 election advising believers to vote for the list of (Citizen) led by cleric Ammar Al-Hakeem. At the same time, he spoke ill of PM Noori Al-Maliki and said voting for his list (SoL) was religiously unacceptable. The fatwa/opinion was aired by many television channels opposed to Al-Maliki.[21]

Notwithstanding the fatwa, SoL increased its parliamentary seats by four, from 89 to 93. In contrast, the 'Citizen List', in whose favour the fatwa was issued, almost doubled its parliamentary membership, from 17 to 31.[22] Najafi's followers would have voted according to his guidance; therefore, some of the extra seats can be attributed to the fatwa.

Shia religious leaders usually issue guidelines to their followers on how they should conduct their lives. The faithful are told if they follow these guidelines, God will reward them in heaven. If not, they will attract His wrath. That's why they refer to their 'maraji' in every issue they are not sure about, while the religious leaders have to provide answers for any question asked. They advise their followers on public issues such as jihad, among other things.

If the spiritual leader's authority is extended to politics, Shia voters, especially the devout ones, would consult their 'maraji' on political issues. During the last four general elections, many voted according to what they believed their religious leaders wanted. If the 'marji' didn't have a view on political issues, his associates would provide such a service. Every 'marji' has at least one representative in every city, town or village, and these are not necessarily apolitical. When they express their political views, people will take them to mean the views of the 'marji' himself.

One spiritual leader, Ayatullah Muhammed Al-Ya'aqoobi, established a political party, the Islamic Fadheela (Virtue) Party, which all his followers joined and/or voted for in elections.[23] The party got 15 seats in 2005, seven in 2010 and six in 2014. Since the leader is a 'marji', he must be obeyed by those who follow him. When believers vote, they won't be voting their conscience but the clergyman's conscience, as Akeel Abbas puts it.[24]

Khums (tax at 20 per cent)

Khums is an annual religious tax equal to one fifth of people's incomes (after deducting their cost of living) levied on all the Shia faithful. They have to pay it to their spiritual leader or his representatives.[25] The proceeds of the tax, in addition to the proceeds of another tax, zakah, levied at 2.5 per cent on income before the cost of living, are spent in the ways the spiritual leader feels fit. It's mainly spent on religious schools, salaries of students and staff, housing, endowments and so on.

Jawad Shahristani, the main representative of Ayatullah Sistani and his son-in-law, says 50,000 students are supported by religious tax. He heads 27 institutions that are sponsored by Sistani in Iran, including centres for culture, social welfare, medical care, astronomy, translation, and high tech.[26]

These religious taxes have accumulated over the years and turned Shia religious leaders into powerful figures with numerous mosques, hussainiyas, offices, publishing houses, hospitals, schools and even hotels and restaurants under their control.[27] A marji is basically a state within a state. In a democracy, the state is the only one that collects tax from citizens. Most Shia religious leaders bequeath their wealth, most of which is accumulated from khums, to their children, and their successors have to start from scratch. The only known Shia religious leader who has not bequeathed money to his children was Ayatullah Khumaini. In addition, Khumaini barred members of his family from taking up government posts, in a move that was unprecedented.

Jihad

Although jihad has been interpreted as 'holy war' it has a wider meaning, but military action is one of them. In one of the Prophet's hadeeths, he referred to the military action as the 'minor jihad', while the 'major jihad' was to exercise self-discipline.[28] But what really concerns us here is the 'minor' jihad since other forms are personal and peaceful.

Ayatullah Mahmoud Taleqani (1910–1979) an Iranian high-ranking Shia cleric, classified jihad into four categories:

First, jihad waged against foreigners in order to 'remove those obstacles which are placed before those who cannot see the truth'. Second, jihad to protect Islam and Islamic countries, which involves the defence of one's rights and dignity; third, jihad against protected minorities (dhimmi) if they rebel against the Muslim law and 'become hostile (muharib)'; and finally jihad against the despots.[29]

Another Shia scholar, Ayatullah Murtaza Mutahhari (1920–1979), whose teachings have greatly influenced many Shia, including Ayatollah Khomeini, argues that a

purely aggressive war – such as in pursuit of greed, territory, over-ambition, or as a result of a feeling of one's own racial superiority over another group – is incorrect, even evil. However, if a war is undertaken in order to defend one's land, property, freedom, or self-esteem, then war is legitimate, even commended and necessary for human existence.[30]

Abdulaziz Sachedina, a scholar, author and chair of Islamic studies at George Mason university, points out that one Shia interpretation of jihad that dates back to early Islamic times permits the 'jihad of the Sword' even against fellow Muslims 'if the latter are engaged in spreading discord in the earth'.[31]

Jihad can only be declared by religious leaders if and when they see fit. Once they issue the jihad fatwa, it becomes a sacred duty on every able-bodied Muslim to fight the intended enemy. Although jihad is the same among Sunnis and Shia, it becomes more personal and specific among the Shia because every individual has to follow a certain religious leader, in line with the principle of taqleed. If that leader declares jihad, they must obey him. If they don't, the individual becomes a sinner or infidel.[32]

Jihad is declared with no regard to the views or discretion of the government or the law of the land, regardless of whether the government is elected or appointed. It can also be declared against minorities (dhimmi) as Taleqani decreed, or even fellow Muslims according to Sachedina.

In a democracy, only elected leaders can declare war and even then, they are accountable to parliament. Jihad could run counter to the basic principles of democracy and the legal state. An elected government is bound by a constitution and accountable to an elected parliament, and thus, should have the first and final say on declaring war, be it defensive or offensive. Religious leaders are not necessarily aware of political or economic consequences of wars; therefore, it's not in the interest of any state to have individuals acting above the law. Members of an elected government, if they are devout Shia, have to obey fatwas of the religious leaders they follow even if those fatwas run counter to the interests of the state, since they have no right to question a marji's ruling.

Jihad was declared by Ayatullah Sistani against ISIS when it attacked the city of Musil in June 2014 and it was obligatory on all able-bodied Shia who follow him to fight ISIS. The fatwa was issued without any prior consultation with the elected government, although Sistani directed believers to fight within state apparatuses. Many in Iraq believe the jihad fatwa contributed to halting the advance of ISIS terrorists on Baghdad, by galvanizing people's support for the war effort and lifting people's morale. But it was also used by political parties to establish armed militias or declare their existing secret militias publicly and get the state to pay their salaries.

Shrines and religious holidays

These are shrines which are presumed to be burial places for imams and revered persons, the most prominent of which are the Imam Ali Shrine in Najaf, Imam Hussein's and Imam Abbas' in Karbala, Kadhimain in Baghdad and Al-Imamain Al-Askariyyain in Samara. There are many other shrines across Iraq, although they are less important.

The Shia faithful gather in large numbers at these shrines at certain dates of the Islamic year in order to worship and also attend religious sermons. Many Shia across the world regard visiting these shrines as an important pilgrimage at specified dates such as anniversaries of deaths or births of the imams. Iraqi Shia faithful perform these pilgrimages several times a year, and when they can. Not all Sunnis practice this rite; in fact, many of them disagree with it.[33]

Since the fall of the Saddam regime, these pilgrimages have become phenomenal. Millions of people go to these shrines, often on foot, and the state has to provide security for them in difficult circumstances. Terrorist organizations,

Al-Qaeda and ISIS in particular, have targeted pilgrims specifically and hardly a single occasion passed without bloodshed.

But all these terrorist threats did not prevent the faithful from participating in these ritualistic practices. These pilgrimages serve to enhance people's belief in their faith. They also serve to enhance the authority of religious leaders who could measure their influence through these gatherings. Islamist politicians have used these gatherings to rally political support, and almost all of them participate actively in them publicly.

These shrines are so important that devout Shia from other countries go to defend them wherever they are, and even foreign states justify interfering in other states to protect shrines. Iraqis have gone to Syria to defend Shia shrines.[34] Indian volunteers flock to Iraq to defend sacred shrines.[35] The Iranian President, Hassan Rohani, pledged to protect Shia Shrines in Iraq against ISIS.[36] This shows the importance of shrines in Shia Islam. While the Shia regard them as holy, ISIS extremists spare no effort to destroy them and regard the Shia as apostate.[37] Pilgrimage to these shrines has proven to be very disruptive of civil life in major cities. They have caused resentment among the non-religious and members of other sects. Securing millions of pilgrims has also been a costly operation and is never accident-free.

The five Shia beliefs described above do interfere with the application of democracy and infringe on state and government sovereignty (especially jihad and khums). They also cause the state to incur a lot of costs in security and lost labour through paid unofficial holidays for state employees. During religious holidays, devout Shia offer free food and shelter to pilgrims, while many major roads are closed to allow for processions to pass. These activities do affect businesses, especially hotels, restaurants and shops. They cause the state to lose billions of dollars in revenue and working days, as well as delays in delivering essential services.

Sunni doctrines

The Sunnis have four doctrines which are believed to be close to each other theologically. The differences between them do not amount to making any distinction that is relevant to this study; therefore, Sunnis from different doctrines act as one sect since they agree on all important matters regarding politics and governance.

Sunni scholar Muhammed Al-Aloosi regarded Sunnis as one sect.[38] Ordinary Sunnis do not feel there is a difference among themselves since all their practices and beliefs are similar. However, there are significant differences between the attitudes of the followers of Sunni doctrines towards the Shia. While the followers of Shafii and Hanafi doctrines accept the Shia as Muslim brothers, the followers of the Hanbali doctrine, especially the Wahhabi section, regard them as apostate. The Malikis are critical of the Shia but do not go as far as excommunicating them. Whatever the differences between them, Sunnis do not believe in, follow, or practice, the above-mentioned Shia beliefs (except jihad), although one cannot rule out any practice on an individual basis as some Sunnis in Iraq do visit some shrines, although they do not have elaborate rites of visitations as the Shia do. Sunnis in Egypt and Sudan have some closeness to Shia rituals especially with regard to shrines. This is due to the fact that they were ruled by Shia and Sufi rulers.

There are important Sunni shrines in Baghdad such as Imam Al-Gailani and Imam Al-A3tham. They are also full of worshipers during Fridays and religious occasions. Jihad is practiced by Sunnis and all those jihadists who come to Iraq to fight are following this principle. But jihad within Shia Islam is institutionalized and only the highest religious authority can declare it, while within Sunni Islam, any cleric can pass a fatwa of any kind, including declaring jihad. The fundamentalist Armed Islamic Group (GIA) in Algeria killed women and children during their war against the Algerian regime. When they were asked during interrogations how they could justify this heinous act in Islam, they said they had a fatwa from a junior cleric who lived in London, Abu Qatada, who permitted the killing of women and children during jihad.[39] Although Abu Qatada described himself as a 'student of Islamic law, not the Algerian group's mufti', yet his opinions were taken by the GIA to be ultimate fatwas.[40]

Sunni clerics in general do not exercise authority on their followers as their Shia counterparts do, and this is acknowledged even by Sunni scholars such as Ahmed Al-Kubaisi.[41] Nor do they have financial resources to spend on their followers as the Shia leaders do. Sunni imams have traditionally been appointed by governments, thus they are state employees who have to follow official guidelines.

On the other hand, Shia clerics have been, and still are, independent of the government, financially and professionally. This gives them the freedom and open-ended resources they need to a build a large following. One phenomenon that needs attention in Sunni Islam is the spread of extremism and violence. The insurgency in Iraq, explored in Chapter 11, had taken an extreme religious/sectarian orientation and attracted fighters from many countries in the Middle East, Africa, Asia and Europe. Those fighters believe they are performing the religious duty of jihad.

Sunni Arabs

Sunni Arabs in Iraq represent around 20 per cent of the population.[42] They are the only community that is classified by both its ethnic origin and religious affiliations. The reason is that they share their Arab ethnicity with the Shia while they share their Sunni faith with the Kurds and Turcoman who are divided between the two sects, but are politically classified according to their ethnicities. The Shia, although they are largely Arabs, are classified by their religious affiliation alone.

The Arabs (Sunni and Shia) constitute around 80 per cent of the Iraqi population, while the Kurds, Turcoman, Assyrians and others form the rest. Muslims form 97 per cent, but they are divided between Shia (65 per cent) and Sunni (35 per cent).[43]

Islamist parties under democracy

The democratic system, for the time being, seems to be the only means by which all Islamist parties in Iraq could remain in existence, given the fact that there is no single dominant group among them, although every group seeks to achieve such status.

Despite their Islamic rhetoric, Islamists are deeply divided. As we saw earlier, their backgrounds are different and some of them are led by historically rival families (Al-Hakeem and As-Sadr families who lead (SIIC) and (ST) respectively, are a stark example). Also, IFP is an offshoot of (ST), Badr was traditionally the armed wing of SIIC and there is rivalry now between them. IDP is also divided between the original party and the offshoot which is IDP-IO. In addition, there is now rivalry between two wings within the original IDP – Al-Maliki wing and Al-Abadi wing.

We also noted earlier that Sunni and Shia sects are historical rivals and have totally opposing interpretations of history and religion. Any Islamist party will have to be either Shia or Sunni and will have to argue issues in accordance with its doctrinal jurisprudence. This means there is a 'natural' divisiveness in Islamist politics which always raises tension, and worse, it could lead to violence or even civil war as we saw in 2005–2007.

The division among Islamist parties led them to seek alliances with other secular and Kurdish nationalist parties against each other. Following the elections of 2010, Islamists parties such as Sadrists and SIIC among others, were opposed to allowing their fellow Islamist, IDP leader and PM, Noori Al-Maliki a second term in office. It was Iranian pressure on other Shia groups, such as Badr Organization, that persuaded them to unite behind Maliki.[44] In 2012, the Sadrists joined secular and Kurdish nationalist blocs in a collective effort to field a no-confidence vote in the IDP-led government of Noori Al-Maliki.[45] The effort was foiled by the president who is believed to have yielded to pressure from Iran, which supported Al-Maliki.

Current PM, Haider Al-Abadi, is only supported by certain Islamists parties, but a large faction of his SoL list, led by former PM Noori Al-Maliki, seeks to undermine his rule and has managed to unseat his defence and finance ministers in two no-confidence votes that are widely linked to Mr Al-Maliki.[46]

In the 2018 elections, Al-Abadi and Al-Maliki couldn't unite in one list. Instead, they led opposing lists and divided their vote.

On the other hand, secular parties have also remained divided, lacking relevant political programmes and charismatic leaders and thus unattractive to the population at large. Perhaps one of the reasons why Islamists have succeeded is the absence of organized secular parties with clear and relevant programmes. The leading secularist, Ayad Allawi, admits secularists have failed but their failure is not as 'intrinsic' as the Islamists.[47]

Despite their deep differences, Islamist parties, be they Sunni or Shia, can unite and have united in the past, on issues which restrict people's freedoms and deprive women of their rights. On 22 October 2016, parliament passed a law to ban alcohol. Both Sunni and Shia Islamists were united on that. Without the coalescence of the Islamist parliamentary Speaker, Saleem Al-Juboori, of IIP, with IDP, SIIC, IFP and other parties and individuals, the bill would not have become law. The secular Kurdish KDP, whose member, Muhsin Saadoon presides over the parliamentary legal committee, which must have formulated the law, has also connived in this process for short-term political gains, knowing that the law wouldn't be applied in the Kurdish region. Similar actions, such as passing the controversial Jaafari Personal Status Law, could happen in the future which means democracy and civil liberties and freedoms are not safe under Islamists.[48]

Notes

1 Michael Heffernan, 'What's the difference between Shia and Sunni Muslims?' (2015): http://islam.about.com/cs/divisions/f/shia_sunni.htm
2 Syed Husain Jafri, *Origins and Early Development of Shi'a Islam*, Longman. (1979) pp. 27–53.
3 Heffernan (2015) op. cit.
4 Ibid. and also Moojan Momen, *An Introduction to Shi'i Islam: The History and Doctrines of Twelver Shi'ism*, Yale University Press (1985)
5 Rawls (1993,1996, 2005) op. cit. p. 154
6 Ali Mamouri, 'Iraq's religious minorities and Shiite mourning holidays', Al-Monitor 14/11/2013: www.al-monitor.com/pulse/originals/2013/11/shiite-mourning-minorities-iraq.html
7 More on Imamate can be found in the writing of Mohamad Jawad Chirri: https://goo.gl/sfm7Z0
8 Muhammed Al-Alousi, *Shia and Sunna* (Arabic) London, Darul-Hikma Publishers (1992) p. 15. Also Mohamad Jawad Chirri, op. cit.
9 Jassim Hussain, *The Occultation of the Twelfth Imam: A Historical Background*, Muhammadi Trust (1982).
10 Allawi (2007) op. cit. p. 210
11 Rahimi, Babak, 'Ayatollah Sistani and the democratization of post-Ba'athist Iraq', USIP, June 2007: www.usip.org/sites/default/files/sr187.pdf
12 Allawi. (2007) op. cit. p. 208
13 Ibid., p. 209
14 Ruhollah Khomeini, *Islam and Revolution: Writings and Declarations of Imam Khomeini*, Translated and Annotated by Hamid Algar, KPI, London (1985).
15 Sultan Mohammed Al-Nuaymi, Arabian Gulf Centre for Iranian Studies, 21/6/2016: https://goo.gl/IpMprs
16 Haider Al-Khoei, 'War on the Rocks', 8/9/2016: https://goo.gl/iUTOiB
17 Bremer (2006) op. cit. p. 93
18 See Afzal Hoosen Elias: 'Taqleed': https://goo.gl/z6xCTy
19 Interview with Farid Ayar
20 Interview with Hani Fahs
21 Video at this link: www.youtube.com/watch?v=hAjA-5oump8
22 Election Guide, op. cit.: www.electionguide.org/elections/id/2425/
23 Institute for the Study of War: https://goo.gl/KY0AFO
24 Interview with Akeel Abbas
25 More on Khums on Sistani's website: www.sistani.org/english/book/48/2286/
26 Barbara Slavin, 'Mullahs, money, and militias', USIP, June 2008: https://goo.gl/BRFWiZ

27 As-Saha hotels spread in several countries belong to Ayatullah Fadhlallah's Foundation

28 Imam Hassan A. Amin, 'What is this thing called jihad or Islamic Holy War?', The Huffington Post, 11/12/2015: https://goo.gl/hgMHZf

29 Assaf Moghadam, 'The Shi'a perception of jihad', Alnakhla Fall 2003: https://goo.gl/FP38op

30 Ibid.

31 Ibid.

32 Al-Hurr Al-Amili, *The Tools of the Shia in Reaching the Issues of the Sharia*, Jihad: https://alkafeel.net/islamiclibrary/hadith/wasael-15/wasael-15/index.html

33 Michael Lipka and Fatima Ghani, 'Muslim holiday of Ashura brings into focus Shia-Sunni differences', Pew Research Center, 14/11/2013: https://goo.gl/4Fj18Z

34 Suadad Al-Salhy, 'Iraqi Shi'ites flock to Assad's side as sectarian split widens', Reuters, 19/6/2013: https://goo.gl/EwgmZG

35 Iraqi News, '30,000 Indians volunteer to fight in Iraq to defend Shia shrines', 27/6/2014: https://goo.gl/UVox59

36 Rory Donaghy, 'Rouhani vows to protect Iraqi Shia shrines', Middle East Eye, 19/6/2014: https://goo.gl/eDZ4At

37 James Rush, 'Ancient shrines become latest casualties of ISIS rampage', Daily Mail, 7/7/2014: https://goo.gl/m7CpeZ

38 Al-Aloosi (1992) op. cit. pp. 47–72

39 Camille Tawil, *Brothers in Arms*, Al-Saqi Books (2011) chapter 4

40 Ibid., chapter 4, footnote 5

41 Ahmed Al-Kubaisi, Video, www.youtube.com/watch?v=U2E8M81ntnw Second video: www.youtube.com/watch?v=NutTHlG_r5A

42 Chibli Malat estimates Shia between 55–60 per cent, Sunni Arabs at 15–20 per cent and Kurds at 20 per cent, while Shafiq Al-Ghabra has higher figures; Shia 65 per cent, Sunnis (including Kurds) 35 per cent (of 97 per cent of Iraqis). See L. Sadiki (2014) op. cit. p. 464: https://goo.gl/MwqBDl Also, Bremer (2006) op. cit. p. 38

43 Shafeeq N. Ghabra, 'Iraq's culture of violence' pp. 39–41

44 Interview with Sami Al-Askari

45 The Economist, 'No-confidence vote may reveal Mr Maliki's real opponents', 15/6/2012: https://goo.gl/ZQYcpZ

46 The Arab Weekly, 2/10/2016: https://goo.gl/xhr5PA

47 Interview with Ayad Allawi

48 Speak approved the first reading of PSL in November 2017

7 Use of religion for political purposes

Using John Rawls' classification, the Iraqi society can be described as 'not well-ordered' and suffering from 'profound divisions' about constitutional essentials when certain religious arguments were tolerated.[1] Hence, the focus should be on whether the religious convictions of the believers truly contravene the ideal of public reason.[2]

A conception of justice must be 'free standing' which means that it must not refer to any particular doctrine, be it ideological, religious or philosophical.[3] Justice as fairness must not be founded upon any comprehensive doctrine. It must not bear a relationship to any particular doctrine, but it must be articulated in such a way that all or most members of the democratic society in question feel they can relate to it. Its basic idea must be found in the 'public political culture' of that society.[4]

But at the same time, it must not be, wherever possible, in conflict with any reasonable comprehensive doctrine or doctrines so that the followers of these doctrines won't find it conflicting with their beliefs if they adopt such a concept. We know that Islamic religious discourse is divisive, since it divides people into Sunni and Shia immediately because their differences are so deep and extend to history, politics and culture. It also divides people into religious and non-religious, where there are deep differences between the two, from food, drink and dress, to lifestyle and way of thinking.

The Shia traditional religious teaching allows, in fact stipulates, the separation of religion and politics. This is the quietist tradition which current religious leader, Ayatullah Ali Sistani, belonged to before 2003 and still belongs to, in my opinion. On 5 May 2016, Sistani's representative in Karbala, Ahmed Al-Safi, announced that the ayatullah won't be expressing his views on Iraqi political issues as he did in the past.[5] This means he doesn't wish to get involved in politics anymore. It's clear evidence that Sistani still belongs to the quietist trend, not the interventionist trend nor the middle school which some thought he had founded in 2003.[6] The mainstream Sunni teaching has a similar position; in fact, Sunni scholars over the years have preached that people should always obey the ruler, even if he wasn't a Muslim.

Sheikh Ali Abdur-Razik proved that neither the Qura'an nor the Sunnah require an Islamic government and the concept of caliphate/imamate was not

Islamic but a pursuit by rulers to advance their worldly desires using heavenly means.[7] Iranian Shia scholar, Abdulla Nuri, believes 'with the exception of God, nothing is absolute in Islam'.[8] Prominent Lebanese Shia Scholar and religious leader, Muhammed Mahdi Shamsuddeen believed in 'the nation's right to rule itself in the way it sees fit'.[9]

Lebanese Shia leader, Grand Ayatullah Mohammed Hussein Fadhlalla, called for the establishment of 'the state of human beings'.[10] Those religious leaders have called for a non-religious basis for the state. This effectively means there is a religious basis in Islamic theology for excluding religious discourse from public debate. However, since Iraqi society is 'not well-ordered', there can be a space for religious discourse but only if it supports public reason and doesn't cause disagreement or violence among people who have different religions or doctrines. In other words, any religious discourse must belong to the national political culture and must not be in conflict with any other reasonable doctrine.

Many observers and participants in the Iraqi political process, including former Islamists, have blamed the use of religion for political purposes for the failure of the democratic process. The main parties which have won elections in the last ten years have been Islamist, be they Shia or Sunni. These parties are not committed to democracy and some have actually been anti-democratic in theory and practice.

They have not shrunk from declaring their rejection of democracy because it 'violates the Qura'anic text'.

Why do Islamists reject democracy?

Dia Ash-Shakarchi, who was a cleric during the 1990s and became MP for IDP in 2005, before he turned secular, identified three reasons for Islamists' rejection of democracy: First: 'Democracy means the rule of the people and this contradicts their belief of 'the rule of God' which is one of the necessities of monotheism according to verse 44 of chapter 5 of the Qura'an.

Second is a social/ethical reason. One necessity for democracy is for the state to guarantee general and private freedoms. Islamists believe the social aspects of democracy have 'corruptive consequences', according to their understanding of corruption. Third is a political reason, which is fear of competition. Non-Islamist political forces may oust them from power if democracy prevails. They fear they cannot monopolize power in a democracy. Pluralism in the framework of an Islamic state will confine competition to the parties of political Islam, excluding secular or 'civil' forces.[11]

The religious rhetoric in the first and second elections in 2005 has induced large sections of the electorate to vote for the Islamist list under the pretext of being the one 'sanctioned by the religious authority'. Although the religious leader Ayatullah Sistani himself never publicly declared his position, he only urged people to vote for the right candidate, but four of his representatives stood with UIA in the first elections of 30 January 2005. This made large segments of the Shia electorate believe that Sistani supported UIA, and this was used by UIA candidates to claim they enjoy the Ayatullah's support. UIA had publicly used large posters of Sistani for electioneering purposes across Iraq in the first and second elections in 2005.[12]

Their list number in the first election, 169, was emblazoned on these photos to further deepen the impression that he supported UIA. In the second election of 15 December 2005, UIA candidates claimed they still enjoy Sistani's support since it's the same list that he endorsed only ten months earlier. Their posters carried the picture of Sistani with their list number, 555, emblazoned on them.

Secularists accuse Islamists of not believing in democracy, while Islamists say, albeit reluctantly, they do and got to power through democratic 'mechanisms'. Farid Ayar, member and spokesman of IHEC, admits that Islamist parties have violated the rules right from the first elections, but it wasn't easy to find them guilty because they used tactics that made them not liable legally, such as claiming that those who used religious symbols were their supporters and they have no control over them.[13]

IHEC was and has been weak and incapable of enforcing its regulations. Several serious violations during the first and second elections were reported, but IHEC failed to take action. Over 2000 complaints were submitted and some were very serious.[14] Islamists have not hidden their violations either. They used religious symbols, places of worship and fiery sectarian and religious speeches publicly. SIIC/SCIRI for example is the most overt in the use of religious symbols. They printed the names of the Prophet and his descendants at the back of their posters to make sure devout Muslims do not throw them away, since it would be disrespectful of these holy figures to do so.[15]

All UIA candidates claimed they were supported by the religious leader, Ayatullah Sistani, although he never acknowledged that officially.[16] The interim PM and leader of IDP, Ibrahim Al-Ja'afari, used a prayer book emblazoned with his photo showing him praying to promote himself as a pious man. Also, mosques, religious centres and supportive clerics were used to promote the UIA. Many of their candidates were clerics who lead prayers and perform religious duties at mosques and religious centres and used them to promote their list.[17] On top of that, there were many candidates who wore religious cloth and this is a strikingly obvious religious symbol.

Religious parties' manipulation of sect and religion to their favour, and violation of the rules contributed to the failure of democratic consolidation in post-2003 Iraq. This is confirmed by elite interviewees who pointed to the numerous advantages that Islamists have over secularists, especially the use of mosques, religious centres and religious cloth and slogans for election and political campaigning. Islamic personalities, especially clerics, are largely immune from blame or criticism due to their religious status. Their mistakes would go unchecked since they are revered by ordinary people and any criticism by rival candidates can backfire on them.

Religious immunity

Corruption under Islamist parties has intensified and it's difficult for the press, people, and even judges, to question them due to their 'religious immunity', political power and protection of the military wings in their parties. There is no single instance in which a cleric was charged of any wrongdoing, including those accused of murder and kidnapping. Some of their followers are extremists and can take matters into their hands and even kill those who criticize them. Their militias are also active and feared by people. There are several instances of killings and assassinations, such as that of journalist Hadi Al-Mahdi on 8 September 2011, in his flat in Baghdad by 'unknown' assailants. Al-Mahdi was an outspoken critic of Islamists and many observers believe his assassination was planned.[18] Kamil Shyaa, the advisor at the Ministry of Culture, was assassinated by armed men as he was going home on 23 August 2008.[19] Many candidates were assassinated or targeted.[20] Journalists were killed through targeting rather than combat.[21] The battle between candidates in Iraqi elections was not between equals; Islamists always had the upper hand. It was between the powerful and the weak, the armed and the armless, the civilized and the savage, the educated and the illiterate, the revered and the not-so-religious or perhaps the 'infidel'.

Religion was used to immunize Islamist politicians from criticism, and they were able to win due to this undeclared immunity and reverence. The situation has slightly changed, and it's possible now to criticize some religious parties and some of their leaders, but it might be a bit late to have any effect. They are now established, rich, organized and powerful, while their opponents are weak, poor, dispersed divided and frightened.

If Islamism has impeded democracy and protected inept leaders from criticism and kept them in power, can it be argued that democracy needs a secular system to progress?

Shia religious scholar Sayyid Hani Fahs said that the only way to 'activate the humanitarian dimension of religion is through a civil state'.[22] Fahs says he avoids using the word 'secularism', even though he means it, because 'secularism has bad connotations in our countries'. The aim of democracy is to 'reach secularism', and 'secularism without democracy is not really secularism', he asserts. He further contends that 'the principle of separation of religion and politics needs to be applied in the East'. 'Enlightenment is the solution, not Islam' Fahs concludes.[23] This undermines the very basics of the ideology of Islamist parties.

Enlightenment, Fahs contends, means 'creating a state for individuals, a legal state where individuals have free choice and human rights to which we add from our peculiarities without annulling any of their original qualities'.[24] Human rights are one concept even though it has a variety of interpretations, he explains.

Fahs approves of religious parties' participation in the political system although with the qualifications 'under the ceiling of the law'. He calls for 'an administrative and epistemological system that forbids religious parties, peacefully and through democratic means, from forming a religious state'. This statement clearly says a lot. A religious state is not acceptable to him, and it should not be allowed. Fahs invokes the European experience and says Western democracies didn't ban religious parties, but they imposed the democratic system and culture on them whereby they can be developed through democracy, and this is how Western religious parties were matured.

Fahs warns of the dangers of religious government for religion. He examines the Iranian example and asks, 'if the people are not happy with their religious government, they would seek to topple it and this would mean "toppling religion"'.[25] This is an eventuality that he doesn't wish to see happen anywhere because he fears for the fate of religion. 'We must nurture democratic persuasion through dialogue', he avers.[26]

Fahs reveals the taqleed principle (emulation) is limited to religious issues and cannot be extended to political matters. A religious leader can encourage people to vote. If he supports a particular candidate, he will 'lose his comprehensiveness and fall'. He acknowledges that 'people do not differentiate between fatwa, encouragement or opinion'. Therefore, they can take one to mean the other. He also regards Sistani's representatives standing in the elections of 2005 as a mistake.

Fahs clearly states, 'When religion interferes in the making of a state, it corrupts it as much as it interferes in it. When the state interferes in the production of religion, it corrupts it as much as it interferes in it'. He asserts that 'those who wear religious cloth should not engage in politics' and this 'must be enacted within the law'.

Former minister, Samir Sumaidaie, accuses Shia Islamist parties of not believing in democracy but they found an opportunity to grab power through democracy. 'For them it's simply a ladder to get on top'.[27] It's noticeable that Islamist politicians do not even mention the word 'democracy'; instead, they use 'mechanism'.

Sumaidaie doesn't mince his words. 'The efforts made by the Americans to help install democratic structures ... were hijacked, sabotaged, and used as a stepping stone to jump to a position of power. Once that was achieved, power was consolidated using non-democratic means'. This reveals the real fear for democracy in Iraq. Some former Islamists, such as Dia Ash-Shakarchi and Sharwan Al-Waeli, left Islamist parties because of this trend.

Coexistence is possible!

Sumaidaie contends it's possible for democracy and Islam to coexist. 'Islam is no more reactionary and anti-democratic than Christianity', he says. 'Democracy could not have been established in Europe without forcing the Church out of the political arena. The same has to happen with Islam'. But why should there be religious reforms? Isn't it easier to separate religion and politics as all democratic countries have done? This way, politics can progress without the hurdle of religious interference while religion can be reformed when and if its leaders find it necessary or possible.

Sumaidaie explains what reforms are needed:

> Reforming Islam in such a manner that the more extreme interpretations of its tenets are banished and its softer, more humane and accommodating elements are promoted to a dominant position and the acceptance of the principle of the separation of religion from the state.

He goes on to say, 'Only then will democracy take root and thrive in Islamic societies'.

Many have tried to reform Islam, including Ali Abdur-Razik, but as reformists appear they attract calls to go back to basics. Any religious reform has to be done from within the religious establishment.

It's easier, as many intellectuals have argued, including John Stuart Mill, John Rawls, Ali Abdur-Razik and Hani Fahs, if politicians agree on a political system that respects all religions but operates independently of all, serving citizens of all faiths and creeds in matters that concern their lives, leaving what concerns the afterlife to individual believers to manage and religious and philosophical debates to civil society.

Sumaidaie, and others, in comparing democratization in Iraq to what happened in Europe when the church was forced out of politics; they are in effect calling for the establishment of a secular system for democratization to succeed. He rules out the idea of 'Islamic democracy' because 'under Islamist doctrine, certain principles are considered eternal and unchangeable because they are divine instructions, whilst under a secular doctrine, anything can be changed if that is the will of the people'.

Sumaidaie admits the strength of Islamist parties and their ability to mobilize religion to rally the faithful to gain power. 'Religion is a very potent force especially in conservative societies where education is limited and people are not aware of the ramifications of supporting sectarian religious parties', he explains. But with limited awareness, Islamist parties which Sumaidaie says 'have not been performing according to their ideals and proved to be prone to dishonesty, corruption, misuse of power, negligence and incompetence' still get elected.

Would Islamists, when they are in government, work on developing real education and promote awareness if both lead to shrinking their popularity? Or promote the sorts of education and awareness that suits them and perpetuates their rule and influence? They have done the latter, and religious education is spreading fast in Iraq.[28] Many universities and colleges have been established promoting religious education. People are registering in these institutions and getting degrees from them for several reasons, the most important of which is that state employees get financial rewards for holding university degrees.

Islamists' ideas sound good when they are in opposition, but 'they become empty rhetoric when they are in power' Sumaidaie avers.[29] The problem here is that in a rentier state, they have the means to sustain their power, notwithstanding the fact that 'the administration of a country is highly complex … and requires competent skilled leaders who can use modern tools to achieve specific economic, educational and service results' as Sumaidaie argues. The Muslim Brothers, who 'had no clue what to do' according to Sumaidaie,[30] have been forced out of power by the military; but had 'democracy' prevailed in Egypt, they would have maintained their power for a while, although the fact that Egypt is not a rentier state didn't work in their favour.

Sumaidaie describes Islamists in Turkey as successful. But he associates this with the fact they are 'not acting as an Islamist but rather as a secular party within a secular political framework'.[31] Secularism has been well established in Turkey since Ataturk's time and it would be difficult for the Islamists to change that within a short period of time, although the possibility still exists they may seek to change that. Turkey is an important tourist destination and the application of Sharia law would result in a huge loss of revenue from the tourist sector. Therefore, it serves Islamists well for the time being not to introduce Sharia law.

Prominent sociologist and author Faleh Abdul-Jabbar argues it is difficult to 'marry' Islam with democracy,[32] even though he agrees that there is a space for the religious to live within a democracy, in line with Rawls' theory. 'If tolerance exists, followers of all religions can cohabit peacefully even within a non-democratic state' Abdul-Jabbar asserts.[33] But 'tolerance in the minds of religious persons always comes with 'tacit reserves' even in the most tolerant of countries'.[34] Perhaps it's misguided to hope for mere tolerance in a religious society, especially an Islamic one where there are still extreme interpretations of the Qura'anic text or the Prophet tradition in many Muslim countries. In the last two decades, two caliphates were established; one in Afghanistan, another between Iraq and Syria. The world has witnessed how harshly they have treated the non-religious Muslims, let alone the non-Muslims such as Christians and Yazidis.

The need for tolerance

Abdul-Jabbar affirms tolerance comes before democracy and is necessary for any state, be it democratic or not. 'If there is no tolerance, it's difficult for different people to live together even under democracy'. He maintains that 'democracy is based on one man one vote principle' and this gives all people the right to live in the way they wish without infringement on their rights.

Abdul-Jabbar explains 'there is a difference between creed and its interpretations'. He invokes the thoughts of scholars such as Abdurrahman Al-Kawakibi and Hussein An-Na'eeni who interpreted the Islamic creed as requiring the ruler to be constrained by a constitution. The thoughts of the two prominent Sunni and Shia scholars do accord with modern political thoughts. But Islamic scholars cannot all agree on one course of action regarding politics and governance; hence the need for tolerance.

Although Abdul-Jabbar accepts that ethnic and religious groups can be represented fairly in elections, he warns 'the collapse of national identity and its replacement by sect, class or race, limits democracy and weakens it'. He attributes the difficulty of questioning PM Al-Maliki to his ability to 'persuade others within his sect that any questioning of him would be a questioning of the whole sect'. This has reduced the whole sect to its representatives in government, he contends.

Abdul-Jabbar highlights the position of Iraqi secularists and liberals who stood in elections. They were considered 'infidels', and thus, were forbidden by Islamist parties in government from participating or holding rallies. 'The Islamic formula for sectarianism is to have a monopoly over the sect and prevent any diversity within the group'. He calls this 'monopoly and prevention' and regards it as a serious impediment to democracy. 'To Islamists, a Shia is the one who is politically Shia and this impedes democracy in a serious way'.

He identifies the absence of accountability and the monopoly of representation, by undermining the chances of non-Islamists of representing the sect and depriving them of benefits, as a serious impediment to democracy. 'This is destruction and an economic war, rather, dictatorship of needs'.[35]

Abdul-Jabbar asserts that Article (2A) impedes democracy. The article was inserted by Islamists. Although clause 2B bars enacting laws against democracy, clause A is stronger because the 'constant Islamic rulings' are known and clearly defined, while the 'principles of democracy' are vague and disputed and no documentary reference to refer to if there was a dispute. Democracies across the world have different traditions and applications and this is used by Islamists to say they want their own version of democracy.

Academic and writer Akeel Abbas believes article 2 is self-contradictory because 'it tries to reconcile irreconcilable contradictions'.[36] 'Democracy and religion belong to two diametrically opposed orders of reality'. He goes on:

> The former is based on debate and questioning that leads to following the opinion of the majority, while protecting the rights of the minority whereas the latter is based on holy texts that accept no debate or questioning and pay no attention to the opinions of the majority or minority.

Abbas argues this article 'causes conflict instead of establishing balance and gives a disproportionate role to the clergy as the interpreters of religious texts, whereas there are no codified, binding democratic ideas or texts that can be resorted to'.[37]

There is also the notion of 'different democratic systems' that Islamists always refer to in their arguments. They think this gives them the right to demand a system that 'suits Islamic societies' which might lack fundamental aspects of modern democracy.

Abdul-Jabbar finds it bizarre that the constitution has a stipulation that forbids issuing laws that contravene Islam. But he has words of praise for Ayatullah Sistani. 'The religious establishment has actually made the constitution less extreme (in religious terms) than would have been if left to political Islam'.

Abdul-Jabbar is confident that society has the ultimate say on any restrictions imposed on it. 'Islamists cannot really introduce restrictions against the will of society'. He rules out the possibility of a coup d'état. 'Even the PM cannot launch a coup because he will face resistance from all population centres... A military violent action can be done, but no coup is acceptable'.

Regarding 'dissimulation', and whether it affects democracy, Abdul-Jabbar believes it will only restrict people's freedom of choice if clerics interfere in politics. He agrees that Ayatullah Sistani restricted people's freedom in 2005 when he supported the Shia list of UIA. But in 2010, he told people to vote for whoever they wanted.[38]

Former PM, Ayad Allawi, questions the ability of Islamic countries to establish democracy: 'Where and in which Islamic country is there democracy similar or near to what we see in democratic countries?' He asks rhetorically.[39] He argues there is a problem in understanding religion in Muslim countries; it 'prevents nurturing democracy'. This echoes the views expressed by Samir Sumaidaie who stipulates reforming Islam before democracy can take root in Iraq.

Allawi blames foreign influences, colonialism, occupation, lack of self-determination and domestic reasons for 'severely impairing the evolution of democracy in Islamic countries'. To him there exists a religious impediment to democracy not only in Iraq but in Islamic countries as well.

Local values

'Democracy must take "local values" into account and it should not be a photocopy of the UK, USA or France', Allawi contends. This is similar to Islamist politicians' demand although the aims may be different. While Islamists want to adjust democracy to suit their beliefs and interests, Allawi wants to assure conservatives that democracy doesn't lead to abandoning prevalent national and religious values.

As a secular and Western-educated thinker, Allawi wouldn't accept tribal values or those critical of women's rights or personal freedoms. Democracy can take local nature, and this explains why French democracy is different to British, American, Japanese or Indian ones. But true democracy, in all its versions and manifestations, must incorporate liberal values, freedoms and minority rights. The starting point for the democratic process for Allawi is 'the presence of the rule of law, basic rights of citizens and citizenship, and the presence of institutions that can defend democracy'.

Allawi explains how Islamist parties emerged. 'They started as reactions to foreign involvement, degradation and insults that came with it, but they soon became too sectarian, violent and authoritarian as we see in Egypt, Iraq, Tunisia... etc'. Allawi is clear: 'The state must be secular', with no place for Islamist parties, which he described as prone to violence, authoritarianism and sectarianism.

He highlights another point. 'Islamist parties are political entities, not sacred religious beings, and they have no right to pose as the only ones who know Islam and able to explain it and use it politically'. Islamist parties are political entities, but they are taking advantage of religion and have clerics as political leaders. Ordinary people are confused by this state of affairs. They cannot distinguish between real apolitical religious leaders, and political leaders who pose as religious leaders.

Leaders of Islamist parties perform religious duties such as leading Friday prayers and giving sermons in mosques and religious centres.[40] People consult them on religious matters whether in their political headquarters or in mosques and religious centres. They seize any opportunity to express their political viewpoints and promote them as religious positions and require their followers to obey, follow and support them. They may not have the right, morally and politically, but until there is an enforceable law to stop them exploiting ordinary people, they will continue to take advantage of people's religious feelings and unduly benefit from this practice.

John Stuart Mill states, 'in the modern world, the greater size of political communities, and above all, separation between spiritual and temporal authority … prevented so great an interference by law in the details of private life'.[41] Separation is necessary for the prevalence of freedom, which is necessary for democracy. He interprets the separation of religion and politics as 'placing the direction of men's consciences in other hands than those which controlled their worldly affairs'.[42]

According to Mill,

> the disposition of mankind, whether rulers or fellow citizens, to impose their own opinions and inclinations as a rule of conduct on others, is so energetically supported by some of the best and some of the worst feelings incident to human nature, that it is hardly ever kept under restraint by anything but want of power; and as the power is not declining, but growing, unless a strong barrier of moral conviction can be raised against the mischief, we must expect, in the present circumstances of the world, to see it increase.[43]

He warns of the revival of religion and compares it with bigotry in the uncultivated mind that could provoke people into actively persecuting those whom they have never ceased to think proper objects of persecution.[44]

Although Ayad Allawi admits that secular parties have failed, he distinguishes between their failure and that of the Islamists: 'National and socialist parties have failed after decades of being in power (while) Islamist parties have failed in a much shorter time'. Is there any difference? Allawi replies: 'The failures of Islamist parties are mainly intrinsic while the failures of old secular parties are largely external (e.g. Cold War) as well as intrinsic'.

If Islamists' failure is 'intrinsic', there is no hope for real democracy with them in power since they will fail due to focusing on the wrong issues. Politics is about managing people's affairs and providing services to them. Using religion is merely an attempt to grab power. Samir Sumaidaie puts it eloquently: Islamists' ideal model is 'one man, one vote, one time'.[45]

But once you are in power, you need to succeed; otherwise people will throw you out, if not peacefully, under democracy, then violently. Islamist parties need to focus on how to serve the people and stop interfering in people's personal matters or conduct. Akeel Abbas calls this 'political religiosity', and he believes it can only 'deepen sectarian identities and undermine Iraq's national identity'.[46] He adds 'Religion in Iraq is essentially sectarian, hence divisive instead of uniting'. Ali Allawi argues 'people's mood could change and if religion is useful now, it may not be so in the future'.[47]

Democratic mechanism

Islamist MP Walid Al-Hilli thinks of democracy as a 'mechanism' no more. He seems to confuse democracy with the Islamic principle of 'shura', which means consultation.[48] This shows he has some objection to 'democracy'. Akeel Abbas contends that

> even those pro-democracy enlightened clergymen and Islamists cannot cite from Islamic teachings any real evidence in support of democracy beyond the reference to the shura principle which merely involves consultation among the elite about state decisions and policies (little to do with democracy as people's real participation in selecting their representatives and rulers).[49]

As a member of IDP leadership, Al-Hilli has been participating fully in the democratic process in Iraq since its inception. Many suspect he and his party are seeking a different political system than a liberal democracy when they are questioned in depth. He emphasized 'shura' and 'democratic mechanism'. He clearly believes in a system other than democracy. 'Shura' is non-obligatory advice to the ruler. In line with this tradition, the Iranian parliament is called (Majlis Shura Islami) or Islamic Consultative Assembly. Al-Hilli asserts that 'the practice of Shura in Islam preceded the introduction of "democratic mechanisms" in the West by hundreds of years'. To him, both democracy and shura refer to the 'necessity to consult the nation (umma)'.

Obviously, there is a great deal of difference between democracy and consultation. Democracy is mandatory, while consultation is optional. When people vote in a democracy, they in effect 'appoint' new leaders and 'sack' old ones, or renew the mandate for old ones and reject the new seekers of power. It's people's decision. In a consultation, there is no decision taken by the consulted. It's the ruler who initiates the consultation and the advice is not obligatory.

Al-Hilli even went as far back in history as the era of King Solomon to give examples for democracy! He invokes the story of the 'Queen of Sheba' and how she consulted her people on how to respond to a letter from King Solomon (delivered by a hoopoe). There are no modern instances of democracy in his mind, something that doesn't bode well for democracy.

Al-Hilli contends that Islam encourages 'consulting' people and it gives incentives for it, which is 'the great reward in heaven'. This sort of encouragement, according to him, makes people committed to the idea in contrasts with Western democracy which 'has no incentives'. 'Shura is subject to the principles

and moral values which direct all Muslims towards the aims that satisfy God'
while 'democracy differs from Russia's to America's and European countries',
each understands it differently'.[50] So democracy and shura are two different concepts now, although they are substitutes except shura is better since it has 'incentives'. Worse still, democracy is not one and the same thing since 'it differs from
one country to another' according to Dr Al-Hilli, and this means that 'Iraq can
have its own democracy designed especially for it which will be different from
the democracy prevalent elsewhere'.

Using Islam to deceive people!

However, Al-Hilli makes a distinction between different Islamist parties since
'they believe in different political principles'. 'Their problem stems from their
(mis)understanding of Islamic creed'. He acknowledges, however, that there are
parties that use religion for political purposes. 'They are nationalist, sectarian or
liberal but they use Islam to deceive people'. He also acknowledges that some
Islamist parties made big mistakes, but he blames this on 'their lack of experience and lack of openness to Islam with its wide concepts'.[51] Does this mean that
politicians can use Islam for deception? This is another reason to choose a
secular system.

Al-Hilli agrees that extremism and the use of 'takfeer' [excommunication] is
a problem, in addition to 'narrow horizon' and failed political programme. But
he maintains there is a need for Islamist parties 'as much as there is a need for
non-Islamist parties'.

Al-Hilli argues:

> shura and democracy and the diversification of views all help to diversify
> parties in performing their roles. We don't fear the multiplicity of Islamic or
> secular parties and their different programmes, but we do fear the infiltration
> of these parties by intelligence agencies of this country or that, making the
> party a platform for this country or that country or its intelligence agency.[52]

What is worrying for many in Iraq about positions like Al-Hilli's is the open
rejection of democracy. This is a serious impediment to establishing democracy
since Al-Hilli's views represent a trend prevalent in Islamist parties that currently dominate Iraq. If moderate Islamist parties, such as IDP, do not believe in
democracy, the hardliners are certainly hostile to it. If democracy is to be established for real, it is imperative to remove this impediment. Political parties must
declare their commitment to democracy, as opposed to consultation. The public
must be educated that the only democracy that can serve the people is the one
that is recognized in established democracies in Western Europe, North America,
and Japan. Other versions, if they existed, are modified to serve the interests of
certain classes and parties; the poor and ordinary are not among them.

Economist Kadom Shubber argues it's difficult to restrain Muslim scholars
from expressing their views on issues they feel strongly about. He calls for a

'civilised dialogue to instill the ingredients of a healthy and functioning democracy' and as a result he expects all interlocutors, including religious and tribal leaders, to respect the decisions of the representatives of the people.[53]

Shubber agrees that politicians shouldn't wear religious cloths in order not to give the wrong impression. He affirms that 'for a democracy to function effectively, those in power must regard themselves essentially as takers from the voters who put them in their positions, if this happens the electorate would be free to exercise their power'.

But religious parties tend to oblige people morally and religiously to vote for them. The electorate are now takers from politicians and those in power due to the use of religion and the position of Iraq as a rentier state.

Author and academic Kanan Makiya says, when he authored his two famous books, *The Republic of Fear* and *Cruelty and Silence*, he thought 'anyone would be better than Saddam Hussein in the leadership of Iraq'. But he is disappointed now with the rule of the religious parties whom he labels as a 'thieving mafia' because they 'distribute state posts on the basis of stealing the state'.[54] These are strong words from Makiya on the religious parties which came to power in part due to his oppositional activities to the Saddam regime and persuasive lobbying of the Bush administration.

Like Sumaidaie and Allawi, Makiya believes that Islam can and must change, as happened in Judaism and Christianity. 'Catholics jettisoned a lot of their religious practices in order to accord with modernity'.[55] He can even see 'signs for rationalism' in Islamic thinking, especially among the young generation. He sees a crisis within Islam, but he believes the 'new Islamists' will be able to change that and argues there is a sector of society that is determined to 'rethink everything'.

These modernizing and reformist trends cannot really face violent Salafist trends, such as Al-Qaeda, ISIS, Nusra Front, Taliban, Boko Haram, Ash-Shabab, and others in different parts of the Muslim world, so they are silenced by the sheer power and brutality of the violent trends. Violent religious trends must be defeated first before any modernizing can take place. Makiya believes that within the Shia doctrine 'there is a room for flexibility'. In this he agrees with Faleh Abdul-Jabbar who indicates that there are 'large islands of liberalism' within the Shia doctrine in comparison to small ones within Sunni Islam.[56]

Makiya maintains that 'change is possible and Islamic tolerance is possible'. He regards tolerance as a temporary substitute to secularism. He argues tolerance is easier to achieve than secularism; yet, like Hani Fahs, he regards 'the separation of state and religion as necessity for religion'. It might well be good for religion to be independent of politics, but what most people are concerned about is the state and society. Reforming religion should be the exclusive realm of religious leaders and scholars. 'We are talking of natural developments that will happen eventually, not necessarily now' he explains. Makiya blames Iran for whatever is happening to Iraq. 'It's Iran which supported the religious parties. Without Iran they would have had no influence'.[57]

Hussein Al-Hindawi asserts that religion has played certain roles against the application of democracy, even in Europe. But he reckons that this is not always the case. 'Religion can play a role in favour of democracy'. 'Religious leaders can present Islamic ideas which serve democracy but do not contravene Islam'.[58] He finds common ground between Islam and democracy: 'Islam favours a just rule and democratic rule is just … it's fair with all people'.

Islamic democracy

Al-Hindawi doesn't explain why a religious leader should promote democracy when he doesn't believe in it. They must believe the application of democracy is in their interest. They may do so once they come under popular pressure. In Lebanon, religious leaders such as Muhammed-Mahdi Shamsuddeen believed in the mandate of the nation on its destiny.[59] Hani Fahs believed in the separation of state and religion.[60] Muhammed Hussein Fadhlalla believed in establishing the 'state of human beings' bereft of any ideology.[61] Al-Kawakibi and Al-Na'eeni before them believed in restricting the ruler.[62]

In Tunisia, there is a moderate Islamist movement led by Rachid El-Ghannouchi, who believes in diversity. Ghannouchi has recently adopted 'Islamic democracy'. 'Ennahda has moved beyond its origins as an Islamist party and has fully embraced a new identity as a party of Muslim democrats' Ghannouchi wrote in Foreign Affairs.[63] Not only that but he announced that his Islamist party has given up all its social and religious activities and will focus on political activities only. This is because there is a popular culture to support these ideas, as Hani Fahs had explained, and those religious leaders have read this culture accurately.[64]

Al-Hindawi distinguishes between different religious scholars, depending on their positions on secularism. He says Ayatullah Kadhim Al-Haeri, who lives in Iran but has Iraqi followers, is against secularism, while others have no problem with it.[65] Al-Hindawi charges that religious parties exploited religious scholars who have no political project. This is largely true since they claimed Sistani supported them while he has no political project except in exceptional circumstances.[66]

Al-Hindawi elaborates that the Shia project in 2003 was to 'return the rule of Iraq to the majority and this was done during the first elections'. He thinks they should have stopped at that and built a modern state based on democracy. 'Some clerics have no problem with building a modern state', he maintains. The religious authority 'can take a corrective position' on politics he advises. 'Imam Khoei believed in the separation of religion and politics'. Al-Hindawi affirms Shia religious scholars are not hostile towards democracy since building a just state is in the interest of the Shia and the Muslims at large.[67]

He demands that religious leaders should explain their positions and declare whether those Islamist political parties represent them. They should forbid them from using their names. He maintains that religious parties are not democratic nor are their constitutions. But 'they have become more professional in using democratic language and democratic game for their interests' he admits.[68]

Dia Ash-Shakarchi attributes the difficulties of democratization in Iraq to the 'prevalence of strict and closed-minded religiosity and the weakness of the culture of religious tolerance especially among the religious or those who possess an emotional loyalty to the sect'.[69] Shakarchi, like Hani Fahs, blames the 'prevalence of a wrong, distorted and warped conception of secularism' in Iraq and the Muslim world where it is regarded as anti-religious.

Shakarchi regards a religious fatwa in political affairs as a serious impediment to democratic transition and calls for the practice of issuing fatwas in political affairs to be banned in order for the democratic process to succeed. However, he realizes this would clash with the 'emotional religious zeal' and this will require laying cultural foundations which will take decades. Even a fatwa that has a positive impact on the democratic process 'will have a negative effect when it becomes an absolute criterion that is not subject to discussion, criticism, refutation and disagreement' as the latter four criteria are important in a democratic system, he contends.

This view of Shakarchi may be too extreme, since a fatwa in favour of democracy from an influential religious leader would be very effective in pushing the democratic process forward. As Faleh Abdul-Jabbar indicated, if it were not for the moderating force of Sistani, Islamist parties would have written a more extreme constitution in 2005.

Shakarchi regards a secular party as 'fairer and more democratic than a religious one', although he stipulates it must be democratic. 'The secularism we call for can only be realized when it is associated with democracy'.[70] This is in line with Hani Fahs' opinion that there is no true secularism unless it is associated with democracy. A secular political system would protect the non-religious from the repression of radical Islamists. Shakarchi calls for banning parties established on a religious or sectarian basis. 'They are the antithesis of the principle of citizenship which is a basic pillar for the democratic system', he declares.[71]

He summarizes Iraq's problems into two: political Islam and political sectarianism and insists democracy must be based on secularism and this means the non-interference of clerics in politics. He even calls for a law to ban politicians from discharging the tasks of a clergyman. 'If clerics want to work in politics, they should drop the religious cloth and refrain from any activity that is usually practiced by clerics. If a politician wants to be a cleric, then he should quit politics'. Shakarchi himself was a man of the cloth when he entered parliament in 2005. He gave up wearing the cloth after he engaged in active politics. He is categorical about the influence of religious dress on ordinary religious individuals, although he concedes many people have changed their views about clerics and do not revere them as they did years ago.

'Secularism defends the freedom of the atheists as much as it defends the freedom of the religious and the freedom of religiosity', he declares. He calls for a social campaign to educate the public that 'secularism is more suitable for the country and religion itself'. He also identifies 'hypocrisy' as a social problem and he believes Islamists practice it more because 'they try to portray themselves as democrats when they are not'. He maintains that Islamists 'rode democracy when they saw there is no other way to achieve their dreams of establishing an Islamic state'.[72]

Shakarchi asserts that the politicization of religion and political sectarianism have indeed contributed to bringing unqualified officials 'who concealed their lack of knowledge and experience behind religious rhetoric'. He charges that not only are they unqualified, but also lack integrity: 'Corruption was strengthened through hiding behind religious and sectarian slogans'. He blames 'Islamist and sectarian parties and unqualified politicians' for the failure of the democratic transition.

Shakarchi now affirms 'foisting religion into politics, or even into public affairs, to any degree, represents an impediment to the process of democratic transition'. He insists this is mostly the case in a 'society where religion plays an influential role in it, and has not gone through a democratic experiment before'.

Islamist politician Adil Abdur-Raheem asserts that establishing a democratic system that depends on 'proper democratic mechanisms and respects the cultural values of the people' won't have a problem with religious values. He admits problems with such a system may arise with religious groups for political motives. We notice the use of 'democratic mechanisms' again by another Islamist.[73] It shows Islamists only believe in 'democratic mechanisms' which are also used in Iran where candidates are vetted before they stand for elections and they must believe in the principle of 'Islamic Jurisprudence' and be loyal to the Islamic Republic regime.[74]

Abdur-Raheem argues the effect of a fatwa depends on the (stature of) the issuing authority and the number of followers, with the existence of a space that is not affected by fatwa. There are people who don't follow fatwas, but those who follow religious guidance are not so few in Iraq. Some religious leaders are more influential than others and, consequently, their fatwa/guidance are followed by more people, but, in principle, a politically motivated religious fatwa/opinion, does compel the devout, no matter how few, to vote in line with it, instead of voting according to their conscience, without the interference of mentors. Any such fatwa will influence election results, in varying degrees, of course. It's definitely a distortion of democracy and can bring undemocratic groups into power and influence. The least these undemocratic forces can do is to impede the course of democracy or at least disrupt the proceedings.

Abdur-Raheem states that religious and secular parties in Iraq 'share a common culture; that is the culture of monopoly of power, exclusion, and marginalization (of rivals)'. He asserts this phenomenon is prevalent and 'Iraqi political activism has been suffering from it for decades'. It's true that Iraqis have a common culture, but what differentiates secular parties from religious ones is the former uses political means and economic programmes to attract voters, while religious parties rely on religious and sectarian rhetoric to rally their supporters and immune themselves to criticism.

Abdur-Raheem asserts that democracy should give 'equal opportunities for all', arguing that religious parties may also be 'interested in the economic side of politics while secular parties could turn to sectarian rhetoric'. The latter point highlights the danger of sectarian discourse in politics, not forgetting that religious parties are political parties that use religion to further their aims.

Abdur-Raheem agrees that wearing the religious cloth 'enables candidates to gain votes' but he regards this benefit as limited 'due to the existence of sections of society that are not influenced by the religious discourse'. But many individuals would not have made it to parliament or government without the religious connection because of their political incompetence and he acknowledged this. Some have been serving in parliament for the last ten years, with no contribution.

Ali Allawi points to religious impediments, such as arguments that 'Islamic political authority cannot be based on simply the views and positions of a political majority'. He contends that political choices 'must necessarily be constrained by religious injunctions that are above and supersede the will of a majority'.[75]

Strikingly, he does not regard a fatwa as an impediment to the democratic process. On the contrary, he finds the position of the religious authority as 'consolidating' to democracy. He invokes the position of the Catholic Church in post-war Europe which consolidated 'the democratic process in the face of a communist alternative'.

But is the example of the Catholic Church in Europe relevant to Iraq and the role of religion in Iraqi politics? Christianity is different from Islam, and many Muslims believe Prophet Muhammed was a ruler and they want to emulate him. That was not the case with Christ. Many Muslim scholars do not give people the right to legislate for themselves since 'this is the role of God and all matters are laid down in the Holy Scripture; the Qura'an', and this was alluded to by Mr Allawi himself. Also, the role of the Church that Allawi is talking about came after the Church was stripped of most of its political power.

Allawi, a practicing Muslim, believes that a secular party is 'better placed to be fairer and more democratic' than a religious one, 'unless it turns secularism into another religion, as had happened in Turkey and Tunisia' (during the reins of Ataturk and Bourguiba). This practically means that applying any idea religiously in politics impedes democracy, even if it's secularism.

Allawi agrees that 'wearing the religious garb' is useful politically today. But he remembers 'thirty years ago, it was ridiculed and those wearing it were not only powerless but were considered reactionary outcasts'. So, the current power of religion may not last long or remain as potent.

Democracy requires the absence of any compulsion in politics, while using religion involves compelling believers to vote in a certain way even if it means they are voting against their interests. Allawi admits that the religious discourse does help politicians get votes but 'Iraqis are prone to radical shifts and there might be a mass migration away from the use of religious rhetoric and symbols'.[76] In principle, Allawi argues that 'only good can emerge from a politics rooted in ethics, which includes ethics based on the idea of religious virtues and values'. Allawi, however, concedes that the political class is 'unprincipled' and uses 'the politics of fear, marginalisation and anxieties of dispossession' in order to 'push people into primary identities that are antithetical to the politics of enhancing the public interest'.

Former Islamist minister, Sharwan Al-Waeli, now believes that there should be a separation between politics and religion. 'Harm comes out of mixing religion and politics. There was a terrible exploitation of religion in politics, as it was used for the promotion and marketing of parties and persons', he contends.[77]

He points out that politicians have used religion to 'market themselves' and he particularly blames those who 'belong to political Islam'. He vindicates the position of the religious authority. 'Unlike the political parties, the marja3iyyah was the only party that kept its distance from benefitting from religion and acted as the sponsor of the national project'.

He justifies the position of the religious authority in allowing its representatives to stand in the first elections and says this was to 'save a project and not for personal gains'. But he acknowledges 'there are those who claimed, in whispering tones or insinuation, to enjoy its support, or spoke out on its behalf, but the marja3iyya did not interfere'.[78] Al-Waeli distinguishes between the main religious authority of Ayatullah Sistani and other religious leaders who may have different positions in support of other parties or lists.

He warns that 'religious and sectarian loyalty is harmful to the democratic process', and contends 'religious parties have exploited people's religious and sectarian emotions'. But he is not sure if secular parties are fairer than religious ones 'because we have not tried their rule so far'. But if only harm can come out of mixing religion and politics, as he pointed out earlier, it would be logical to conclude that it's less harmful if secular parties came to power since they do not mix religion and politics.

Mr Al-Wa'eli expects secular parties to have a better chance in the future because 'religious parties began to field secular and religiously non-practicing personalities among their candidates'. Also, 'they began to talk about the 'civic state'. They have been trying to market their traditional personalities in order to get votes this way. Religious parties resorted to talking about the civic state because they have failed. He reads this as a 'change' in Iraqi society away from religious parties.

He charges that big blocs 'came to prominence because of their sectarian and religious rhetoric', which he believes to have been 'extreme and focused' in the last elections. 'Those who resorted to sectarian and religious rhetoric got many and incredible votes'. Mr Al-Wa'eli expects that the results of the last elections will convey the following negative message to new members of parliament: 'if you are sectarian and able to collect money (illegally), you will win'. He maintains that 'religiosity is not a condition for integrity or efficiency'. He emphasizes the need to get capable people who could benefit society, 'not those who pray and fast in front of people'.[79]

He acknowledges that the political process brought non-qualified people 'either because they belong to a religious family or a religious party or they have a relation with this or that individual'. He reveals that 13 people from the Shia Endowment Office became members of the National Assembly in 2005 'because of their contacts'.[80]

Intrinsic failure

Maysoon Aldmaluji doesn't rule out a role for Islam. 'A moderate version of Islam could live peacefully alongside a democratic system'. But she has her stipulations for this type of Islam. 'It does not take an active part in everyday politics, yet monitors the overall process and takes part in forming public opinion'.[81] She identifies the values of democracy as follows: 'human rights, women's rights, minority rights, freedom of speech, freedom of conscience and religion'. She contends that democracy is indivisible and cannot be divided into Islamic and Western.

She argues that Islamist parties 'identify themselves with ancient historic events. They use the Qura'an as their reference in legislative, executive and judicial matters. They do not recognize any example outside this framework'. She admits, however, while secularists 'identify themselves with national symbols, and use international declarations, agreements and protocols as their references, Islamist parties' symbolism is easily identified with the populace'.[82]

She says of Islamists, 'They have the advantage of Western and regional support. I am totally convinced that the Bush administration gave weight to Islamist parties in forming the Governing Council'. Like Hussein Al-Hindawi, Aldamluji believes the Americans abided by the Shia religious leadership's views in drafting the constitution. She charges the timing of the first elections was set to suit Islamist parties. This is true due to the fact that Islamist parties were better organized than secular groups, which were new and centred around individuals such as Ayad Allawi and Ahmed Al-Chalabi. Had the elections been held a few years later, secular parties may have had better chances of winning power, given the fact that Iraq in general has been secular politically.

Aldamluji accuses Islamist parties of an 'inability to deliver the justice they promised'. Like Ayad Allawi, she believes the failure of Islamist parties is intrinsic. Iraq is a 'complicated state with a complicated social system', she argues, and 'Islamist parties did not set out to build a democratic state'. This view conforms to their tendency to reject democracy and only accept its mechanisms. Aldamluji doesn't see any need for religious parties, accusing them of causing sectarian conflicts and failing to run the state. 'They claim to speak on behalf of God according to their interpretation of the Qura'an'.[83]

She is adamant that democracy cannot exist under religious or totalitarian parties, even if they were secular: 'Democracy … is a set of modern values that recognize the freedom of individuals and rights of groups (women, children, elderly, etc.). I do not believe that democracy can be identified as Islamic or Western'.

Aldamluji argues that Islamist parties have impeded democracy on more than one level:

> they stick to Islamic doctrine on personal affairs, allowing children to marry at the age of 9 or less, they discriminate against women in inheritance and allow women to be beaten up by their spouses and siblings as a measure of

discipline. A woman's testimony is not allowed in a court of law. They encourage sectarianism and permit religious discrimination against non-Muslims.[84]

Former IHEC spokesman, Farid Ayar, reveals that '4 million Shia went to the polls to elect Shia representatives without any real electoral programmes nor any guarantee from those they would elect for freedom of speech afterwards'. Other communities were equally guilty of voting based on sub-national ethnic or sectarian affiliations. 'Two million Kurds voted on an ethnic basis', Ayar goes on to say. 'Two million Sunnis and Christians and others also voted on the same bases'.[85] He contends that those elections were not conducted properly because 'the level of awareness of the Iraqi people was not up to the standard of realising the meaning of democracy'.

John Stuart Mill describes this humorously: 'He who lets the world, or his portion of it, choose his plan of life for him, has no need of any other faculty than the ape-like one of imitation'.[86]

Ayar invokes the voting patterns in established democracies. 'In a proper democracy, voting must be on the basis of the political projects and programmes presented by the candidates, parties or political groupings'. This did not happen in Iraq. He regards voting on the basis of sect, religion or ethnicity as 'based on compulsion not freedom'. He gives examples. 'A Shia cleric can order a thousand Shia voters to vote for one candidate who is not known to them. This is voting not electing and there is a difference between the two' he declares. He firmly believes this is an impediment to democracy.

In Ayar's view, the formation of the first government was not democratic because 'those who were elected were not afraid of the electorate withdrawing their support from them since they voted for them because they were Shia, and, as long as they remain Shia, they will vote for them again'. He describes the current democracy in Iraq as 'fragile' and this is because it's 'based on ethnic, religious and sectarian bigotry'.

He affirms secular parties 'serve democracy more than religious parties which do not believe in democracy to begin with and regard it as a "despicable satanic act"', quoting some 'prominent' Islamic writers.

Regarding religious symbols, Ayar reveals: 'We (IHEC) had banned the use of religious symbols but religious parties managed to manipulate the ban in a very strange way': 'They were printing many publications bearing the pictures of religious leaders, sheikhs and sayyids, and when we would hold them to account, they would deny having done so and attribute it to their supporters'.

Ayar calls for the banning of parties established on the basis of religion and he believes this doesn't breach the principles of democracy. 'If we allow them to work, the voter would be under the influence of the clergy and this restricts his freedom. In fact, his freedom would be non-existent because of his connection to religion'.[87]

He affirms that the religious discourse encourages the making of false claims, hypocrisy and opportunism. He reveals many people became MPs and officials as a result of using a religious discourse while they were Marxists in the past. 'The road to power is now through opportunism and the use of religion', he laments.

It might be argued that opportunism is always associated with politics and business in all countries. But the danger for democracy might be the exploitation of religion for political purposes and the effects this has on the country as a whole. Ayar warns of this phenomenon in a very serious way. 'This double (deceitful) fanatic religious, sectarian discourse has created the bigotry and back-wardness in all dimensions of life that is currently happening in Iraq'.

He blames the same religious discourse for bringing unqualified persons to parliament, government and leadership in the country. 'This is the reason why the country has reached this decadent stage on all levels', he explains.

Akeel Abbas agrees that there are religious impediments hindering the estab-lishment of a fully democratic system. He observes that clergymen, clerical insti-tutions, and Islamist parties look suspiciously at democracy, considering it a 'Western invention that has no basis in Islamic teachings'.[88] He maintains that the lack of evidence from the Qura'an or Islamic thought to support the estab-lishment of democracy poses a dilemma even for those pro-democracy, enlight-ened clergymen and Islamists.

Religious fatwa, real or imagined, undermines the very notion of elections 'as one's voting his/her own conscience' Abbas avers. He adds: 'It becomes rather voting the clergyman's conscience by thousands or millions of his followers'. There are other negative aspects to this phenomenon. 'It stops individual voters from developing the necessary skills to examine the electoral platforms of the different candidates'.

Voters can become enlightened and educated through the process of 'exam-ining and comparing different platforms and making a personal voting decision based on it'. According to Abbas, this enables people to think independently, not as followers who vote based on voting decisions made by their religious leaders.

He agrees that religious dress and rhetoric bring electoral benefits. Because 'religion is the dominant way of thinking in Iraq currently, many voters attach special value to politicians' acts, displaying signs of religious loyalty or affili-ation'. A secular party, Abbas contends, is better placed to be 'fairer and more democratic' than a religious party. This is because 'a religious party, particu-larly in Iraq, is tied to pre-modern loyalty and understanding of human affairs, instead of the modern interests of the voting public'. There is another issue which Abbass points to in this regard. 'A genuinely secular party has the potential to appeal to the interests of Iraqis, regardless of ethnicity and faith, whereas religious parties inherently appeal to the interests of particular groups'.[89]

Abbas calls for an electoral system that includes only secular parties because 'it's definitely better for the country'. He sees benefits in this for the consolida-tion of a trans-communal national identity. 'Without secular parties that tran-scend sects and ethnicities, Iraq will continue to be prey to sectarian and ethnic strife'.

Abbas also draws an important comparison between the religious and non-religious parties:

> Because religious rhetoric helps politicians get more votes, this encourages the non-religious to pretend to be religious in order to get more votes, even though they are not religious in actual life. Common voting appeals and patterns are religious in nature, something that leaves non-religious parties at a clear disadvantage. These parties sometimes find themselves 'forced' to adopt religious gestures and rhetoric which, in turn, gives the entire political and electoral process a religious character that is not genuine or truly representative.[90]

This can only create double standards which he believes will 'promote a false spirit of political religiosity that will deepen sectarian identities and undermine Iraq's national identity'.

The use of religious and sectarian slogans has negative effects for the country and the democratic process in general because 'they have definitely helped bring unqualified officials who may have hidden their inabilities behind their religious rhetoric', Abbas warns. He also provides the evidence. 'It is very clear from the abysmally poor performance of the state machinery, particularly in its upper echelons and decision-making bodies'. He reckons that this is because 'a large portion of the general public tends to evaluate public officials based on their religious ethics, not on professional competence'.

Democratization in Iraq has partially, not fully, failed, according to Dr Abbas. Elections 'as a periodical mechanism to renew or rescind the trust in the sitting government has been somewhat deeply established in Iraq over the past 11 years'. But 'the entire election process is unfairly skewed in the interest of religious parties', he adds.[91]

Economist Kamal Field expects the influence of religious leaderships and others to remain strong until 'a breakthrough occurs in the level of education and general knowledge of the people'.[92]

But the reverse is happening on the ground. Religious education has been enhanced many folds with so many religious schools and universities opening across Iraq under Islamists.[93] Field argues that democracy 'didn't come as a result of mass desire'. 'It's actually like a plant that was growing in a hostile environment'. This is true as far as the change in 2003 is concerned. But Iraqis did rebel against tyranny in 1991, seeking freedom and hoping for a democratic system, but they were brutally suppressed before the eyes of the world.[94]

Democracy may be growing in a hostile environment, but this is because religious parties are educating people to believe that it's Western and anti-Islamic.

Field rejects the classification of parties as 'secular and religious'. Instead, he classifies them as 'believing in good governance or not believing in good governance'. 'The best party will be the one which believes in the principles of good governance', he declares.[95] He agrees that wearing the cloth has an influence on 'simple people', but he, like Ali Allawi, contends that this is a short-term phenomenon.

He agrees that 'religious rhetoric helps politicians get more votes', and adds, 'it encourages the non-religious to jump on the religious bandwagon in order to get more votes', but he reckons this is not peculiar to Iraq.

Voting on religious basis

Field agrees that people in Iraq have voted according to their religious and sectarian affiliations. This is 'because they do not trust or know any alternative'. He also agrees with the notion that 'using religious and sectarian slogans has helped to bring to power unqualified officials who may have hidden their inabilities behind their religious rhetoric'.

Writer Abdulkhaliq Hussein agrees that a fatwa, even if it was false, impedes the democratic process. 'I believe religion and politics should not be mixed'.[96] He invokes the European experience in which the political problems were not solved until 'they had separated religion from politics'. He believes that Iraqi religious leaders 'have not issued any fatwa in favour of any religious or political group'. Strictly speaking, this is true since no statement under the title 'fatwa' has been issued by a serious religious leader. But religious leaders and clerics have expressed opinions in favour of UIA.[97] This was acknowledged by Islamist politicians Sami Al-Askari[98] and Sharwan Al-Waeli.[99] People cannot differentiate between a fatwa and an opinion since both are opinions originating from senior religious leaders. They regard any such opinion as obligatory direction that must be followed.

Hussein admits implicitly that some politicians have given a false impression that their parties are favoured by the religious leader. But he is 'confident' that these politicians 'will fail' and 'their attempts will be counterproductive'. His view has not been borne out in reality. Those politicians and their parties won elections after elections and have become prominent through these false claims.

He affirms 'religion is deeply rooted' in Iraq, and it's advantageous 'if a religious leader can encourage people to cast their votes without bias to any political party'.

Although Hussein supported Islamist PM Noori Al-Maliki, and this was clear in numerous articles that he has written in recent years, he admits that 'a secular party is better placed to be fairer and more democratic than a religious one'. But he qualifies this. 'Democracy means to use ballots instead of bullets to choose the government. What about if the religious party wins? Are we going to revoke democracy and the results of the ballot boxes and install an unelected secular government?' This would be dictatorship, he asserts. The solution, in his opinion, is to 're-educate the people about democracy'. He invokes Robert Lowe's saying, 'we must educate our masters'.[100]

He explains that even if religious parties were to be banned, 'religious politicians would establish parties under secular names'. He cites the experience of the Turkish Islamists as a case in point. He concludes it's difficult in a democracy to ban religious parties.

The idea of secularism is not to ban the political activities of religious people as their involvement in politics is important since they form a large section of the population, but it's to limit the use of religion in politics since modern societies are characterized by pluralism, debate and dissensus and people do not follow one religious or philosophical doctrine.[101] Therefore, religious discourse is divisive and doesn't appeal to all citizens.

With regards to wearing the cloth, Hussein doesn't believe that they are significant in getting more votes. He brings the case of Ayad Jamaluddeen, who wears religious clothes but still lost in the elections of 2010 and 2014. But Jamaluddeen is a 'diehard secular' despite his religious garb. Why should religious voters vote for someone who is openly calling for distancing religion from politics and who is alleged to be non-religious on personal basis?

Jamaluddeen was MP in 2005–2010 and his religious status (and garb) must have played a part in getting him there. He joined a secular list (Al-Wataniyya) which wanted to have men of the cloth to prove it wasn't anti-religious.

He acknowledges 'only a very small minority voted for a candidate from an opposite sect or religion'. He accepts that 'religious and sectarian slogans have helped to bring unqualified officials' but he argues 'time is the best healer' and 'unqualified officials will be exposed'.[102]

Adnan Al-Janabi regards a fatwa in favour of or against any participant in the political process as an impediment to democracy 'since democracy depends largely on the free will of individuals to vote for their preferred party'.[103] Not only does he believe a secular party is 'better placed to be fairer and more democratic than a religious one', but he also calls for the banning of religious parties altogether. He agrees that 'wearing the religious cloth or using religious rhetoric helps politicians get more votes in a religious society such as the Iraqi one. This makes the non-religious pretend to be religious in order to get more votes'.[104]

Al-Janabi expects the double standard, which politicians practice, will 'lead to what Iraq is now: a failed state on the verge of civil war'. He observes that people have been voting according to 'their religious and sectarian affiliation' in the previous elections. Religious rhetoric, in his opinion, has helped bring unqualified officials who have hidden their inabilities behind their religious rhetoric. Al-Janabi concludes 'democracy has failed'.

Bassim Jameel Anton argues one impediment to establishing a democratic system is using religion to stop the spread of democracy. This is an important point. Not only is religion used to get to power, but also to stop the spread of democracy.

Anton argues that a fatwa can affect elections and impede democracy especially when there is a large percentage of Iraqis who 'go to the ballot box influenced by emotions not wisdom'.[105] He further argues that religious parties only appeal to people's 'sense of religiosity' and they 'provoke sectarian loyalties' instead of presenting their economic programmes and pledging to their supporters to implement them.

Anton calls for a law to ban religious parties from standing in elections in order to 'prevent the exploitation of the emotions of simple people and the manipulation of religions for electoral purposes'. He has evidence that wearing religious cloths or using religious rhetoric 'helps politicians to get more votes' and this is manifested in pushing some secular politicians to join religious lists to win elections and 'it worked for them'.

This use of religious and sectarian slogans, according to Anton, 'has helped to bring unqualified and inefficient officials who were able to hide their professional deficiencies behind the religious rhetoric and the proof is parliament's failure to produce economic laws'. He lists a few impediments which contributed to the (partial) failure of the democratic transition. Among them are the dominance of the religious portfolio (on Iraqi politics) and the (undue) strength of the religious parties.

Shorouq Al-Abayachi contends there are many religious impediments to democracy which have been 'accumulating over the long decades of modern Iraqi history without any serious remedies by any social, political or cultural institution'.[106]

She regards a 'fatwa in favour of one candidate or against another an impediment to democracy, even if it was imagined and not true'. She states she has experienced it directly during past elections:

> The religious emotions of people were exploited for the benefit of parties and individuals who worked for their personal, party or sectarian interests without the real enforcement of democratic practices and without serving the interests of the people who elected them.

She is alarmed that these people were elected once again despite all their shortcomings.

Al-Abayachi regards a secular party as 'more just than the religious one' because secular parties believe in the principle of citizenship and the separation of religion and state 'in a way that guarantees the non-exploitation of religious emotions for sectarian and ethnic purposes'. The logical upshot of this view is to call for a secular political system based on the separation of religion and state that guarantees the application of the principles of equality and justice for all citizens regardless of their sub-identities. This, in her opinion, is required 'due to the pluralistic nature of Iraqi society'.

She agrees that wearing the religious cloth and using a religious discourse to help politicians get more votes, 'especially in rural societies where illiteracy, poverty and ignorance are prevalent'. In her estimation, this has fostered 'the practices of religious pretence' because candidates seek to get to high positions or to win additional votes. She says this has sometimes meant indulging in 'agitating sectarian emotions among the Sunni and Shia'. This supports what has been argued by others such as Dia Shakarchi, that Islamist parties are automatically divisive since they are either Sunni or Shia.

Ms Al-Abayachi blames 'political and religious hypocrisy' for the failure in building state institutions on the basis of the right criteria of propriety and competence. This hypocrisy has also 'entrenched ignorance and retarded concepts' in Iraqi society. She observes that 'incompetent and unqualified officials' prevail in most Iraqi governmental institutions and this is a result of the use of sectarian and religious slogans. 'The political manipulation of religion and sectarianism is also another problem which impedes democracy. This has 'enhanced warlords and militarism instead of civility and openness'. The proliferation of religion-based militias and armed groups supports this view.

Ms Wahda Al-Jumaili expresses hope that 'a civil state that believes in human beings before loyalty to religion or sect' can be built, although she thinks this is premature in Iraq 'where religious parties have climbed to power on the back of religious feelings of Iraqis'.

She argues that fatwas have been instrumental in the last ten years and they have changed the direction of elections, but acknowledges the religious authority has now distanced itself from politics. She laments religious parties for climbing to power on the back of religious feelings of ordinary people. She reckons the benefit of using religious discourse or wearing religious cloth is decreasing after 'the exposure of the falsehood of those who claim to be religious'.

This view can only be ascertained in future elections. How wide-spread is this 'exposure of falsehood'? Are the electorates now really immune from religious influences during elections? There is disillusionment among many people and this can be seen in the social media and continuous protests and demonstrations in Iraqi cities over government failures, but it's not clear whether this will be translated into votes.

Politics based on religion is a serious impediment to democracy. This is because religious discourse is divisive since not all people affirm one religious or philosophical doctrine. Religion belongs to the sphere of holy texts that do not accept any debate, while democracy is based on pluralism, debate and cohabitation between different peoples. Democracy is the zeitgeist in most of the world with no major contestant as a political system (with the exception of the reinvigorated fundamentalism in the Islamic cultural community).[107] As we saw above, the evidence is overwhelming that democracy can only exist and consolidate under a pluralistic secular system that allows people to live together in dignity and choose their representatives with no compulsion of any kind.

Notes

1   Rawls (1993,1996, 2005) op. cit. p. 249
2   Public reason is an idea developed by John Rawls which requires the adoption of a standard by which moral or political rules can be assessed. It also requires people to refrain from advocating or supporting rules that cannot be justified to those on whom they would be imposed. Only rules that can be justified by appeal to suitably shared or public considerations, such as freedom and equality, should be accepted. At the same time, there must be an abstention from appealing to religious arguments, or other controversial views over which reasonable people are assumed to disagree. For more on public reason, see: https://plato.stanford.edu/entries/public-reason/
3   Ibid. p. 12
4   Ibid. p. 9
5   Erem News (Arabic), 5/5/2016: www.eremnews.com/news/arab-world/427976
6   Allawi (2007) op. cit. p. 208
7   Razik (1925) op. cit. (chapter 5)

8 Asef Bayat, *Making Islam Democratic*, Stanford University Press (2007) p. 92

9 Interview with Hani Fahs

10 Saleem Deghash-Fadhlalla, 'Theory on state for human being', Bayanat.org 9/10/2015: http://arabic.bayynat.org/ArticlePage.aspx?id=19169

11 Interview with Dia Shakarchi

12 Appendices 5, 6 and 7

13 Interview with Farid Ayar

14 John Hardin Young, International Election Principles, American Bar Association (2009) p. 196

15 Missy Ryan, Reuters, 22/1/2009: https://goo.gl/YCd0OI

16 Faraj Al-Haidari quoted by Reuters, ibid.

17 Sheikh Jalal As-Sagheer, UIA parliamentary leader (2006–2010) is the imam of Buratha mosque: www.theguardian.com/world/2016/feb/22/iraqis-take-a-bite-out-of-no-chocolate-cleric

18 Committee for the Protection of Journalists (CPJ) 8/9/2008: https://goo.gl/dOL29L. Also, Annie Gowen and Aziz Alwan, Washington Post, 9/9/2008: https://goo.gl/LK0CFL

19 High Beam Research, 23/8/2008: www.highbeam.com/doc/1G1-183573773.html

20 Omar Al-Jaffal, 'Iraqi elections marred by hit squads targeting candidates', Al-Monitor, 30/4/2104 https://goo.gl/wKGe1S

21 Mark Smyth, 'CPJ-Iraq war and news media: A look inside the death toll', March 2013: https://cpj.org/blog/2013/03/iraq-war-and-news-media-a-look-inside-the-death-to.php

22 Interview with Hani Fahs

23 Ibid.

24 Ibid.

25 Ibid.

26 Ibid.

27 Interview with Samir Sumaidaie

28 Adnan Abuzeed, 'Iraq State Education increasingly religious', Al-Monitor 5/5/2014: https://goo.gl/M661aD

29 Interview with Samir Sumaidaie

30 Ibid.

31 Ibid.

32 Ibid., p. 27

33 Ibid.

34 Mill (2002) op. cit. p. 7

35 Interview with Faleh Abdul-Jabbar

36 Interview with Dr Akeel Abbas

37 Ibid.

38 Interview with Faleh Abdul-Jabbar

39 Interview with Ayad Allawi

40 Ayatullah Muhammed Al-Yaqoobi (IFP), Muqtada As-Sadr (ST), Ammar Al-Hakeem (SIIC/Hikma), Jalal As-Sagheer (SIIC), Sadruddeen Al-Qubbanchi (SIIC), Ali Al-Allag (IDP) Abdul-Haleem Az-Zuhairi (IDP), Khudair Al-Khuzaei (IDP-IO/DA), Khalid Al-Atiyya (SoL), Muhammed Al-Hindawi, Dhia-Uldeen Al-Fayyadh (SIIC), Hameed Mualla (SIIC/Hikma), Hussain Al-Assadi (IDP), Humam Hammoudi (SIIC) among others are clerics who wear religious cloth and perform religious duties in addition to being political leaders.

41 Mill (2002) op. cit. p. 11

42 Ibid., p. 11

43 Ibid., pp. 11–12

44 Ibid., pp. 25–26

45 Interview with Akeel Abbas

46 Interview with Ali Allawi
47 Ibid.
48 Interview with Walid Al-Hilli
49 Interview with Akeel Abbas
50 Interview with Walid Al-Hilli
51 Ibid.
52 Ibid.
53 Interview with Kadom Shubber
54 Interview with Kanan Makiya
55 Ibid.
56 Interview with Faleh Abdul-Jabbar
57 Interview with Kanan Makiya
58 Interview with Hussein Al-Hindawi
59 Interview with Hani Fahs
60 Ibid.
61 Deghash (2015) op. cit.
62 Interview with Faleh Abdul-Jabbar
63 Foreign Affairs, September/October 2016: https://goo.gl/xDMgGA
64 Interview with Hani Fahs
65 Interview with Hussen Al-Hindawi
66 Rahimi (2007) op. cit.
67 Interview with Hussein Al-Hindawi
68 Ibid.
69 Interview with Dia Ash-Shakarchi
70 Ibid.
71 Ibid.
72 Ibid.
73 Interview with Adil Abur-Raheem
74 Michael J. Totten, 'No, Iran is not a democracy', World Affairs Journal 16/2/2006: https://goo.gl/SDvvwG. Also: Colin Freeman, 'Iran's "democratic elections" only missing one thing – choice', *Telegraph*, 8/6/2013: https://goo.gl/igDcj6
75 Interview with Ali Allawi
76 Ibid.
77 Interview with Sharwan Al-Waeli
78 Ibid.
79 Ibid.
80 Ibid.
81 Interview with Maysoon Aldamluji
82 Ibid.
83 Ibid.
84 Ibid.
85 Interview with Farid Ayar
86 Mill. (2002) op. cit. p. 49
87 Interview with Farid Ayar
88 Interview with Akeel Abbas
89 Ibid.
90 Ibid.
91 Ibid.
92 Interview with Kamal Field
93 Adnan Abuzeed, Al-Monitor, 27/1/2015. (op. cit.)
94 Hamid Alkifaey, *Routledge Handbook of the Arab Spring*, London, Routledge, (2015)
95 Interview with Kamal Field
96 Interview with Abdulkhaliq Hussein

97 Appendix 1
98 Interview with Sami Al-Askari
99 Interview with Sharwan Al-Waeli
100 Interview with Abdulkhaliq Hussein
101 Rawls (1993, 1996, 2005) op. cit. p. 9; also p. xvi
102 Interview with Abdulkhaliq Hussein
103 Interview with Adnan Al-Janabi
104 Ibid.
105 Interview with Bassim Jameel Anton
106 Interview with Shorouq Al-Abayachi
107 Linz and Stepan (1996) op. cit. p. 75

8 Sectarianism

Prologue

One of the problems that hurt Iraq as a state, let alone the current process of democratization, is sectarianism. It's not a new problem; the British faced it when they were trying to establish the new state back in the 1920s. The Shia opposed the British occupation and fought alongside their former oppressors, the Ottomans, against the British occupiers who were regarded as 'infidels' while the Ottomans were their coreligionists.[1] At the outset of WWI, in November 1914, Shia religious leaders (mujtahids) issued fatwas declaring jihad against the British in defence of the Ottoman Empire. Following the war and dismemberment of the Ottoman Empire, the Shia of Iraq rose up in an armed rebellion against the British. Sunni scholar Muhammed Al-Aloosi regards the Shia position as 'honourable' and describes the Ottoman Empire's policy as 'extremist in (pursuing) ignorant Sunnism' and as a result, the Shia situation was 'no good' due to sectarian directions of state policy.[2]

Having crushed the mainly Shia 1920 rebellion, the British didn't pay enough attention to the sectarian makeup of Iraq when forming the first government of Abdur-Rahman An-Naqeeb, who was not an ordinary Sunni citizen but a Sunni sect leader. He was the head of the Gailani religious clan, the decedents of Imam Abdul-Qadir Al-Gailani, a revered Sunni Imam and leader of a Sufi order, with a big shrine in Bagdad. His name, An-Naqeeb, meaning the head, clearly reveals he is the head of this distinguished religious Sunni family as well as all the ashraf (Sunni nobles) of Baghdad. His mere presence as the leader of the new government of Iraq, especially when it came immediately after the bitter defeat of the Shia 1920 revolution, gave the mainstream Iraqi Shia the impression that the British were in effect building a Sunni state and were penalizing them for their opposition to their rule.[3]

When the first Iraqi government was formed by An-Naqeeb, the Sunnis dominated and held the most important posts.[4] An-Naqeeb was known to have disdain for Shia clerics and for those who participated in the 1920 revolution against the British.[5] He also had a lot of admiration for the English as he told Amin Rihani, the Lebanese writer and poet.[6] 'The English have the knowledge, wealth and wisdom. What do the (Iraqi) nationalists have? Do they love the country more than us, when it's our country before it's theirs? Most of them are still foreigners'.[7]

Due to these critical views of his fellow countrymen, An-Naqeeb's reputation among Iraqis deteriorated considerably, and the British were soon trying to find a replacement leader for all Iraqis. King Feisal, before them was not happy with him and sought to replace him and he was replaced against his wishes, by Abdul-Muhsin As-Sadoon.[8]

Some senior Iraqi politicians of the monarchy era believed the British preferred to deal with the Sunni minority because 'they will always need to rely on a (foreign) power for support, and they were always ready to cooperate with it'.[9] The Sunnis, who had accumulated lots of administrative experience during the Ottoman period, also provided the British with a bureaucratic class capable of running the administrative bodies of the new state.[10]

The Shia, in contrast, were disadvantaged in this regard as they were marginalized under the Ottomans, who distrusted them and practiced systematic discrimination against them in many ways, while Sunnis were selected for virtually all administrative posts in the governorates which would be merged to become Iraq following WWI, namely Basra, Baghdad and Mosul. By appointing An-Naqeeb's cabinet, which had some Shia ministers, the British followed in the Ottomans' footsteps, although there was a difference in the sense that the Shia rose against the British, not the Ottomans.[11]

The British followed this by bringing a non-Iraqi Sunni king, Feisal, the son of Hussein bin Ali, the Hashemite Sharif of Mecca and leader of the anti-Ottoman Arab Revolt (1916–1918), to rule Iraq where the Shia constitute more than half of population.[12] Some Shia notables, including those hosted by Sharif Hussein in Mecca, such as Noor Al-Yassiri, welcomed the selection of the Sharif's son as king of Iraq.[13] They joined Sunni community leaders in sending letters to Sharif Hussein requesting that one of his sons become the king of Iraq.[14]

Sunni dominance

After the installation of the monarchy on 23 August 1921, the ruling class in Iraq in the following years was dominated by Sunnis. Most governments were led by Sunni politicians, the most prominent of whom was long-serving PM Noori As-Saeed.[15]

The Shia felt disenfranchised and thus there were calls among Shia clerics to boycott the government and its institutions. The Shia clerics who made these calls were distrustful of taking part in government not only because of the disenfranchisement of their community but also because of traditional theological Shia arguments which reject the legitimacy of any government not headed by one of the 12 imams of Shiaism, whom the Shia believe to be infallible.[16] Their non-participation has other reasons in the view of Abdul-Kareem Al-Uzri, a Shia minister of finance in the monarchy era.

Al-Uzri contends that 'the British were unable to reach agreement with Shia political leaders, first among whom were the religious scholars, whose position was intransigent and uncompromising, insisting on complete independence'.[17] He acknowledges that the British had one option left available to them in the face of Shia intransigence which was to deal with the group that was willing to cooperate and reach a political settlement with them and that was the Ottoman Sunni officers and civil servants who worked in the former Ottoman administration.[18]

There was a feeling of discrimination among the Shia population throughout the period between 1921 and 2003, except perhaps during the rule of Brigadier Abdul-Karim Qassim (1958–1963), who sympathized with the poor, of whom the majority were Shia. This has created friction and distrust between the two main sects in the country. Any move towards establishing a strong political system by any politician was viewed with suspicion by the Shia.

Khalil Osman shares Al-Uzri's view on the Shia intransigence:

> Political marginalization under the monarchy accentuated the sense of collective identity among the Shi'ites who tried to renegotiate their inclusion in the national polity. But the rigidity of the political system restricted the possibility of accommodating their demands.[19]

General Qassim gained the trust of the Shia because he had balanced views regarding Shia-Sunni differences. He was of mixed parentage; Sunni father and Shia mother.[20] Qassim was seen as 'fair' by the Shia public and even his political opponents, such as Hassan Al-Alawi, later admitted that Qassim was patriotic and fair and he expressed regret for opposing him.[21] Qassim attempted to redress the grievances of the masses of impoverished Shia peasants through a land reform program which sought to take agricultural land from the feudal lords, including Shia tribal chiefs, and distribute it among the poor Shia farmers in the south.[22]

Most of the major landowners were Shia (23 Shia, 14 Sunni, nine Kurds).[23] Qassim also introduced laws that were seen to be fair and built cities for the poor, the most noteworthy of which is what is now called Sadr City, formerly known as Revolution City, the name Qassim had given to the populous district of Baghdad.[24]

However, Sunni Arab nationalists, by and large, didn't like Qassim because his policies were designed to empower the poor which were mainly in the Shia south. The Sunnis were mostly inclined towards, and sympathetic with, Arab nationalism. This was at odds with Qassim's Iraqist streak which was promoted by the Iraqi Communist Party, which was very popular among the Shia youth.[25] But Arab nationalism was regarded by some experts on Iraq as internally divisive and externally irredentist and destabilizing force in Iraq.[26]

Since the army was dominated by disgruntled Sunni officers, Qassim constantly faced coup attempts, mutinies and assassination attempts until he was toppled at the hands of Arab nationalist army officers (mainly Sunnis) led by his erstwhile revolutionary partner, Colonel Abdu-Salam Arif, helped by BP led by Colonel Ahmed Hassan Al-Bakir, among others.[27] Arif became president and Al-Bakir Prime Minister. Qassim was summarily executed with a number of his colleagues at the Baghdad radio station on 9 February 1963.[28] Fifty years on, Qassim is still popular in Iraq, especially among the poor Shia. They celebrate the 14th of July coup, and remember his execution on 9 February.

Discrimination under Ba'ath

Arif had soon betrayed his divided Ba'athist allies and turned against them, forcing them out of power in November 1963, after nine months of fragile partnership. But he didn't stay for long, as he was killed three years later in a mysterious plane crash in the south of Iraq. His brother, Abdu-Rahman, took over as president. The latter was weak, and this led to his dismissal in a coup led by the Ba'athists on 17 July 1968. Ahmed Hassan Al-Bakir and Saddam Hussein, both Sunnis and relatives from Tikrit, dominated the scene. It was clear from the outset, as Charles Tripp states, that the new regime was dominated by the clan of Sunni army officers, not too dissimilar to those who had governed Iraq a decade ago.[29] After 11 years in power, Al-Bakir resigned in July 1979 to be succeeded by Saddam Hussein.[30] Saddam ruled with an iron fist for 24 years until he was toppled by an American military invasion on 9 April 2003.

During these years, the government was dominated by Sunni Arabs.[31] While some Shia did participate in the Ba'ath government, they were not trusted by the establishment, especially after the Iranian Revolution of 1979, which overtly opposed the Saddam regime, accusing it of sectarianism and pursuing anti-Islamic policies. More and more Shia were imprisoned, executed and fled the country, escaping a new wave of repression and crackdown. Many Shia religious leaders were executed under the pretext of alleged Iranian loyalties.[32] This brutal repression pushed the Shia more towards Iran. Underground Shia organizations, which looked up to the Iranian Revolution as a role model in facing up to their repressive government, took up arms as the regime escalated its repression against Shia activists and religious leaders.

Shia Islamist activists engaged in bomb attacks and assassination attempts against senior BP officials. There were also calls by leaders in the Iranian revolutionary regime on the Iraqis to rise up and topple BP rule. This only led to more brutal and repressive measures by the regime. Through the use of excessive and brutal force, the Ba'ath government managed to crush the Shia Islamist threat but at a very high price in lives.[33]

Many Shia felt discriminated against by the Sunni-dominated government; although the regime was secular, it was regarded as Sunni based on the family background of its influential leaders. Saddam's violent reaction to those who hold different views to his made it difficult for him to build any bridges with Iraqis in general. Although BP had many Shia among its membership, some in senior levels, those who had real power were Sunnis close to the two Sunni presidents, Al-Bakir and Saddam Hussein, who came from the same village and were close relatives.[34]

The important ministry of defence was almost always occupied by a Sunni minister from Tikrit. (It was first occupied by Hardan At-Tikriti, then Hammad

Shihab, then Saddam's cousin and brother-in-law, Adnan Khairulla Tilfah, then Saddam's cousin Ali Hassan Al-Majeed). There was hardly any Shia member in the Revolutionary Command Council, the highest authority in the land, from 1968–2003, and even when the number was increased to include non-Sunnis, it was reduced again to five members in 1977, all of whom were Sunnis.[35] The five members were Ahmed Hassan Al-Bakir, Saddam Hussein, Sa'adoon Ghaidan, Izzat Ad-Doori and Taha Al-Jazrawi.[36]

Many Shia of Iranian and Kurdish origins were regarded as 'foreigners' and they got 'deported' from their own country in the 1970s and 80s and their belongings were confiscated under the pretext that they were originally foreigners.[37] On the top of that, their sons were imprisoned or executed.[38]

Shia, in Iraq and across the world, saw this as an act of sectarian cleansing. The friction between the two sects, which was brewing under the surface, came out into the open during the Iraq-Iran war in the 80s. Many Shia soldiers and officers defected to Iran or Syria, whereas many Shia civilians left the country and sought refuge elsewhere. Those who stayed had to prove their loyalty to the regime in many ways, either by joining BP or any of the numerous security apparatuses, and work hard to please the regime through submitting reports, false or true, on their fellow countrymen. Sectarian distrust among the people grew further following the 1991 post-Gulf War uprising.[39]

This episode was characterized by the use of brutal force by the regime to suppress the uprising, which spread to 14 of Iraq's 18 provinces, including the shelling of Shia shrines, as well as the use of Shia rhetoric and religious symbols by the rebels, who also engaged in violent activities against those they suspected of belonging to BP or the state's security services.[40] Khalil Osman states:

> The rebellion in southern Iraq was marked by a vigorous assertion of Shi'ite identity, featuring overtly Shi'ite religious symbolism and rhetoric.... But the passionate and strident assertion of Shi'ite identity vis-à-vis the despotic Ba'athist state gave rise to fears and feelings of exclusion among Sunnis, which resulted in their loss of sympathy for the rebellion.[41]

By 2003, the main Shia Islamist parties and other ordinary Shia, secular or Islamist, were determined that no Sunni domination of the government should be allowed once again and were equally determined that they, being the majority in the country, must play an active role in politics and be the ruling class of the country. But the Sunnis were not to give up power easily. They resisted the American occupation which led to their ouster from power and the establishment of a Shia-dominated regime. The Sunni population, especially in the capital, Baghdad, and the provinces of Anbar, Musil, Salahuddeen and Diyala, boycotted the political process, hardly participated in the first elections of January 2005 and heavily rejected the constitution, which was mainly written by Shia and Kurds, helped by the Americans and the British, with some Sunni participation.[42]

The prevalent view among the Shia is that Iraqi Sunnis have never settled and accepted Shia rule. This view is enhanced by the fact that Sunni fighters from other parts of the Arab and Islamic worlds flooded the Sunni provinces of Anbar, Musil, Salahuddeen and Diyala, as well as the capital Baghdad, and began to blow up government offices, street markets, mosques and religious centres, killing tens of thousands of innocent civilians. Although the Sunnis did participate heavily in both the December 2005 and March 2010 elections, Sunni unrest continued unabated, fuelled by continued feelings of marginalization. In fact, the regime change in Iraq in 2003 gave rise to a crisis of identity among Sunnis who found it difficult to cope with their loss of power and influence. Insurgent groups used these feelings of discontent and anger among Sunnis to gain sympathy and recruit fighters.[43]

Sectarian politics, which may have been covertly practiced before 2003, became the order of the day. As American forces left Iraq in December 2011, the provincial council in the Sunni province of Salahudden demanded a federal region, and submitted a request to Central government to conduct a plebiscite in the province over federalism. The government declined to carry out the plebiscite, saying it will lead the Ba'athists across the country to assemble in the province. PM Al-Maliki refused to instruct the Independent High Electoral Commission (IHEC) to conduct the referendum in violation of Law 13 (2008), which states the government has to refer the request to IHEC within 15 days.

Sunni displeasure

The former Speaker of Parliament, Usama An-Nujaifi, a Sunni from Musil and leader of the main Sunni list 'Muttahidoon', declared during a visit to the US in 2012 that Sunnis in Iraq were unhappy with the current arrangement and wanted a federal entity. That was the first time he mentioned such a demand based on sectarian grounds. In January 2013 a protest began in the western Sunni province of Anbar which lasted solidly for a year, until it was dispersed by the Iraqi army which entered the province to chase outlawed armed groups which took over some parts of the province. The Shia-dominated government of PM Al-Maliki, which grew more distrustful of Sunnis, was reluctant to meet their demands because it felt they were nothing but an attempt to weaken their grip on power and to restore their influence. Tension between the government and Sunni population reached its height at that time and didn't calm down until Al-Maliki was forced to relinquish power in mid-August 2014. Nujaifi repeated the demand for a Sunni federal entity recently.[44]

It's established that people voted largely on sectarian grounds in all elections held in the post-2003 period. This is clear from the fact that reflected the country's sectarian distribution. Also, many politicians, academics and independent observers acknowledged it. This meant that those candidates with high sectarian rhetoric stood a better chance of being elected. Parliament became dominated by sectarian figures from both sects. Political programmes hardly existed and the main issue became which sect governs the country. If it couldn't, it should at least impede the other from governing.

The main political parties were those that expressed the interests of sectarian and ethnic groups and sought to maximize the shares of their respective communities and party members and supporters in power. In the 2014 parliamentary election, Hanan Al-Fatlawi, a Shia female physician and lawmaker known for her vociferous sectarian views, was re-elected with over 90,000 votes in the Babylon Province.[45] This is a high number of voters, considering that she is a woman. Only 22 female candidates, out of 83, were elected without the help of the gender quota law in the 2014 elections.[46]

Islamist parties sought to aggravate sectarian fear within their communities to guarantee that they maintain a large electoral base of support. Sectarianism has been connected to power politics. It occurred under the influence of multiple struggles over power, resources and socio-political developments, set into motion by the creation of the nation-state.[47]

Sectarianism subverts democracy as Iraqi politics in the last ten years has shown and as Iraqi politicians and academics have pointed out in exclusive interviews. It thwarts the power of the electorate to choose between competing political programs. Within the charged sectarian atmosphere of Iraq, elections became occasions for exacerbating intercommunal tensions, rather than a means through which citizens participate in shaping government and its policies. Voting became an exercise in which community members flex numerical muscles to obstruct the claims to the state's power and other resources made also at the ballot box by other communities.

Under these circumstances, the electorates of various communities have tended to use their voting strength to defend the shares of their respective communities in power rather than to contribute to the process of making policies that address the interests of all citizens irrespective of their sectarian background. This state of affairs made the peaceful rotation of power, a key mechanism in a democracy, more difficult as evidenced by the political crises surrounding the formation of governments in the post-2003 period.

Nowhere did sectarianism in post-2003 Iraq subvert democracy more than in the distorted version of majority rule that it nurtured. Under Iraqi sectarianism, the democratic principle of majority rule has no longer been a rule by a political majority. It has rather been translated into the rule of sectarian communities. As such, majority rule as a means to decide on public issues based on political programmes that address the interests of the broader citizenry and on the principle of citizenship was lost. Amid the heated competition between large sectarian groups over power resources, feelings of marginalization among minorities were reinforced and heightened. This shook the twin pillars of democratic governance represented by the principles of majority rule and protection of minority rights.

Sectarianism has also undermined the emergence of competent governance. It contravenes basic democratic principles since voters should be free of all pressures to vote for their preferred candidates who should be chosen on the basis of their suitability and their political and economic programmes. If sectarian politics prevails, then people's choices will be limited and those individuals who pursue militant sectarian policies and use radical rhetoric are likely to be elected.

Officials elected on their shrill sectarian rhetoric are rarely efficient or competent. This is confirmed by the views of distinguished interviewees.

Holding elected officials accountable in such a system has been highly problematic. Government accountability, in the sense that those enjoying executive powers ought to explain their policies to the elected representatives, could not be practiced. Former PM Noori Al-Maliki and ministers from his bloc refused to appear before parliament to explain certain policies or policy failures.

At times, anti-corruption measures have become a tool in the hands of the executive branch to marginalize and score points against political rivals. At other times, efforts to bring corrupt officials to justice for wrongdoing have been aborted by outcry from their communities and political parties claiming that they had been targeted for sectarian reasons. This undermined the rule of law which is a fundamental pillar of democracy. It's defined as 'the sovereignty of law over the people and elected officials'.[48]

When a country moves from a non-democratic to a democratic system, those in power should implement the law and be punished for their wrongdoing. People in a democracy expect and have the right to have fair rulers, not tyrants whose actions are not bound by the law.

Democratization entails the expansion of accountability, the independence of the judiciary, and the public protection of property rights.[49] This expansion can happen when there is rule of law. This is also important for justice, equality, social stability and economic development, which are essential in a successful democracy. When the rule of law expands in a country, democracy becomes consolidated. When sectarianism undermines the rule of law, democracy and democratic governance are undermined.

Sectarianism in post-2003 Iraq has made government less responsive to the will of the public. Elected and non-elected officials, who win their public offices based on power-sharing arrangements that restrictively allocate posts based on sectarian and partisan affiliation, have been more inclined to respond to the aspirations of their communities rather than the demands that cut across communal lines and benefit the broader citizenry. As such, citizenship built on a foundation of equality of citizens, in rights, dignity and respect, regardless of their sectarian identity, lost its meaningfulness in Iraq.

Sectarianism has become a source of polarization, prejudice and intolerance which contributed to undermining social peace between Iraqi communities, turning diversity into an arena of inter-communal rivalry and discord rather than serving as an indicator of cultural richness and an opportunity for building networks of inter-communal harmony, dialogue and cooperation.

It has also contributed to the creation of a dysfunctional state and democratic system. Contaminated by sectarianism, the institution of democratic politics in Iraq became a source for political instability rather than a mechanism for channeling societal interests and meaningful citizen participation in the selection of government and determining its policy.

Sectarianism impedes democracy

Prominent Iraqi sociologist Faleh Abdul-Jabbar explains that sectarianism impedes democracy in three serious ways:

1   It negates accountability, and this has a destructive result.
2   It limits representation, since this becomes the right of sectarian politicians to represent the sect they belong to.
3   Sectarian officials deprive those who disagree with them of benefits using economic tools to force citizens to comply with the diktats of the rulers (the dictatorship of needs).[50]

Abdul-Jabbar regards the Islamic formula for sectarianism a 'monopoly over the sect' since it prevents diversity within the group. It is 'monopoly and prevention' that renders a Shia 'the one who is politically Shia' and the same goes for others. He regards it as a serious impediment to democracy. 'To Islamists, a Shia is the one who is politically Shia and this impedes democracy in a serious way'.[51]

The absence of accountability and monopoly of representation, through the prevention of non-Islamists from representing the sect and depriving them of benefits is an economic war or 'dictatorship of needs' according to Abdul-Jabbar.[52] This way, democracy becomes a dictatorship.

When there are few work opportunities outside the state, since the rentier state owns the economy, citizens are forced to belong to the ruling party (or parties) and would be inclined to obey the government of the day. This weakens democratic institutions since it limits people's freedom.

Former Iraqi PM, Ayad Allawi, regards sectarianism as one of the reasons for the failure of Iraqi democracy so far.[53] However, he reckons the pluralism of Islamic parties in Iraq doesn't make them sectarian; only if there is one party, will it be sectarian.[54] But this opinion is at odds with realities on the ground, according to Khalil Osman.[55] Allawi admits, however, that Islamist parties, which he believes were created as a reaction to foreign interference and domination, have become 'too sectarian, violent and authoritarian' and this contradicts his earlier assertion that the multiplicity of Islamist parties prevents sectarianism.[56]

There is a multiplicity of Islamist parties in Iraq (IDP, IFP, IIP, SIIC, BO, Hikma, ST, RT, IDM among others), yet sectarianism has intensified, perhaps because sectarian parties compete among themselves in their sectarian discourse. Islamist parties can unite on certain issues as they did in 2005 to oust Allawi from the premiership, and in 2010 when they backed Noori Al-Maliki for PM even though Allawi had more seats. In October 2016, they united to pass a law banning alcohol. This means they can act as one party at crucial times for themselves.

Dia Shakarchi blames 'political sectarianism' for impeding democracy.[57] He regards the feeling of belonging to a sect as 'the biggest impediment to the process of democratic transition' followed by belonging to religion, ethnicity and region.[58] He goes further by claiming that Islamist parties are necessarily sectarian because they have to be either Sunni or Shia. 'There is no trans-sectarian Islamist party, neither in Iraq nor anywhere else'.[59]

Although most Islamist parties claim to be 'for all Muslims', in reality, there are no Sunni members in the Shia parties of IDP, IFP, SIIC, BO, Hikma or ST and no Shia members in IIP. When one asks them for the reason, as I have, they would say their parties are open to members of both sects but no one from the other sect has crossed the boundary 'due to sectarian polarization'! Shakarchi also blames corruption on sectarianism. 'Corruption was strengthened through hiding behind religious and sectarian slogans'.[60]

Shakarchi estimates that 90 per cent of voters voted on sectarian basis and explains:

> Most parties or electoral coalitions are either Sunni or Shia, and each side insinuates to its audience from among its respective sect that it's the pro-tector of the sect from the 'terrorism' of the other sect, or the protector of the latter sect from marginalization and repression at the hands of the former.[61]

Ali Allawi affirms sectarian bias 'impedes democratisation in Iraq'. 'Primary identities overshadow the democratic process' he asserts.[62] He acknowledges that people did vote in the last elections according to their sectarian rather than religious affiliations.

Kanan Makiya regards as sectarianism a huge hurdle in the face of any pro-gress. He has even called for a 'fatwa' against sectarianism.[63] Maysoon Aldam-luji cites sectarianism as one of the factors that caused the failure of the Iraqi democratic experiment so far.[64] She is adamant that Islamist parties 'encourage sectarianism and permit religious discrimination against non-Muslims'.[65] She blames them for 'causing sectarian conflicts in Iraq and failing to run the state'.[66]

Akeel Abbas, who authored a book about the subject, regards sectarianism as one of the impediments to democratization. It resulted in sectarian strife, which 'made people resort more to their sectarian identities, seeking protection in sect-based militias that are more trusted and effective than the state itself'.[67] He explains that sect-based parties, by their nature, are 'not pluralistic and have in mind the interests of their sect followers' not all the citizens as modern parties have. He con-cluded that 'sectarianism and tribalism are structurally anti-democratic'.[68]

Hussein Al-Hindawi regards the current Iraqi state as sectarian, just like the previous one.[69] Adnan Al-Janabi,[70] Bassim Anton,[71] Kamal Field,[72] Adil Abdur-Raheem,[73] Sharwan Al-Waeli,[74] Farid Ayar,[75] Shorouq Al-Abayachi,[76] Waleed Al-Hilli[78] and Wahda Al-Jumaili[77] – who complained of Shia discrimination against Sunnis – have all highlighted the negative influence of sectarianism on democracy and society as a whole.

Abdulkhaliq Hussein described it as 'entrenched' and he reckons it may take a generation to disappear but he blames this on the Sunnis, 'who found them-selves no longer dominant in the newly found democratic regime, while the Shia find themselves threatened by Sunni extremists'.[79] Dr Ayar says our current democracy is fragile because it's based on 'sectarian bigotry'.[80]

Kurdish writer, Kamran Qaradaghi, blames 'sectarian polarization' for deepening 'the principle of belonging to the community, whether ethnic or sectarian, before belonging to the state'.[81] Adil Abdur-Raheem acknowledged that religious parties used sectarian rhetoric although he charges that secular parties could turn to sectarian rhetoric.[82] Sharwan Al-Waelil acknowledges that sectarian loyalty is widespread in Iraq. He adds: 'religious and sectarian loyalty is harmful to the democratic process' and 'religious parties have exploited people's religious and sectarian emotions'. 'The citizen has reached a stage where he cannot compromise on the sectarian identity even though he is hungry, unemployed and his rights are taken away. This trend is harmful to society', he declares.[83]

Wahda Al-Jumaili lists 'favouring sub-identities over national identity' as an impediment to democracy and she blames it on the 'failing of politicians'.[84]

Shorouq Al-Abayachi argues that electoral popularity is linked to a high tone of sectarianism.[85] This explains why some candidates have increased the dose of sectarianism in their discourse during elections. Hanan Al-Fatlawi went as far as saying she would like to see seven Sunnis (killed) in place of every seven Shia killed in fighting terrorism.[86] She got over 90,000 votes in Babylon in the subsequent election.[87]

Al-Abayachi has observed that the electorate in Iraq voted in the last four elections on the basis of religious and sectarian loyalties. She singles out the elections of 2005, although she admits the density of this trend has decreased in the elections of 2010, but returned in full force in 2014.[88] This is corroborated by Sherwan Al-Wa'eli who said sectarianism was very high in the election of 2014.[89]

Al-Jumaili argues that sectarianism is back because of the weakness of the state and affirms sectarian loyalties were the basis of voting since 2005. Sami Al-Askari admits sectarian agitation has been prevalent in Iraq since the fall of the Saddam regime and it has contributed to 'pushing the electorate into specific directions'.[90]

Sectarian divisions have prevented the emergence of an Iraqi national leader who is able to unify the country and have a vision for the future. Ali Allawi states, 'The search for the will-o'-the-wisp, the Iraqi national leader, predictably got nowhere, there were only Shia, Sunni and Kurdish politicians, a smattering of self-styled liberals and secularists, each determined to push their particular agenda forward'.[91]

Sociologist Ibrahim Al-Haidari affirms sectarian loyalty always conflicts with loyalty to the national identity and constitutes an impediment to practicing democracy, which requires a belief in pluralism and respect for the other. 'Sectarianism impedes achieving democracy because it divides the national identity and breaks it up, while democracy unifies sub-identities in one national identity because it's based on the concept of citizenship and respect for the other'.[92]

Sectarianism is a form of group discrimination that contravenes the basic principles of democracy, which are based on freedom of the individual and respect for the law. It constitutes a serious impediment to democracy and progress. If democratization is to succeed in Iraq, there must be a complete eradication of sectarianism from state institutions. This could have been done with some support from the democracy sponsor, the US, back in 2004/2005.

Parties should not have been allowed to form on the basis of sectarian identity, not just theoretically but also practically. All parties say they are not sectarian, but when all their members come from one sect, they become sectarian automatically. This should not have been allowed right from the outset. The American sponsors could have insisted on it and they would have had wide support even among non-political religious scholars who are against sectarianism. But they chose to tolerate it which has led to its intensification.

Sectarian vocabulary should have been banned from the political discourse in the Transitional Administrative Law in 2004 and then the permanent constitution in 2005. Again, the Americans could have insisted on it when they were running Iraq directly. It has become a lot harder later on since it will need some concerted effort to rid Iraq of sectarianism which may not be easy, especially when current sectarian forces are in government, and not prepared to give up their only weapon to stay in power. In the 2018 elections, parties have moved away from sectarianism and this is due to the fact that people have come to find the sectarian rhetoric empty and harmful. However, one candidate for the 'Conquest' list, Wajeeh Abbas, used flagrant sectarian jibes and was elected. His remarks were widely condemned, but he was elected. This means that sectarianism is still alive and firm action needs to be taken against it.

Notes

1 Yatzhak Nakash, *The Shi'is of Iraq*, Princeton University Press (1994) pp. 60–61
2 Al-Aloosi (1992) op. cit. p. 114
3 Al-Uzri (1991) op. cit. p. 349
4 Charles Tripp, *A History of Iraq*, Cambridge University Press (2000) p. 45
5 Ali Al-Wardi, *Glimpses of Iraq Recent History* (Arabic) Islamic Publishing House (2005) vol. 6, p. 24; also Amin Al-Rihani, *Kings of Arabia* (Arabic) Al-Rihani Printing House, Beirut (1959) pp. 397–398
6 Nijmeh Salim Hajjar, *Political and Social Thoughts of Amin Rihani*, Tauris Academic Studies (2010) London
7 Al-Rihani (1951) op. cit. pp. 397–398
8 Al-Wardi (2005) vol. 6, pp. 204–207
9 Abul-Kareem Al-Uzri (1991) op. cit. p. 350
10 Kamil Al-Chaderchi, *From the Papers of Kamil Al-Chadirchi*, Beirut, Al-Talee'ah Printing and Publishing (1971) p. 80; also see Al-Uzri, *History of Iraq in Memoirs*, [1930–1958] 1st edn, Beirut, no publisher (1982)
11 Al-Uzri (1991) op. cit. pp. 347–348
12 A British population census conducted in 1919 put the Shia population at 55 per cent: Abdallah Fahad Al-Nafisi, *The Role of the Shia in the Political Development of Modern Iraq* (1973), Al-Nahar Publishing, Beirut, p. 167
13 Al-Wardi (2005) op. cit. volume 5, part 2, p. 189
14 For more on Faisal, see Ali Allawi, *Faisal I of Iraq* (2014) Yale University Press
15 Khalil Osman, *Sectarianism in Iraq: The Making of State and Nation since 1920*, Routledge (2014) pp. 117–128

16 Joseph Eliash, 'Misconceptions regarding the juridical status of the Iranian "Ulamā"', International Journal of Middle East Studies, volume 10, issue 1 (1979) pp. 9–25

17 Al-Uzri (1991) op. cit. p. 349

18 Ibid., pp. 348–352

19 Osman (2014) op. cit. p. 92

20 Hassan Al-Alawi, *Abdul-Kareem Qassim, a Vision after the Twenty*, Azzawraa Publishing House, London (1983) pp. 13–14

21 Ibid. The entire book is dedicated to the life of Abdul-Karim Qassim, his fairness and balanced views

22 Ronny E Gabbay, *Communism and Agrarian Reform in Iraq*, Taylor & Francis, (1978) pp. 108–151

23 Hanna Batatu, *The Old Social Classes and the Revolutionary Movements of Iraq*, (2004) Al-Saqi Books (Arabic) London, p. 87

24 Baghdad government puts the population of Sadr City at 2,995,750, Almada Press, 'Convert Al-Sadr City to a governorate' (Baghdad 2014); IRIN says the population is 2.5 million in 2008

25 On the Iraqist-Arab nationalist rift in the Iraqi intellectual circles, see Eric Davis, *Memories of State: Politics, History, and Collective Identity in Modern Iraq*, University of California Press (2005) pp. 55–81

26 Abbas Kelidar, ed. Eisenstadt and Mathewson (2003) op. cit. p. 36

27 Uriel Dann, *Iraq under Qassem: A Political History, 1958–1963*, New York, Praeger (1969); and Hanna Batatu, *The Old Social Classes and the Revolutionary Movements of Iraq: A Study of Iraq's Old Landed and Commercial Classes and of Its Communists, Ba'athists and Free Officers* (1978) pp. 764–1026

28 Ali Kareem Saeed, *The Iraq of 8th February: From the Dialogue of Concepts to the Dialogue of Blood*, (1999) Beirut, Alkunooz Printing House, pp. 104–106

29 Tripp. (2007) op. cit. p. 194

30 Talib Hussein Ash-Shibeeb, a leading Ba'athist and former Iraqi foreign minister, believed that Al-Bakir was removed from power and later poisoned by Saddam Hussein (Ali Kareem Saeed [1999] op. cit. p. 391); Tahir Tawfiq Al-Ani revealed (in an interview with Russia Today published on 24–25/7/2016, op. cit.) that Saddam Hussein was behind Al-Bakir's resignation: https://goo.gl/py0FqT

31 Osman (2014) op. cit. chapter 3

32 Adil Ra'uf, *Islamic Activism in Iraq between the Marja'iyah and Party Affiliation: A Critical Reading of the March of Half a Century* (1950–2000), Damascus, Iraqi Center for Media and Studies (2000)

33 Osman (2014) op. cit. pp. 79–82

34 Batatu (1978) op. cit. p. 399

35 Ibid., p. 400

36 Ibid., footnote 26

37 Osman (2014) op. cit. pp. 232–236

38 VOA, 27/10/2009: www.voanews.com/a/a-13-a-2003-05-06-31-an-66851487/375890.html

39 Fanar Haddad, *Sectarianism in Iraq: Antagonistic Visions of Unity*, Oxford University Press (2011); and Phoebe Marr, *The Modern History of Iraq*, Westview Press (1985) pp. 227–232

40 Osman (2014) op. cit. pp. 83–84; and Kanan Makiya, *Cruelty and Silence: War, Tyranny, Uprising, and the Arab World*, W.W. Norton (1994) p. 66

41 Osman (2014) op. cit. p. 84

42 Marr (1985) op. cit. pp. 287–296

43 Ahmed Hashim, *Insurgency and Counter-Insurgency in Iraq*, Cornell University Press (2005) pp. 60–108

44 Suadad Al-Salhy, Middle East Eye, 20/2/2016: https://goo.gl/VKxs4z

45 IHEC's election results for the province of Babylon 2014 published online and accessed in June 2014
46 Rabih Nader, 'Iraqi women make gains in parliamentary elections', Al-Monitor, 12/6/2014: https://goo.gl/CO041u
47 Osman (2014) op. cit. p. 269
48 Patrick O'Neil, *Essentials of Comparative Politics*, W.W. Norton (2007)
49 Matteo Cervellati, Piergiuseppe Fortunato and Uwe Sunde, 'Democratization and the rule of law', (2009): www.wto.org/English/res_e/reser_e/gtdw_e/wkshop10_e/fortunato_e.pdf
50 Interview with Faleh Abdul–Jabbar
51 Ibid.
52 Ibid.
53 Interview with Ayad Allawi
54 Ibid.
55 Interview with Khalil Osman
56 Interview with Ayad Allawi
57 Interview with Dia Shakarchi
58 Ibid.
59 Ibid.
60 Ibid., p. 58
61 Ibid., p. 59
62 Interview with Ali Allawi
63 Interview with Kanan Makiya
64 Interview with Maysoon Aldamaluji
65 Ibid.
66 Ibid.
67 Interview with Akeel Abbas
68 Ibid.
69 Interview with Hussein Al-Hindawi
70 Interview
71 Interview
72 Interview
73 Interview
74 Interview
75 Interview
76 Interview
77 Interview
78 Interview
79 Interview with Abdulkhaliq Hussein
80 Interview with Farid Ayar
81 Interview with Kamran Qaradaghi
82 Interview with Adil Abdur-Raheem
83 Interview with Sharwan Al-Waeli
84 Interview with Wahda Al-Jumaili
85 Interview with Shorouq Al-Abayachi
86 Diana Moukalled, Al-Arabia.net, 11/4/2014: https://goo.gl/qYeUcA
87 Rabih Nader (12/6/2014) Al-Monitor, op. cit.
88 Interview with Shorouq Al-Abayachi
89 Interview with Sharwan Al-Waeli
90 Interview with Sami Al-Askari
91 Allawi (2007) op. cit. p. 460
92 Interview with Ibrahim Al-Haidari

9   Lack of democratic tradition

Many people talk of the lack of democratic tradition as one of the reasons for the failure or lack of progress in the democratization process in Iraq. Others talk of the need to blend democracy with local values in order to make the new system familiar and more acceptable to people. While some others say democracy is a new system and it has to be taken in its entirety since it's indivisible. There is a valid argument for both views.

Samuel Huntington predicted 'democracy could become a dominant feature of the Middle East and North Africa in 1990s'.[1] His prophecy didn't materialize, although Iraqis did rise against the dictatorship in 1991 demanding democracy and reforms, but they were brutally suppressed. Also, the Arab Spring broke out in the second decade of the twenty-first century, although it has not produced a stable democracy yet despite the fact that it has managed to change regimes in Tunisia, Egypt, Libya and Yemen.

But even then, Huntington identified the obstacle for democracy in Islamic countries as 'cultural'.[2] But he rejected the notion that certain cultures are permanent obstacles to development in one direction or another. He regards cultural obstacles as limited.[3]

Iraqi sociologist, Ali Al-Wardi, saw democracy and democratic values as 'social rather than political virtues'.[4] Al-Wardi emphasized the 'disjointed' nature of Iraqi society, but he was not 'fatalist' regarding the possibilities of change. Rather, he insisted that 'no social or political project could succeed if it didn't take a realistic account of the country's history'.[5] Al-Wardi did come out in favour of a form of democracy based on both recognition of the country's diversity and proportional representation. He maintained that

> Iraqi people are divided against themselves and their sectarian, ethnic, and tribal struggles exceed those of any other Arab people and there is no way of resolving this condition better than adopting a democratic system, where each group can participate in power according to its proportional number.[6]

Lebanese Islamic thinker and author, Hani Fahs, asserts that social realities must be taken into consideration when devising a political system.[7] He invokes the experience of the late Lebanese religious leader Muhammed Mehdi

Shamsuldeen, Tunisian religious leader, Rachid Al-Ghannouchi, and Sudanese religious leader, Hassan At-Turabi who adapted their ideas to suit the local culture. 'They realised the importance of accepting social realities'.

Fahs expected the Muslim Brothers in Egypt to fail when they were in power, and this was on the record in September 2012. They were toppled by the army on 30 June 2013. He explained that 'they started doing all sorts of unacceptable practices'. He argues they introduced a culture that had no relation to the 'pluralistic Egyptian society where the Copts, Muslims and the non-religious, lived together'. 'If Muhammed Mursi cannot become president of all Egyptians, he should abandon politics altogether', Fahs asserted.

Fahs reveals that 'there are religious jurisprudents who do not abide by the conditions of their religious mandate. They want to interfere in the very fine details on whim'. 'A sultan, and by that I mean ministers, managers, governors, presidents and rulers, must not wear a (jubba)', he declares.[8] He expected Iraqi Islamists to reflect what they have learnt in exile in their performance in government.

In his criticism of the Iraqi experiment, Samir Sumaidaie cites 'the lack of democratic culture' among the political leaders and most of the electorate as an impediment. This makes it 'democracy without democrats', he declares.[9] Sumaidaie argues that a functioning, robust and durable democratic system cannot happen by chance but through evolution and struggle between forces with political power, which they do not wish to relinquish, and other forces which struggle to devolve political power and make it accountable to the people. He affirms parts of the structure of the dictatorship (cultural, financial, and social) remained potent and resistant to the new order, which threatened their dominance.

He insists that there is a need for a 'democratic culture' to prevail, not necessarily among the people, but at least among the 'ruling elite'.[10] It's a valid point, but how can this be achieved in a democracy where the ruling class is elected by the people and they are bound to be of the same culture? Voters wouldn't elect people of a different culture. Culture does take a long time to form and it may develop in a way that is not necessarily conducive to enhancing democracy.

Novelty of experiment

Sumaidaie suggests a few steps to accelerate democratization, such as: Organizing a democratic movement, pushing forward the process of education and enlightenment, launching an ideological battle with anti-democratic forces, encouraging openness to the world through travel and cultural and other forms of exchanges, and enlisting and leveraging the help of international organizations and interested world powers.

If sectarian conflict in the region deepens, it will entrench sectarian forces in Iraq, while if the Iranian theocratic regime suffers from an internal crisis and collapses, it would have a positive impact on democracy in Iraq. If the situation in the Gulf, and in Saudi Arabia, in particular, changes dramatically, it would have a profound influence on the whole region.[11] Sumaidaie's views sound well-thought out, but linking establishing democracy to reforming Islam means it may take a long time if it ever happens.

Faleh Abdul Jabbar defines the principles that govern impediments to democracy: 'democracy is based on the free choice of the individual and whatever impedes this freedom impedes democracy'.[12] This must extend to the social, tribal, familial, religious and cultural restrictions imposed on individuals which restrain their electoral choices.

Sami Al-Askari also blames the slow progress of the democratization process on the novelty of the experiment 'after decades of dictatorship and oppression'.[13] He goes a lot farther by saying 'our Islamic societies, Iraq is no exception, have not known anything but the culture of despotism through centuries. Freedom of expression was reserved for the strong only'.[14] He affirms Iraqi society is dominated by tribal values and these values do not accord with the spirit of democracy and personal freedom.

Al-Askari emphasizes the need for freedom of expression to prevail first and in a gradual manner, benefitting from different factors, while it is 'getting freed from tribal and clerical restraints'. To him, democracy in Iraq existed 'in theory' over the last eight years where elections were free and voters did vote for candidates of their choice, except in some cases. But he contends there are influential factors such as social structure and the novelty of democratic experience and the 'role played by the religious establishment in political and social life', have all contributed to 'pushing the electorate into specific directions which were designed earlier'.[15]

But Al-Askari argues this happens in any democracy. 'Talking of an electorate that makes its own choices without external influences is really academic', he asserts.[16] His last assertion is not supported by facts since the electorates, by and large, examine the different political programmes and evaluate different political views before making informed voting decisions.

Al-Askari admits that wealth and belonging to certain families do play an effective role in winning elections in Iraq. 'Elections are like a staircase where some people can climb but taking the staircase is not available for everyone'. He again gives an example from the West: 'The rich in Western democracies are the ones who can get to decision making positions and prominent families in America inherit the presidency and seats of Congress'.[17] In the Iraqi context, the last statement must mean that those who were able to snatch money and positions now will stay in power for generations, since people in a democracy are influenced by money and familial prominence! This must also mean the current phenomena that came as a result of corruption, violence and despotism will have a lasting effect. It's interesting that Al-Askari spoke about rich US families 'inheriting' the presidency and seats of Congress when then-US president, Barack Obama, comes from a very humble background with a foreign African father.

Walid Al-Hilli blames the past political culture of despotism under the former regime for being an impediment to the progress of democracy. He also blames 'the racist feelings' of some people who are 'biased' against members of the other race.[18]

Al-Hilli insists that the biggest impediments to democracy, whatever the form of democracy he believes in, are 'education and culture' or the lack of them. He contends that the problem is 'the absence of the desire to understand the requirements for democratic mechanisms'. He reckons that many people didn't understand democracy but 'they started singing democracy's praise according to their whim and not as it should be'.

Al-Hilli is hopeful that democracy in Iraq 'will develop in the future'. He doesn't claim success, although his party, IDP, has been in power since 2005 and the last three PMs were members of its politburo.

Kadom Shubber states that tribalism in Iraq is 'deep-rooted' and it's difficult to dismantle tribal networks, and the religious authority is revered, and this has led to elections resulting in a 'poor expression of the true popular will'.[19] Civil rights, he contends, are normally acquired as a consequence of 'hard-fought struggles by those who demand them'. They are not given to them 'on a silver plate'![20] He lists certain requirements for the success of a democratically based political system. First, 'people need to recognise that the system is both necessary and fair, in order for them to be motivated to utilize it and respect its outcomes'.

Second, top leaders 'must show flexibility and mutual respect for one another'. 'No political system is fool-proof, and loopholes might spring up at any time. The onus is on societal leaders to find speedy remedies'. Third, the system must have proper and adequate safeguards. These involve legal and security elements designed to ensure the system's smooth functioning, as well as adjudicate when disputes arise.[21]

Those conditions, Shubber explains, do not exist in Iraq. He gives his reasons: 'this is a nation that had been ruled ruthlessly by a brutal dictatorship for over 30 years'. He cites 'antiquated bureaucracy, no acceptable legal system nor transparent or just enforcement framework and violent state apparatuses'. Ordinary people have come to understand that the 'only effective deterrent to malpractice, crime, corruption and other wrongdoing was harsh punishment or the prospect of it', he explains. Shubber contends that most Iraqis were 'ill-prepared for the positive changes in their political system post 2003'. Also, the changes that came about 'became the target of some criticism from most ordinary people'.

The president of the first electoral commission (2004–2008), Hussein Al-Hindawi, cites some historical and cultural hurdles to democracy in Iraq. '40 years of retarded totalitarian regime left its mark on Iraq'.[22] He regards the Saddam regime as 'particularly bad' in comparison with other totalitarian regimes such as Spain's Franco, whom he described as 'anti-communism and that's it'.[23] He credits Franco for establishing a real democratic system in Spain. 'He was a true believer in democracy but he thought the time wasn't right for it'. The last statement is controversial. Franco was a dictator who headed an authoritarian regime which, as we saw in Chapter 4, by its nature allows the development of democratic forces.

Al-Hindawi speaks of difficulties presented to Iraqi democracy by 'the absence of democratic tradition'. He says it made it difficult for people to understand democracy. 'A blanket given to the voter by a candidate persuades him to vote for that candidate'. He describes such a voter as 'having no respect for his opinion'.[24] But when people lack the basic necessities of life, such actions are not surprising. Hindawi highlights another cultural problem. 'The political class has no respect for democracy'. 'There is no single person who has any respect for the concept of democracy among Iraqi politicians', he contends. It's a damning statement from the president of the first electoral commission who was tasked by the UN with administering the democratic system. It's difficult to establish a democracy when politicians do not respect it or believe in it. This is a real impediment.

Al-Hindawi excludes one person of his sweeping statement: 'Perhaps Ahmed Al-Chalabi has more understanding of democracy than others because he lived abroad'. But Chalabi never won an election on his own. He had to be part of an Islamist list to win a seat. Al-Hindawi is categorical that 'none of the elite who lived abroad is democratic; on the contrary, they think that democracy is a (deceit)'.[25]

He explains that those who believed in democracy during the opposition era did that 'because they were weak'. In other words, they did it because they wanted help from other countries for 'toppling Saddam Hussein and establishing a democratic regime in its place'. They used democracy in their discourse because the world would sympathize with this cause. But once the dictator was removed, they went back to their old ideas. Hindawi's last statement accords with Adam Przeworski's view that not all who engaged in opposing the authoritarian regime are necessarily pro-democratic. Some use the democracy slogan as a step toward 'devouring their authoritarian opponents and their allies in the struggle against the old authoritarian regime'.[26]

Al-Hindawi reveals that among the Iraqi diaspora, estimated to number 2–4 million, 'most of those who went back to Iraq were the ones who lived in non-democratic countries such as Syria and Iran'.[27] This is largely true, since most people who immigrated to Western countries stayed there, with a few exceptions, largely politicians who travelled between Iraq and their new countries, and some others who couldn't succeed in the West due to their lack of skills or understanding of language and culture. Very few among those who returned to Iraq were people who lived, worked and achieved in the West. But even those few who have retuned, 'have actually lived in their own narrow societies and hence didn't understand the European experience' according to Hindawi.[28] Many of those Hindawi referred to didn't speak the language of the countries they lived in, nor did they understand their cultures.

Dia Shakarchi has a long list of reasons for the difficulties the democratic experiment in Iraq is facing. The first impediment to democracy, in his opinion, is the absence, or the low level, of the requisite of democratic culture, which includes the 'culture of citizenship'. 'This culture, or awareness of it, denotes the feeling of belonging to the nation of Iraq, and also the belief in freedoms and equality and respecting other opinions'.[29] He identifies another impediment, that is 'the culture of focusing on the role of the individual (leader) and the failure of the culture of institutional action to take root'. Shakarchi is actually criticizing the absence of collective and establishmentarian action in Iraqi culture.

He notes the absence of peaceful transfer of power in Iraq, even in the ranks of 'democratic secular parties'. This sounds like a contradiction in terms since democracy stipulates the practice of 'peaceful transfer of power' to the winner in elections. But those secular parties which have made it their mission to introduce democracy to Iraq have not practiced democracy within their parties to prove that they are democratic. Most party leaders have remained in their positions since their establishment as the mechanism to replace leaders has not been activated. Worse still is bequeathing leadership positions to sons and siblings as happened in SCIRI/SIIC/Hikma when Ammar Al-Hakim inherited his current position from his father who in turn inherited it from his brother.

Another problem Shakarchi highlights is 'double standards' which, he charges that the political elite are 'infected' with.[30] He is also adamant that tribal, regional and sectarian loyalties do impede democracy.

Adil Abdur-Raheem identifies the prevalent culture in Iraqi society as the culture of 'religious, partisan, tribal, sectarian or regional loyalties'. He says 'Some candidates were chosen despite not possessing parliamentary qualifications'.[31]

The only criterion or 'qualification' in a democracy, however, is the choice of the people. What he means is that the candidates were not fit to be members of parliament. In other words, the wrong people were elected due to the confusion, misinformation and lack of clear political programmes. But this might also be attributed to the lack of awareness among the electorate. As for educational qualifications, the law in Iraq stipulates that no one can stand for parliament unless they possess an international Baccalaureate (successful completion of secondary school education).

He identifies 'well-entrenched loyalty' in Iraqi culture as a problem: 'It brings weak people to state institutions and is one of the factors that impede democracy'. What is meant by loyalty here is not political affiliation but sectarian, tribal and ethnic affiliation. He confirms that loyalty, be it religious, tribal, partisan or sectarian, 'was the basis for voting in the previous period'.

Ali Allawi also cites cultural impediments to democracy. The prevalence of tribal and patriarchal values 'reduce[s] the scope for individual action, thereby limiting or undermining one of the principal premises of democracy', he asserts. He also alludes to the idea of lack of democratic culture in Iraq. 'Very few Iraqis have been steeped into the liberal democratic politics', he states.[32]

He adds sectarian, tribal and regional affiliation or bias to the cultural values that impede democracy. These primordial identities 'overshadow the democratic process', he asserts. He agrees that hypocrisy by politicians and the electorate necessarily has an adverse effect on the performance and efficiency of the political class.[33]

Sharwan Al-Wa'eli identifies a common problem, too, which is Iraqi democracy is not indigenous. He argues it 'was built abroad and this has led to real misunderstanding or misreading of the realities inside Iraq since the internal situation was not taken into consideration'. He identifies 'giving freedoms' too soon as problematic, and the transformation of the country 'by 180 degrees was done all [of] a sudden'. This, he contends, has made the Iraqi democratic transition 'immature'.[34]

He contends 'the transformation from a centralized totalitarian system that had legal rules for everything to a chaotic system in every sense has led to distorting the understanding of democracy'. 'Standardised global views on democracy' were bound to fail in Iraq since democracy is not just ideas and procedures, in his opinion, but it's a practice as well. His interpretation is that both the political class and the people had misunderstandings about democracy. For the political class, it's 'monopoly of power', while the people need 'cultural concepts that raise their standard to the point where they can apply democracy in practice'.[35]

Al-Wa'eli associates the exploitation of the electorate by politicians with poverty in the country. He charges that politicians played with the emotions of the electorate for political purposes. 'Political parties have exploited the citizen and his need to get a job and other simple needs, especially where 37 per cent of the population is poor. Politicians have played with people's emotions and stole their votes'.[36] With regard to tribal loyalty, Al-Waeli notices it's not strong in cities but is still strong in villages.[37]

Historical example

Maysoon Aldamluji laments that Iraq was given a 'strenuous opportunity to turn into a democracy' but the experiment has not been successful. 'In many aspects, Iraqis today are not better off than they were before 2003'.[38] Aldamluji lists poor historic examples of democratic tradition, absence of democratic institutions, weak judicial system and lack of vision among the ruling elite as obstacles to democracy.[39]

She explains why a historical example is necessary for the establishment of democracy in Iraq: 'Historic examples apply to all countries … that begin the process of democratization for the first time, not just Iraq. A nation builds up its democratic traditions through accumulating collective experience'.[40]

Farid Ayar has a very different explanation about the suitability of democracy for Iraq. It's especially significant when it comes from a member of the electoral commission that organized the first two elections and the referendum on the permanent constitution. Ayar is adamant that 'democracy is not an ideal idea for Iraq'. 'It's a good system for those who appreciate what democracy is all about'. 'Therefore we need to specify the nature of the people or human groups where democracy is to be applied'.[41]

Ayar does not hesitate to speak up. 'I believe democracy doesn't benefit Iraq currently and we must find a new idea or a system other than democracy'. He must have damning evidence, which must have come after his four-year stint with IHEC that made him reach this drastic conclusion. It was Farid Ayar who explained it all for politicians on a personal level and to the public through the media and public meetings. Based on his study of the first elections held in Iraq, he asserts the application of democracy is neither 'good nor right in the sense it's prevalent now'.

One can sense his anger, regret and disappointment as he goes on to describe the electoral scene during the first two elections. While admitting that there is a free press in Iraq now, Ayar argues the proliferation of the media 'doesn't lead to progress nor to guiding the people towards their basic issues because the channels are mostly religious and they broadcast material that soils the reputation of the Iraqi people'.[42]

Ayar has a point there since writers such as Jack Snyder also believe the media can play a role that is anti-democratic. Snyder states that the media provide political elites opposed to, or who feel threatened by, democratization, with the wherewithal to win the public over to their anti-democratic cause. He notes that the elites in newly democratizing states

> often retain partial monopoly control over the media, and the market is divided into segments by national identity. This kind of imperfectly competitive market may yield the worst of both worlds. On the one hand, elites have no alternative but to compete intensely for the mobilization of mass support. On the other, by targeting captive ethnic or national market segments, they can avoid debating in a common forum where ideas are publicly and rigorously scrutinized by competitors and expert evaluators.[43]

Ayar makes clear that 'religious, ethnic and regional fanaticism flies in the face of democracy and impedes its application'.[44] However, he disagrees with the current system which treats all voters on the same footing. He contends that people are not the same and, therefore, should not be treated in the same way. 'There are illiterate people who go to vote, and beside them stand educated people who are graduates of renowned universities. There is a huge difference between the two. How can they be equal?'[45]

Notwithstanding Ayar's insistence that this is not a matter of discrimination, this view clearly has no basis in democracy and flies in the face of international law and the principle of the citizens' fundamental equality of rights and duties under the law, which constitutes the bedrock of the concept of citizenship.

Ayar concludes that all these aspects of democracy, such as elections and parliaments, 'are of no benefit to third world countries presently because peoples are in need of a just rule associated with ruthlessness'. He marvels at the fact that in many cases ruthlessness seems to yield benefits for third world countries while democracy does not.

He doesn't seem to question the legitimacy of the undemocratic regime he is proposing. 'That legitimacy comes through the ballot boxes alone is an incomplete statement', he opines; 'the "brain boxes" are the ones which bring legitimacy'.[46] He argues the army should be given a role in cementing democracy, although he doesn't trust the current army, which he regards as weak, and blames democracy for this weakness.

Effectively, Ayar's argument stipulates that the consolidation of democracy depends in part on the role played by the army, but as democracy is consolidated, the army is enfeebled, and therefore the consolidation of democracy is weakened as a result. According to this reasoning, democracy appears caught in a vicious circle from which it cannot break free.

Ayar's worst fear stems from the prospect of the breakup of Iraq. 'I reject division even if it comes through democracy in which my belief has been shaken'. He regards the reign of Brigadier Abdul-Kareem Qassim as the 'only real democratic regime in Iraq'. 'The country was more beautiful, cleaner and better, and the people were comfortable', he notes.[47] Clearly, Ayar's understanding of democracy differs hugely from reality. He associates democracy with successful policies and strong government and economy. Although this would be the aim of a democratic government, it may not be the end result. Government failure doesn't make it undemocratic.

Undemocratic culture

According to John Rawls' theory, there are three types of societies, depending on the political circumstances they live under, each of which needs a different approach.[48] The first one is a society that is 'well-ordered and its members recognise a firm overlapping consensus of reasonable doctrines and it's not stirred by deep disputes'. In such a society, religious discourse should not be allowed in the public domain but be relegated to civil society. The second type is also 'well-ordered' but it's subject to serious dispute with respect to applying one of its principles of justice. In this society certain religious arguments should be tolerated on a limited scale.

The third type is a society that is not well-ordered and where there are serious divisions about constitutional essentials when certain religious arguments have to be tolerated.[49] Iraqi society must fall into the third category, since it's deeply divided and not well-ordered.

Diamond (2005) stated the existence of several issues that Iraqis were divided about, and he described them as 'different cultural groups'.[50]

Among the reasons that Akeel Abbas lists for the failure of the democratic experiment is 'a dominant, mainstream culture that is essentially undemocratic in its basic values and system of meaning'. Another one is 'the weakness of civil society organizations and secular parties'.[51] He affirms tribal and sectarian affiliations or biases impede democratization because 'they feed into collective, hierarchal thinking, instead of individualistic thinking that is usually the basis of any genuine democratic process'.

Abbas regards tribal and sectarian affiliations as 'structurally anti-democratic', although he makes a distinction between them and regional, sub-national affiliations which he doesn't believe to be impediments to democracy.

He points to the lack of knowledge or practice in Iraq of 'individualism and genuine respect for pluralism' which he considers as one of the 'fundamental pillars of any effective democracy'.

Abbas contends the challenges to democratization in Iraq are 'primarily cultural'. 'The non-democratic culture will have to democratize to allow the emergence of a genuine democratic experience'. He advises that this requires reforms in the areas of education, law and state performance. 'It is a generational project that would probably take 20–30 years to materialize, if everything runs relatively well'.[52]

Kamal Field sees progress through the idea of 'good governance'. He agrees that tribal, sectarian or regional affiliations or biases impede democratization, but only if 'the values of the tribe are contradictory to the values of democracy or good governance'.[53] It's established that biases of any kind do affect and impede good governance which depends on fairness, equality and transparency, and this ultimately affects democracy. Field compares the influence of Iraqi political leaders on the political system with other advanced countries. 'In Iraq the personality of the political leader plays a role in creating the character of the political system. In advanced countries ... leaders have a limited role in exploiting the leadership position'.[54]

Field contends that the 'general cultural and educational standards do not currently accord with the democratic option', and this is one of the difficulties for democracy.[55] But isn't this because voters felt they were under religious obligations to do so due to intensive campaigning by Islamists? If a breakthrough in education is the only possibility for democracy to succeed, a breakthrough is now far-fetched, as religious education has been enhanced under Islamists, with so many religious schools and universities opening.[56]

Abdul-Khaliq Hussein blames the long decades of the despotic Saddam regime for what he calls the 'chaos' which he says was inevitable after the collapse of the regime. He explains the current difficulties in historical perspectives and how other nations faced similar upheavals. He referred to the 'Thirty Years' War [1618–1648] in Europe' between Catholics and Protestants, which ended with the Treaty of Westphalia in 1648, where 'nearly 20 per cent of the European populations were annihilated'. He also referred to 'the sectarian wars' in Britain.[57]

Despite this gloomy picture, a sense of optimism still seeps through as he observes that 'in the end, tolerance prevailed'. This prompts him to sound a hopeful note about the future of democracy as well as social and inter-communal peace in Iraq. 'Eventually, the Iraqi people will learn how to live together in peace, and come to cherish a democratic regime' he says. 'But no one ... knows how long this eventuality will take to arrive'.

One difficulty he alludes to is cultural. It's the fact that 'the loser cannot accept defeat'. Still, he has an explanation for this: 'That's how democracy started in the West. Eventually democracy and acceptance of the results of elections have become an integral part of their cultures. Iraqi people are no different'.[58]

He asserts that democracy 'has never been born fully developed anywhere in the world and those who expected that Iraq would become Sweden or Britain immediately after Saddam's downfall were mistaken'. Hussein stresses that democracy needs time to flourish 'particularly in a country that has no history of democracy prior to 2003'. It shows he also attaches importance to the prior existence of 'democratic culture'. Although he strongly believes there are cultural and religious obstacles to democracy, he is hopeful because 'the situation is not hopeless'. The problems Iraq faces are not peculiar to Iraq, in his opinion. 'Almost all the great European democracies have faced such problems', he avers. He identifies Iraqi culture as 'a mixture of modernity and Bedouin [values]' coupled with the effects of sectarian and racial conflicts. He argues the 'pluralistic nature of Iraqi society' requires a democratic system.[59]

Adnan Al-Janabi, a tribal sheikh, explains that Iraq is a 'tribal society with a "Bedouin" mentality which has no respect for representative governance'.[60] This is selfless politics that a tribal sheikh who rallies on his tribesmen to vote for him in elections, admits is an impediment. Al-Janabi also regards regional affiliations or biases as hurdles to the development of democracy.

Mr Bassim Anton argues that tribal, sectarian and regional loyalties do impede democracy and the evidence is 'many educated people didn't even get 10 per cent of the tribal voters'. He contends that secular parties are 'mostly fairer and more democratic' because 'they usually have high percentage of educated and cultured people among their membership'.[61]

He doesn't believe the democratic transition has completely failed: 'the democratic culture has spread, even though in a distorted way sometimes'.[62] However, he lists a few impediments which contributed to the partial failure of the democratic transition, among which is 'the weakness of democratic culture'.

He argues that society, parliament and government ministries were divided on sectarian basis because most voters in the last three or four elections voted on the basis of their religious and sectarian loyalties. He points to the 'initial weakness of politicians and rulers at the beginning stages', 'the sectarian division' of the Governing Council, 'the dominance of personal interests of politicians and rulers and financial and administrative corruption'.[63]

Shorouq Al-Abayachi regards 'the patriarchal fatherly, tribal male mentality' as the most important cultural impediment that has been enforced through increasingly failed governmental policies since the beginning of the 1990s.[64] She also lists as impediments 'the collapse of the middle class and the disappearance of its civilized values', which acted as a 'nurturing environment' for the cultural and sectarian diversity. Al-Abayachi links democracy and tolerance to the existence of the middle class.

She believes the spread of illiteracy and ignorance in Iraq is due to the collapse of the educational institutions and the spread of poverty that's, in turn, responsible for creating this situation. She also blames wars, dictatorships and later sectarian conflicts for enforcing the attitudes and mentality she mentioned. Al-Abayachi also lists tribalism and regional loyalties among impediments to democracy. 'These sub-identities have contributed to the loss of the Iraqi national identity'.[65]

She argues these loyalties have contributed to enforcing 'submission to the clerics and the clergy in general and to tribal and regional personalities', while real democracy 'depends on the spirit of citizenship and the horizontal extension of responsibilities according to competence and talents and based on equality between citizens without any consideration of their religious, sectarian and regional backgrounds'.[66]

Wahda Al-Jumaili acknowledges the existence of tribalism but doesn't regard it an impediment to democratization. She explains it was an option that people resorted to. 'The nature of Iraqi people is tribal, and when the state is weak, the citizen resorts to any other refuge that can protect him which is the tribe, region or sect'.[67]

Al-Jumaili contends the culture of society and politicians promotes a 'central system, a ruling party and despotism', so democracy is alien to Iraqi culture. Among the challenges to democracy, in her opinion, are the discord, division and weakness of social peace and favouring sub-identities over national identity. She pins this on 'the failing of politicians who are decision makers'.

Kamran Qaradaghi also attributes the failure to establish the institutions required for a democratic state to the 'absence of democratic culture'.[68]

Kamal Field avers there is an absence of 'the norms of coexistence' between people of different opinions or beliefs in Iraq. He explains this reflects the lack of equality in rights and duties.[69] He regards this as an impediment to establishing democracy.

Sociologist Ibrahim Al-Haidari believes democracy 'cannot grow in a country where there are no democrats and democratic culture'. He states that 'we still haven't learnt democratic ethics and are not trained to practice democracy on sound basis and in a way that contributes to our progress'.[70] He identifies a serious social problem regarding democracy:

> When an opportunity to exercise freedom arises, we quickly exploit this margin of freedom and democracy so that it turns into chaos. The individual only knows the negative side of freedom; that is the excessive audacity in speaking and acting, the taking of the right[s] by force without any regards for the state and the law and without respecting the [rights of the] different other. On the contrary, the other is insulted and exploited, and acts that reflect shallowness of culture and ethics are performed.[71]

He regards what he calls 'Pastist culture' as 'parental, patriarchal, auditory, oral, non-written' and contends it 'stands against democracy at the level of praxis because it is neither liberal nor informed'. He regards this as the reason why most of the electorates vote on the basis of their religious, sectarian, tribal, partisan affiliations as well as private interests. Furthermore, Al-Haidari contends that 'the use of democratic mechanisms to hold elections in an atmosphere where individuals do not enjoy complete social/political awareness, nor self-independence, aborts the democratic process and facilitates the ascendance of non-democrats to power'. He attributes this to the 'weakness of the state and the spirit of citizenship, the split identity and the non-development of real and effective democratic forces in society'. He argues it strengthens the tribal, sectarian and regional spirit and consolidates it at the expense of the homeland, citizenship and democracy.

Al-Haidari has a final piece of advice:

> We must learn about freedom, the individual's independence and a real democratic culture, then we can practice them as values and behaviour in daily social life starting from the family, through civil society establishments which are independent of the state, till we reach the top of the pyramid of power. This is the only way to rid ourselves of backwardness, despotism, violence and terrorism. If democracy is a culture, then it must grow automatically and spontaneously and from within.[72]

Samuel Huntington regarded the weakness of democratic values among key elite groups as well as the general public a contributing factor to the first and second reverses.[73]

In conclusion, as we have learnt above, democracy is alien to Iraqi culture, Iraqis are new to it and they need to learn about it in order to practice it. It came to Iraqis all of a sudden and it requires some education in order to consolidate. This will take time and effort.

Notes

1 Huntington (1991) op. cit. p. 315
2 Ibid.
3 Ibid., p. 310
4 Allawi (2007) op. cit. p. 15
5 Ibid.
6 Ibid.
7 Interview with Hani Fahs
8 Islamic religious garb
9 Interview with Samir Sumaidaie
10 Ibid.
11 Ibid.
12 Interview with Faleh Abdul-Jabbar
13 Interview with Sami Al-Askari
14 Ibid.
15 Ibid.
16 Ibid.
17 Ibid
18 Interview with Walid Al-Hilli
19 Interview with Kadom Shubber
20 Ibid.
21 Ibid.
22 Interview with Hussein Al-Hindawi
23 Ibid.
24 Ibid.

25 Ibid.
26 Przeworski (1991) pp. 94–95
27 Interview with Hussein Al-Hindawi
28 Ibid.
29 Interview with Dia Shakarchi
30 Ibid.
31 Interview with Adil Abdur-Raheem
32 Allawi (2007) op. cit. p. 135
33 Interview with Ali Allawi
34 Interview with Sharwan Al-Waeli
35 Ibid.
36 Ibid.
37 Ibid.
38 Interview with Maysoon Aldamaluji
39 Ibid.
40 Ibid.
41 Interview with Farid Ayar
42 Ibid.
43 Snyder (2000) op. cit. p. 58
44 Interview with Farid Ayar
45 Ibid.
46 Ibid.
47 Ibid.
48 Rawls (1993, 1996, 2005) op. cit. p. 248
49 Ibid., p. 249
50 Diamond (2005) op. cit. p. 128
51 Interview with Akeel Abbas
52 Ibid.
53 Interview with Kamal Field
54 Ibid.
55 Interview with Abdulkhaliq Hussein
56 Adnan Abuzeed (5/5/2014) op. cit.
57 Interview with Abdulkhaliq Hussein
58 Ibid.
59 Ibid.
60 Interview with Adnan Al-Janabi
61 Interview with Bassim Anton
62 Ibid.
63 Ibid.
64 Interview with Shorouq Al-Abayachi
65 Ibid.
66 Ibid.
67 Interview with Wahda Al-Jumaili
68 Interview with Kamran Qaradaghi
69 Interview with Kadom Shubber
70 Interview with Ibrahim Al-Haidari
71 Ibid.
72 Ibid.
73 Huntington (1991) op. cit. p. 290

10 Political and administrative errors

De-Ba'athification

The Ba'ath Party (BP) had two million members; at least that's what it claims and what the US has acknowledged.[1] It's true that most of them were not necessarily believers in its ideology nor enthusiastic for its policies, but under the rule of Saddam Hussein everyone needed to join BP in order to get on in life, to get a job anywhere in the civil service or an education, or because he/she was coerced.[2] Some joined to progress in their career or just to feel safe from persecution. In the army, everyone had to join. The same goes for education.[3] Students could not be admitted to certain universities and colleges unless they joined BP; most of them did. The media profession was only open to Ba'athists.[4] Only those who work in the private sector could escape joining because they didn't need to, although they still had to show support in other ways, such as contributing large sums of money to Ba'ath Party causes, joining professional bodies linked to the party, attending public rallies to support BP policies and attending BP events and celebrations.

Even if 10 per cent of the two million members were true believers, this amounts to 200,000. It's a huge number of people to alienate when you are trying to build a democracy from scratch.

On 16 April 2003, General Franks, the Commander of the US forces in Iraq, banned BP in his 'freedom message'.[5] On the top of banning BP from political participation, Bremer signed Order number 1, the 'De-Ba'athification of Iraqi Society' on 16 May 2003. The order basically excluded the four top ranks of the party from holding any public sector jobs in the highest three layers of responsibility. He estimated the number to be 20,000 members and most of them are Sunni Arabs.[6]

Larry Diamond estimated the number of Ba'athists affected by the decision to be between 30,000 and 50,000 individuals.[7] He even thinks the final number is a lot higher. This created the feeling of discrimination since a particular section of society is hurt more than others. The instruction from the US Secretary of Defence Donald Rumsfeld, was that the order 'must be carried out even if implementing it causes administrative inconvenience'.[8] So, Americans expected inconvenience as a result of implementing this decree because most state employees were Ba'athists.

In addition, this was done without any consultation with Iraqis or political parties or professional bodies, which may have given them different advice. Bremer told his staff 'we would engage responsible Iraqis' in the de-Ba'athification process. 'We do not know Iraq as well as Iraqis do'.[9] But this Iraqi 'engagement' was kept secret, and no one knows who Bremer consulted, if he ever did. Later, Bremer acknowledged that banning Ba'athists from holding senior official posts was 'a lot more than inconvenient' since 'senior Ba'athists had formed the leadership of every Iraqi ministry or military organization'.[10]

In fact, this policy caused chaos in Iraqi institutions, and it created enemies for the new regime within the Iraqi people, since there was almost no family that didn't have a Ba'athist within its ranks. But it also caused hardship and discord among many people. Bremer admitted it was a mistake to let Iraqi politicians be in charge of the implementation of de-Ba'athification.[11]

Iraqi historian Kanan Makiya called it 'unwise':

> It was by far wiser not to have banned BP after 2003 because of how many people had been members of it and because of the suspicion that would naturally fall upon anyone who had been a member, thus encouraging the politics of 'settling of accounts', which turned out to be one of our biggest problems after the fall of the regime because all the new leaders engaged in it on a very wide scale.[12]

Ayad Allawi, regarded politicizing de-Ba'athification as one of the reasons of the failure of democracy in Iraq.[13] Akeel Abbas asserts this policy is 'wrong-headed and counterproductive' because 'BP has some following among Iraqis who, if BP is barred from politics, will go unrepresented, potentially turning into a disgruntled and angry segment of society.'[14] He adds this policy 'sends BP to the world of the underground with potential resort to violence, instead of making it go away as the de-Ba'athification policy makers envisaged'. That's exactly what happened. BP went underground and violent. Abbas adds 'this has the effect of upsetting the democratic process in Iraq as the past 12 years have shown'. Abbas concludes that BP should be given the choice of disavowing violence, allowing the judicial system to prosecute its members accused of political crimes in fair trials, and, consequently, allowed to enter politics and only if it refuses should it be banned from entering politics.[15]

Kadom Shubber shares Abbas' opinion that banning any party would force it to go underground, adding that this may 'enhance their status in the eyes of the public'. He called for the establishment of a 'Truth & Reconciliation Commission' which allows those who committed crimes to 'repent' and those affected by their crimes to 'forgive them'. This way, 'only a limited damage is done'.[16]

Hussein Al-Hindawi believes the principle to exclude BP was right but the implementation was 'riddled with mistakes, violations, arbitrary decisions, and sometimes self-interested exploitation' that were met with 'collusive silence from the judiciary'. He regards de-Ba'athification as a 'political project, not a law, and herein lies the problem'. He concludes that the aim 'should have been to ban BP since 2004 as a Fascist party opposed to democracy'. Al-Hindawi reveals that Saddam Hussein's brother, Barzan, had asked Saddam to dissolve BP after the invasion of Kuwait because he believed 'it became harmful to the Iraqi people'.[17]

Kamal Field believes there was some justification to 'exclude BP immediately after 2003' because the masses of the party were used directly and indirectly to repress Iraqis, especially those who belonged to other political parties. But he adds this 'should have been reviewed after establishing the new political process in Iraq to give opportunities to all those who have not committed crimes to engage in normal life' and this should have ideally been done in 2010 or at least in 2014.[18]

Maysoon Aldamluji, has a similar view:

> Individual BP members who have not committed crimes, should have been allowed to stand in elections, but not the party as an institution that had monopolized political life in Iraq and manipulated all government and non-government institutions for its interests.[19]

But she brings in another factor: 'External interferences made the elections unequal'. She points out another problem, which is 'the absence of law for political parties' in all the previous elections.[20] Political Parties Law was only passed in late 2015. She concludes by stating that there was enough justification for excluding BP in the first and second elections. But this needs to be reviewed since 'crimes have diversified and they are no longer exclusive to BP'. She affirms 'ending de-Ba'athification will bring some stability to the country'.[21]

Faleh Abdul-Jabbar contends it's fair to exclude BP from the political process because Ba'athists deprived others from their rights. 'They bear moral responsibility, even those who were not in positions of responsibility'.[22] This sounds harsh if we take into considerations what went on in other countries, which democratized after the fall of one-party rule.

Ibrahim Al-Haidari agrees that banning BP left the new regime with so many enemies, but he believes it was necessary. He blames Iraq's problems, past and present, on 'the heavy legacy of BP and its ideology'. But he qualifies his approval of the ban. 'This type of banning needs an alternative social and political philosophy and a real national democratic project, not sectarian power-sharing'. Since he is German-educated, he knows the German experience of Denazification well. He believes it was right and successful, but attributes this to the establishment of a 'constitutional system that is based on respect for the law and supports the reconstruction of what was destroyed in the war'. He alludes this doesn't exist in Iraq, thus, de-Ba'athification was bound to fail.[23]

Samir Sumaidaie agrees BP should be banned because it didn't believe in democracy. The Ba'athists, 'by their words and deeds, declare themselves as having the absolute right to lead. It's the "leading party". Its legitimacy is based not on elections but on "revolutionary legitimacy"'. Sumaidaie believes BP shouldn't be allowed in Iraqi politics even if its members declared their belief in democracy because it would be 'a totally different animal. It cannot be the Ba'ath Party'.[24] He goes further: 'argument about BP applies to Islamist parties'. 'They should be barred from the democratic process because they aim to use democracy to reach power and then utilize it to destroy democracy. Their ideal model is (one man, one vote, one time)'.[25]

Activist Hashem Ganem believes that the political dynamics would have been enhanced if BP was invited to contest the first post-2003 elections. 'All of Iraq's ills would have been leveled at its doorstep during electioneering'. He reckons that BP 'would have not won any seats in parliament, and if they did, it would've been a miserly [sic] number of seats'. Ganem believes allowing BP to partake in the first elections post 2003 would have shown maturity and inclusiveness, which would have been a stunning political manoeuvre, and a serious step towards reconciliation. But, he admits,

> it would have been inconceivable for BP to join the political fray and would have made the same ludicrous demands to return to power, reinstate Saddam, the US to compensate for the war damage and called for Jihad. Then all consequential violence would have been identified so clearly as theirs.[26]

Ayad Jamaluddeen, a Shia cleric and MP (2006–2010) called for dialogue with BP and allowing those Ba'athists 'whose hands have not been stained with the blood of the Iraqi people' to participate in the political process. He in fact called for 'forcing the Iraqi government to conduct a dialogue with the Ba'athists in order to save the blood of Iraqis'. He told Asharq-Alawsat newspaper 'it's a conflict over power between two groups. The one in power now who got there via American tanks and another one that lost power through American tanks'.[27]

Most Iraqis, politicians and security experts across the world blame the security deterioration on Ba'athists or remnants of the previous regime which are known to be fighting alongside terrorist organizations such as ISIS.[28] This is largely caused by their exclusion from political participation.

Examples from other democratic transitions

In Spain, all parties were allowed to participate in the elections, including the Communist Party which was banned under Franco, and more controversially, Herri Batasuna (HB), a party that advocates independence and 'revolutionary change in the Basque Country and doesn't hide its sympathy and indirect support for ETA terrorists'.[29] HB managed to get some representation, but it was contained politically.

Spain allowed even anti-democratic forces such as Fuerza Nueva, a neo-fascist group that was allowed to participate in the 1979 election in which it only attained 2.1 per cent of the total vote, electing only one deputy, and disintegrated as a political force soon afterwards.[30] Even Antonio Tejero, the general who participated in a coup in 1981, was allowed to run a party, Solidaridad Espanola, from his jail in the 1982 election. He only won 0.13 per cent of the total votes.

'Democracy doesn't mean that every citizen supports democracy, nor that anti-democrats should not enjoy democratic freedoms for legal and nonviolent activities'.[31]

Juan Linz and Alfred Stepan (1996) state that 'the defence of democracy is the duty of democratic parties and leaders and ultimately of the voters, making possible government by democrats'.[32] Separatists' violence increased considerably in Spain during the transition to democracy, but this didn't stop the democratic leaders from including anyone in the democratic process.

In Argentina, they dealt with the issue of the crimes of members of the former regime by dividing those potentially guilty into three categories:

1   Those who gave orders to violate human rights
2   Those who carried out the orders
3   Those who engaged in human rights violations beyond the actions they were ordered to take

Those in categories 1 and 3 were indicted and tried, while those in category 2 would be tried only if they knew that the orders were illegitimate.[33]

In Poland, there was no barring of any party. In fact, the Communist and Peasant parties, which were allies during the previous regime, won an absolute majority in the election of September 1993 and could have theoretically drafted and passed the constitution in parliament unilaterally.[34]

In Hungary, there was low societal demand for revolutionary purges, and ex post facto justice was substantially low. Most of the technical experts, and even judges, were considered usable by the new democratic government.[35] Even when parliament passed a 'qualified purge law' the constitutional court overturned it. There was a 'lustration law' passed in 1993, but it was restricted to those who played a coercive role in the 1956 revolution.[36]

There are of course understandable reasons for this tolerance, and perhaps it has to do with the fact that the Communists, at least the moderate faction, had played a role in making the transition possible, especially in the round table negotiations with the moderates of the opposition, which led to the transition. Both sides realized that they could not triumph alone, they both recognized the depth of the social and economic crisis and feared that the repeat of the 1956 would do harm to their future.[37]

This sort of understanding and responsible position was not possible in Iraq, and that is also understandable in light of the suppression and repression that the Ba'athists practiced during their 35-year rule. Neither BP, nor the influential opposition parties, who came to power after the US invasion, perhaps with the exception of INA led by Ayad Allawi, a former Ba'athist himself, had any room for compromise nor a space, no matter how small, of mutual trust.

The lack of cooperation is also due to the nature of the change, which was accomplished by a foreign invasion. There were no negotiations or any understanding between the two acrimonious sides, which remained locked in their historical animosity at the expense of the strength of the Iraqi state and the project of democracy. Even Iraqi opposition parties, which came together to form a leadership council and later participate in a coalition government, lacked serious cooperation, as the US civil administrator of Iraq stated.[38]

Many Iraqis disagree with the de-Ba'athification law (now called the Accountability and Justice), for their different reasons. Former Ba'athists oppose it because it has deprived them of participating in political life and management of the country and excludes a large proportion of them form earning a living as state employees. Sunni politicians disagree with the very principle of political exclusion and have called for abolishing the law and the removal of all its consequences. They also believe it was applied in a sectarian way since it targeted them more than others.

In addition, many Shia disagree with it as a matter of principle. Even those who believe it was right to introduce it, such as Paul Bremer, Ibrahim Al-Haidari, and Hussein Al-Hindawi, say there were serious errors in its application. Others, such as Maysoon Aldamluji, Kamal Field and Akeel Abbas, believe it's time to depart from the politics of exclusion.

De-Ba'athification alienated a large portion of Iraqi society from the political process and barred the most experienced managers from participating in building the new state. It was unfair, and it established a precedent for an unfair treatment of the state to a section of its population. This has weakened both the state and democratization and caused discord among Iraqis and contributed to the destabilization of the country. It has become a serious impediment that has to be removed if democratization is to succeed in Iraq.

Disbanding the Iraqi Army and police

The second order that the US civilian administrator had issued was an order to disband the 715,000 men-strong Iraqi army, together with other security apparatuses.[39] One US official commented on this decision: 'that was the day we made 450,000 enemies in Iraq'.[40] Larry Diamond estimates that over a million more people would be affected if their dependents were counted.[41] That decision created massive unemployment and unnecessary hostility to the new regime among so many people.

Had the army remained in place, or were called to duty under a new command after the fall of the regime, it would have acted as a formidable force to enforce law and order and give the state the reverence it needed among the population. Instead, US and Iraqi officials and institutions relied on private security companies, and there have been an estimated 30,000 private contractors working in Iraq in 2004.[42] According to some data, this number has increased in later years and the number of Pentagon-funded contractors in Iraq was 162,428 in July 2008.[43]

The old Iraqi army, as Bremer acknowledged, 'had some true professionals, and partly for that reason, was distrusted by Saddam'.[44] But it was 'self demobilized' according to the Pentagon after the fall of the regime.[45] 'At liberation, there was not a single Iraqi military unit standing intact anywhere in the country'.[46] The American plan that General Jay Garner was going to implement after the fall of the regime was apparently not to keep the army in place. They planned to employ most of Iraqi soldiers, some 400,000 'Shia soldiers', in construction projects in order to get a living wage.[47] Later on, Bremer acknowledged the need for an Iraqi army: 'we have to find some place in Iraqi society for former soldiers'.[48] But he admitted that bringing back the old Iraqi army would 'run against major policy and practical obstacles'.[49] In fact he called it 'Saddam's army' and considered it as part of the instruments of repression, alongside the infamous Mukhabarat security services and BP.[50]

Security in Iraq was almost non-existent after the fall of the regime and the disappearance of its security apparatuses, including BP, which had a security role. There was almost no presence to be felt for a government in the country, with the exception of US tanks and troops who didn't actually perform any policing duties, nor were they trained or qualified to do so. This was acknowledged by US officials, who realized later the need for Iraqi police officers to go back to their posts as well as bringing in US military police to guard Iraqi police stations.

Around mid-May 2003, over a month after the fall of the regime, Paul Bremer asked the US deputy commander, General John Abizaid, to send more military police to perform security duties, as Bremer put it.[51] Bob Gifford, US advisor to the Iraqi interior ministry, had explained the deteriorating security situation in the country to the new administrator. 'Whatever law and order that existed under Saddam has broken down completely', Gifford told Bremer in his first meeting with him in May 2003.[52]

After 9 April , chaos and looting was the order of the day and world media had widely reported the looting that took place across Iraq. US Secretary of Defence Donald Rumsfeld was alarmed by the numerous reports of looting and violence which overtook any other news on the 'US victory' in Iraq. But Rumsfeld dismissed it as just 'Henny Penny. The sky is falling'.[53]

But it was a fact; chaos and looting were widespread across Iraq. According to Iraq's former defence minister, Ali Allawi, 'nearly every ministry and state institution, including the national museum, were looted and then burnt down'.[54] Looting was unchecked for at least three weeks, according to Gifford. 'It had destroyed many of the government buildings in Baghdad. Only the Oil Ministry was spared because American troops had been ordered to guard it'.[55]

The Iraqi police were nowhere to be seen in the streets. 'They disappeared, like the army', Gifford said.[56] Violent crime was increasing, including armed robbery, kidnapping, sexual assault and murder. The criminals were armed with heavy weapons such as RBGs and AKs since all buildings associated with the army and intelligence agencies were looted and demolished across the country, according to Gifford.[57]

Disbanding the Iraqi army left a dangerous security void that was quickly filled by enemies of the new political order.[58] Even the UN compound, in the Canal Hotel, was lightly protected. This lack of security caused the UN to move its mission to Jordan after it was bombed on 19 August, and 22 of its staff, including UN envoy, Sergio de Mello, were killed.[59] That was a serious setback in the efforts to establish a democratic system in Iraq.

The US forces in Iraq were insufficient to keep the peace in the country. Estimates by military experts such as General Eric Shineski, put the number of troops required to pacify and control Iraq properly at 500,000.[60] In fact Paul Bremer himself admitted ten years later that the US made strategic mistakes in Iraq; one of them was keeping insufficient number of troops. He estimated the required number to be 400,000.[61]

More troops would have improved security in Iraq and at the same time made it easier for pro-democracy forces to have a better chance of succeeding in their efforts to establish a viable democracy and enhance their positions in the new order. According to Ali Allawi, 'A larger force would have given the coalition's local proxies the wherewithal to at least face up to the challenge of the Islamists more forcefully'.[62] Islamists filled the vacuum left after the fall of the regime, and 'nearly all administrations that had been put in place after the war in southern cities and Sadr City in Baghdad, fell apart and power seeped to the newly emergent Islamists and their local allies'.[63]

With a high crime rate, no effective government that can enforce law and order and the existence of many power centres supported by armed militias, it's really difficult to establish democracy since 'a democratic government needs to be able to exercise effectively its claim to the monopoly of legitimate use of force in a territory'.[64]

Paul Bremer acknowledged this difficulty: 'We are not going to rush into elections since Iraq has none of the mechanisms needed for elections – no census, no electoral laws, no political parties and all the related structure we take for granted'.[65] However, the US did proceed with elections on 30 January 2005 without achieving any of the above requirements that Bremer stated from the outset.

Bremer, comparing Iraq to Germany and Japan, admitted that the US and its allies had not taken a job this big since the end of WW2.[66] He also acknowledged the need for political structures for democracy to work:

> Let's keep in mind the lessons of Germany and Japan. Democracies do not work unless the political structures rest on a solid society ... political parties, a free press, an independent judiciary, open accountability for public funds. These are society's shock absorbers. They protect the individual from the state raw power.[67]

It's clear that the necessary ingredients for democracy to stand up were not there.

America's Iraqi allies were weak due to the lack of US forces to back them up, and they were also seen by a large section of the Iraqi population as 'American lackeys' – opportunists and power-seekers who jumped on American tanks for personal gain. For these collective reasons, they were unable to establish a popular power base for themselves, nor get popular acceptance as the new leaders of Iraq.

On the other hand, their Islamic rivals were strong with armed militias to establish their authority and the full financial, logistical, intelligence and military support from a major regional power – Iran. Although the US had warned Islamic militias not to enter Iraq and get organized forces or be treated as enemy combatants,[68] that warning was not heeded; they did get organized forces, although 'they remained undetected by officials appointed by the occupying authorities'.[69] Why were the US forces unable, or perhaps unwilling, to detect those organized forces is another mystery, but it's a failing by all accounts.

Professor Ahmed Hashim is critical of the US counter-insurgency campaign, and he blames it for playing 'a key role in the outbreak and perpetuation of the insurgency'.[70] He accused US decision-makers of taking a 'rigid and inflexible ideological approach' which undermined the chances of implementing policies vital in any successful counter-insurgency strategy. Policies such as measured reactions and minimal use of force, political responses, integrated civil–military operations and rectitude towards civilians and prisoners have been largely absent from the US efforts to suppress the insurgency.

The Iraqi army was one of the most organized, experienced and disciplined armies in the region, despite years of Saddam's dictatorship and disastrous interventions. It could have been reformed gradually to make it modern and effective in order to secure the state and keep it revered and strong.

Disbanding the army was a blunder with disastrous consequences on the political process and was clearly an impediment to establishing a strong democratic system with the tools to enforce law and order and support a democratic government strong enough to impose its authority on all citizens and treat them on an equal basis. It left the state very weak while Islamist parties, all of which had armed militias, were in a very strong position. They became the only political broker in the country with the tools to enforce their agenda and the ability to protect the areas they control and impose their will on the whole country in the end. In addition, they had the full and unwavering support of Iran, the strongest state in the region. Iran found in Iraqi Islamist parties an extension of its power in a neighbouring country.

People could clearly see that the only political forces on the ground with real power, in the middle and south of the country at least, were the Shia Islamists. This persuaded them to deal with them, accepting their authority and voting for them in elections. As we have established earlier in the study, Islamists do not necessarily believe in democracy nor in a modern state. They look up to Iran for emulation and support, not Western democracies.

Unsuitable electoral system

The first Iraqi electoral system according to which the first elections were conducted was proportional representation (PR) where the whole of Iraq was one constituency. But the system was changed in the National Assembly after Islamists won the elections to multiple constituencies but with stipulations to guarantee representation for minorities. PR is the 'most widely used set of electoral systems in the world, and its variants can be found at some level of government in almost every country (including the United States, where some city councils are elected using forms of PR)'.[71]

The electoral system was changed several times, but the changes were all in favour of big parties who are basically able to send unelected persons to parliament while those who get thousands of votes do not become members of parliament. This has made it very difficult for small parties and political minorities to get any representation. The list led by Sharwan Al-Waeli got three seats in the province of Thiqar's local elections, because the electoral system was Saint Laguë (SL), but the same list failed to get any representation in the national elections of 2014 because they were conducted according to Iraqi-Modified Sainte Laguë (MSL).[72]

Reidar Visser, a political analyst and researcher, says 'modified Sainte-Laguë 'gives bigger parties more advantages than a pure Sainte-Laguë would give'. In addition, he believes that Iraq 'has created its own version of modified Sainte-Laguë'.[73] It's worth mentioning here that the Iraqi modification to MSL made the system bereft of its original quality of fairness. The Iraqi version of MSL starts with 1.6, while MSL starts at 1.1 or sometimes 1.3.

Mr Al-Wa'eli calls for more enforceable regulations for elections in order to commit candidates and parties to abide by the law. The 'current law states that no religious symbols, photos, places of worship or state institutions can be used for electoral purposes'. But these conditions were all violated, he says. 'Some parties spent billions (of Iraqi dinars) and no one asked them where they got the money from'.[74]

Many politicians and intellectuals are calling for a new electoral system that only allows secular parties to operate, believing this to be in the best interest of the country. Akeel Abbas affirms

> an electoral system that includes only secular parties is definitely better for the country. Without secular parties that transcend sects and ethnicities, Iraq will continue to be prey to sectarian and ethnic strife. Sect-based parties, by their nature, are not pluralistic and have in mind the interests of their sect followers.[75]

Bassim Anton argues an electoral system that 'allows only secular parties to be active in politics is better for the country than a system which permits religious parties which might appeal to religious sentiment or provoke sectarian loyalties'.[76]

Kadom Shubber, who styles himself as 'Islamist liberal' is also critical of the electoral system which he says 'gave the impression of being half-baked and primarily benefiting those already clinging to political and financial power'.[77] He blames the 'backwardness' of the electorate who have 'little sense of the major factors such as economic variables, international relations, public services, education, and the security problem'. This has led to voting practices being influenced by the 'big boys' and these were party bosses, religious scholars or tribal chiefs, he avers.

Some electoral systems such as First Past the Post (FPP), generate 'unearned majorities out of minority electoral support'.[78] MSL, as applied in Iraq, allows non-elected persons to represent people in parliament while it excludes popular individuals from representing their constituents. Jassim Al-Hilfi, a candidate for the Civil Democratic Alliance (CDA), got over 16,000 votes in Baghdad in 2014, yet he didn't become an MP. The same happened to Haifa Al-Ameen, who got over 8000 votes in Nassiria, yet she failed to get elected, while others made it to parliament with just 2000 votes or less.[79]

Al-Hilfi is now campaigning to reinstate the PR system in cooperation with ST 'in order to put an end to the current unjust law that was enacted to benefit only large blocs'.[80]

Since the first elections of 2005, the electoral system was changed in every election and big parties manipulated it in their favour. They have sent candidates to parliament who haven't won while others who have got thousands of votes were barred by the system such as Ms Haifa Al-Ameen in Thiqar and Mr Jassim Al-Hilfi in Baghdad, both belonging to the secular CDA.[81]

The electoral system is clearly an impediment to democracy since it's not perceived as fair by large sections of society, especially smaller parties, and it doesn't give people in the opposition any hope of winning in the future. Secular INC, for example, had to join forces with Islamist SIIC, RT, ST and IFP in order to win just one seat for its leader, Ahmed Al-Chalabi.

One other antidemocratic aspect of the current system is that people vote for one candidate, yet they get another candidate with very few votes to represent them in parliament! A single constituency PR system is perceived to be fairer and it allows people across the country to vote for their preferred list. It also promotes a national agenda rather than regional or sectarian one.

Partisan Election Commission (IHEC)

Many Iraqis accuse IHEC of being biased since all its members are appointed by major parties. IHEC's former president, Hussein Al-Hindawi, asserts that IHEC is now controlled by political parties, and this distances 'the democratic process from propriety and integrity'.[82]

Former minister, Sharwan Al-Waeli, who leads an election list, asserts that a partisan electoral commission cannot be fair. He charges that 'vote-rigging took place in the last elections [2014] more than any other election and I am a witness to it'. He attributes this to a weak electoral commission. 'When the electoral commission becomes strong and not subject to blackmailing, it would not matter even if the governing party is contesting the elections'.[83]

He is sceptical about IHEC's independence. 'The loyalty of IHEC's members was to the influential parties who are participating in the government, that's why IHEC is now restricted'. He regards the first IHEC as stronger and more independent because it was formed by the UN.[84]

Faleh Abdul-Jabbar regards independent commissions as part of the new division of authority in modern countries, added to the classical division of authority.

'This is the power of independent commissions'. He blames the Iraqi Federal Court for effectively 'abolishing' the independent commissions and regards this role as 'disabling to democracy'.[85]

Sami Al-Askari believes IHEC was never independent. 'Once it got out of the control of UNAMI and US embassy, it entered into partisan quotas. IHEC's former and current members were candidates of political blocs and they represent the interests of their blocs when taking decisions'.[86] Hamdya Al-Husaini was an IHEC commissioner for two terms (2004–2012).[87] She is now MP for the Citizen's List (another name for SCIRI/SIIC/Hikma led by Al-Hakeem family).[88] Qassim Al-Abboudi, was IHEC commissioner 2008–2013.[89] He is now MP for BO which's part of SoL.[90] Faraj Al-Haidari was IHEC's president (2008–2012).[91] He was a member of KDP.[92]

Przeworski (1996) states that 'democratic institutions must be "fair": they must give all the relevant political forces a chance to win'; they must also be effective: 'They must make even losing under democracy more attractive than a future under non-democratic alternatives'.[93] The current IHEC is neither fair to all, because it's partisan, nor effective, because it has not prevented vote rigging nor other violations such as exploiting religious names and using religious symbols and places of worship for political purposes. In fact, many now, even from within, accuse some IHEC members of engaging in vote rigging during the 2018 elections. IHEC member, Saeed Kakaei, resigned in protest in May 2018.

Since Iraq has a diverse society, ethnically, culturally and religiously, and is deeply divided on major issues, elections must be conducted in the highest possible degree of transparency and integrity in order to strengthen people's trust in the results of elections and adherence to the laws and regulations. This requires an IHEC that is not only really independent, but also seen to be independent by participants and voters alike. In the 12 May elections, elector turn-out went down by almost 40 per cent from the 2005 elections. This shows the people's trust in the system has fallen.

Ambiguous and rigid constitution

The constitution was written and ratified in six months and many experts believe it was rushed. This is not conducive to democratic consolidation due to ambiguities, contradictions, vagueness and religious, ethnic and administrative restrictions. Although constitutions are generally compromises between political parties, and obstacles can be overcome if there is a political will, they can be problematic if society is deeply divided.

The Iraqi constitution was written after it was clear that the power relations between different political groups were in favour of the Islamists who had won massively and were, thus, able to include what they wanted in it. Stable constitutions are the ones written when the power relations between different political forces are not settled in favour of some forces at the expense of others. These constitutions are likely to emphasize rights of minorities and give guarantees to potentially weak political forces and reduce the stakes of competition. They are more likely to induce losers to comply with the outcomes of the democratic interplay and are more likely to be stable constitutions.[94]

Faleh Abdul-Jabbar contends the current constitution is an impediment to democratization:

> Many articles in the constitution impede democracy ... article (2A) that says 'No law may be enacted that contradicts the established provisions of Islam' contravenes another article (2B) which says 'No law may be enacted that contradicts the principles of democracy'.

Abdul-Jabbar finds it bizarre that the constitution has a stipulation that forbids the issuing of laws that contravene Islam. He charges there is a legal vacuum in the constitution since there are at least 58 articles that need to be regulated by law. Abdul-Jabbar, with 19 other writers, have written a book in Arabic which discusses the problems in the constitution.[95]

On a positive note, Abdul-Jabbar argues the constitution would have been more extreme if it was left to Islamist parties to write, but Ayatullah Sistani stood in their way.[96] Akeel Abbas argues article 2(A&B) is self-contradictory because 'it tries to reconcile irreconcilable contradictions'.[97] 'Democracy and religion belong to diametrically opposed orders of reality'. He explains:

> The former is based on debate and questioning that leads to following the opinion of the majority, while protecting the rights of the minority whereas the latter is based on holy texts that accept no debate or questioning and pay no attention to the opinions of the majority or minority.

He is confident the article 'causes conflict instead of establishing balance. It also gives a disproportionate role to the clergy as the interpreters of religious texts, whereas there are no codified democratic ideas or texts that can be resorted to'. Hussein Al-Hindawi argues that the group the Americans handed power to, or those they dealt with, 'were totally ignorant in law, even in Islamic law. None of them was like (Ayatullah) Hussein Na'eeni who proposed a constitution to limit the authority of the ruler'.[98]

Ayad Allawi regards the constitution as an impediment to democracy. 'It was written in 2–3 months and an authoritarian regime is developing out of this democracy', he charges.[99] Maysoon Aldamluji reveals that on a number of occasions, Islamist parties attempted to impose Islamic rulings, like banning the sale of alcohol or replacing the Personal Status Law with Islamic jurisdiction (Sharia). 'Every time they did this, they used clause (A) of article 2 of the constitution as reference. Clause (B) of article 2 was no deterrent, as there is no text to refer to'.[100] Only public resistance, backed by the Marjiiya of Ayatullah Sistani in Najaf, stopped those attempts. Imposing Sharia law on the country is not democratic nor is restricting people's rights and freedoms.

Abdulkhaliq Hussein believes the constitution is democratic but with defects.[101] Bassim Anton regards the constitution as one of the challenges facing democracy because it is brittle and vague and this 'renders it subject to different interpretations'.[102]

Sami Al-Askari, who was a member of the National Assembly that wrote and approved the constitution, acknowledges there are restrictions imposed on the constitution, but they are 'an embodiment of the culture of society in its current stages. On the one hand it preserves the constant features of Islamic culture, and on the other, it is committed to the criteria of the democratic system'.[103]

Dia Shakarchi, who was a member of the constitutional drafting committee in the National Assembly, says the gap between himself and members of UIA was widening due to 'their strict Islamism and their insistence on emphasising their Shia sectarian identity and their attempt to add as much as they can of religious and sectarian colour to the constitution'.[104]

Constitutions that are observed and last for a long time are those 'which reduce the stakes of political battles. Pretenders to office can expect to reach it while losers can expect to come back'.[105] Napoleon was alleged to have said that constitutions that can last are the ones which are 'short and vague'. They only 'define the scope of the government and establish the rules of competition leaving substantive outcomes to the political interplay'.[106] But the Iraqi constitution was clear regarding restrictions but ambiguous with rules and rights.

It's difficult to amend the constitution since this requires consensus among the three main components (Shia, Sunni and Kurds). Any constitutional amendment requires the non-opposition of two thirds of the electorate in three provinces according to article 142-fourth.[107] This would be very difficult to achieve. This stipulation was inserted by the Kurds in the TAL. It was also adopted in the permanent constitution. It may be advantageous for the Kurds, because it blocks any amendment they disapprove of, but it's a disadvantage to the country and the Kurds as a consequence, since they are and will continue to be part of Iraq in the foreseeable future. But the Kurds have always based their strategic plans on their ambition of establishing an independent state. In fact, they have acted since 1991 as if this Kurdish state was already in existence.

Successful democracies are those where the institutions make it difficult to fortify a temporary advantage.[108] This advantage that the Kurds have gained during times of disunity and ambiguity is being fortified by this stipulation in the constitution which makes it almost impossible to amend the constitution since the Kurds would never voluntarily agree to removing it as this will reduce their leverage on the political process. But the stipulation flies in the face of article (2B) because it ignores the democratic wishes of the majority of the Iraqi people. A possible way to remove it is perhaps through Federal Court as it could annul it on the basis of being contradictory with an earlier article (2B) in the constitution.

A stable democratic government must have two opposing characteristics. It must be 'strong enough to govern effectively but weak enough not to be able to govern against important interests'.[109]

Achilles' Heel

It's now clear that the current Iraqi constitution is one of the impediments to the consolidation of democracy because it is advantageous to the Kurdish separatists and Islamists parties. It's also difficult, if not impossible, to amend, even though there is an article in it, article 142, that required amendment within four months of the first session of parliament. Kurdish separatists would oppose any amendment that reduces their power and influence over Iraq.

The constitution also contains articles that threaten civil liberties and freedoms which form the basis of a consolidated democracy, especially Article 2. They were used to introduce laws based on Sharia law such as the Jaafari PSL and alcohol ban. It has proven to be the Achilles' heel of the Iraqi democracy.

Notes

1 Bremer (2006) op. cit. p. 39
2 Ibid., pp. 39–40
3 Hamid Alkifaey, 'Staying above the soil', *Guardian*, 16/5/2003: https://goo.gl/YW989R
4 Jean Sasson, *Mayyada the Daughter of Iraq*, Bantam Books (2004) p. 2003: https://goo.gl/A0dQG0
5 Bremer (2006) op. cit. p. 39
6 Ibid., p. 40
7 Diamond (2005) op. cit. p. 39
8 Bremer (2006) op. cit. p. 39
9 Ibid., p. 42
10 Ibid., p. 40
11 Paul Martin, interview, *Independent*, 18/3/2013: https://goo.gl/qwe6oU
12 Interview with Kanan Makiya
13 Interview with Ayad Allawi
14 Interview with Akeel Abbas
15 Ibid.
16 Interview with Kadom Shubber
17 Interview with Hussein Al-Hindawi
18 Interview with Kamal Field
19 Interview with Maysoon Aldamluji
20 Ibid.
21 Ibid.
22 Interview with Faleh Abdul-Jabbar
23 Interview with Ibrahim Al-Haidari
24 Interview with Samir Sumaidaie
25 Ibid.
26 Interview with Hashem Ganem
27 Ayad Jamaluddeen, interview by Shatha Aljuboori, Alsharq Alawsat newspaper, 14/12/2009: https://goo.gl/R1APkF
28 International Coalition for the Responsibility to Protect: https://goo.gl/ZnKdjB
29 Linz and Stepan (1996) op. cit. p. 98
30 Ibid.
31 Ibid.
32 Ibid.
33 Huntingdon (1991) op. cit. pp. 219–220

34 Linz and Stepan (1996) op. cit. p. 291
35 Ibid., p. 313
36 Ibid.
37 Ibid., p. 306
38 Bremer (2006) op. cit. p. 49
39 Ibid., p. 26
40 Diamond (2005) op. cit. p. 39
41 Ibid.
42 Patrick Radden Keefe, *Iraq: America's Private Armies*, quoted by Eric Hobsbawm, *Globalization, Democracy and Terrorism*, Abacus (2007) p. 37
43 Marcus Weisgerber, 'Back to Iraq: US military contractors return in droves', Defense One, 23/11/2016: https://goo.gl/PKKbyf
44 Bremer (2006) op. cit. p. 52
45 Ibid., p. 27
46 Ibid.
47 Ibid., p. 26
48 Ibid., p. 54
49 Ibid., p. 53
50 Ibid., p. 54
51 Ibid., p. 32
52 Ibid., p. 18
53 Ibid., p. 14
54 Allawi (2007) op. cit. p. 94
55 Bremer (2006) op. cit. p. 18
56 Ibid., p. 19
57 Ibid.
58 Adeed Dawisha, *Iraq: A Political History from Independence to Occupation*, Princeton University Press (2009) p. 2
59 Ibid., p. 46
60 Allawi (2007) op. cit. p. 91
61 Paul Martin, interview with Paul Bremer, *Independent*, 18/3/2013, op. cit.
62 Allawi (2007) op. cit. p. 91
63 Ibid.
64 Linz and Stepan (1996) op. cit. p. 11
65 Bremer (2006) op. cit. p. 19
66 Ibid., p. 17
67 Ibid., p. 19
68 Allawi (2007), op. cit. pp. 89–90
69 Ibid., p. 91
70 Hashim (2006) op. cit. p. 275
71 Charles King, Georgetown University (2000): http://faculty.georgetown.edu/kingch/Electoral_Systems.htm
72 Interview with Sharwan Al-Waeli
73 Mustafa Habeeb, 'New Iraqi electoral law has many holes', Niqash, 14/11/2013: www.niqash.org/en/articles/politics/3327/
74 Interview with Sharwan Al-Waeli
75 Interview with Akeel Abbas
76 Interview with Bassim Anton
77 Interview with Kadom Shubber
78 Przeworski (1991) op. cit. p. 28
79 Mithal Al-Aloosi, 'CDA's number of seats isn't fair', Alghad Press, 20/5/2014: https://goo.gl/YQCP5I
80 Omar Sattar, Al-Monitor, 10/10/2016: https://goo.gl/X0ZO7G
81 IHEC, election results, 2014

82 Interview with Hussein Al-Hindawi
83 Ibid.
84 Interview with Sharwan Al-Waeli
85 Interview with Faleh Abdul-Jabbar
86 Ibid., p. 21
87 Rudaw, 10/5/2016: http://rudaw.net/arabic/middleeast/iraq/1005201613
88 SIIC splintered late in 2017 into two groups, as its leader, Ammar Al-Hakeem, left the party and formed his own group under the name of 'Hikma'. The name refers people to Al-Hakim family and shows this group is family-based, even more than SIIC.
89 *Telegraph*, 18/11/2009: https://goo.gl/eOluO9
90 *Baghdad Times*: https://goo.gl/mEZQKY
91 *NY Times*, 16/4/2012: https://goo.gl/pCL3Il
92 IWPR, 'IHEC under fire', August 2009: https://goo.gl/zX7K0z
93 Przeworski (1991) op. cit. p. 33
94 Przeworski (1991) op. cit. p. 88
95 The Constitution's Dilemma, Institute of Strategic Studies, Beirut, 2006
96 Interview with Faleh Abdul-Jabbar
97 Ibid., p. 138
98 Interview with Hussein Al-Hindawi
99 Interview with Ayad Allawi
100 Interview with Maysoon Aldamluji
101 Interview with Abdulkhaliq Hussein
102 Interview with Bassim Anton
103 Interview with Sami Al-Askari
104 Interview with Dia Shakarchi
105 Przeworski (1991) op. cit. p. 36
106 Ibid.
107 Iraqi Constitution: www.constituteproject.org/constitution/Iraq_2005.pdf?lang=en
108 Przeworski (1991) op. cit. p. 36
109 Ibid., p. 37

11 Exogenous factors

Weak sponsor commitment

Among the impediments to democracy in Iraq is the lack of commitment by the main sponsor for democracy, the United States. Although the US has tried to establish a truly democratic system, it had weak plans and no effective partners in Iraq to help build such a democratic system. Many of the secular elite who should have been natural partners of the US blame the failure of the democratic experience on the lack of resolve by the US to back, with vigour, the establishment of a genuine democratic system.

Initially the Americans appointed a US general, Jay Garner, who lacked deep knowledge of Iraqi politics and culture, as head of an organization that was tasked with overseeing the transition into democracy. Garner mishandled the whole thing and in the words of Larry Diamond, 'cut a poor image for the United States'.[1]

The US then went to the UN and obtained Resolution 1483, which recognized the US as an occupying force. The idea of occupation didn't go well with Iraqis. It led many of them to believe that the US was not really serious about democracy since democracy and occupation do not go together. At the beginning, many Iraqis (43 per cent according to one survey) saw the Americans as liberators. But six months later, two thirds of Iraqis saw coalition forces as occupiers.[2] The UN was against the idea of occupation and it tried hard to convey this to the US administration to allow an interim Iraqi government, but to no avail. In an article published on 22 June 2003 at Alhayat newspaper, I warned that the Americans would be making a grave mistake if they decided to stay as an occupying force since they would lose the current support among Iraqis who would turn against them if they became occupiers.[3] Prior to that, I resigned from a senior post in the Iraqi media on the day the UN adopted Resolution 1483, which regarded the US as an occupying force. I could not be part of an institution that was part of an occupation authority nor was I able to justify to the Iraqi people the continuation of the US and UK as occupying forces when their declared aim was to remove a dictatorial oppressive regime and replace it with a democratic one. Resolution 1483 didn't specify how long this occupation will last.

The tool of the occupation powers in Iraq, CPA, used the UN as a cover of legitimacy but it didn't listen to it after it approved the formation of the Governing

Council. The UN envoy, Sergio De Mello, was very frustrated and bitter before he was killed in an attack on the UN headquarters in Baghdad on 19 August 2003.[4] The compound, in the Canal Hotel, was lightly protected.[5] That incident drove the UN to move its UNAMI mission to neighbouring Jordan after it suffered 'the most devastating tragedy in its history'.[6]

A strong and leading UN role in the political process would have enhanced Iraqi and Arab popular belief that the democratic change was serious since it had international backing. Iraqis' faith in the US was seriously shaken after their intifada against Saddam Hussein in 1991 when the US called upon the Iraqi people to 'take matters into their own hands and force Saddam Hussein, the dictator, to step aside' but only to abandon them to their fate.[7]

It was clear the Islamists, some of whom the US had sought hard to assemble in the London conference in December 2002 and later in the governing council in July 2003, were intent on establishing an Islamic state rather than a democratic one. Ayatullah Baqir Al-Hakim, the leader of SCIRI, made this clear upon his arrival in Najaf in May 2003. He called for a 'constitutional government where Islamic values and precepts would be honoured'.[8] He spoke of a tolerant and just society, but in Islamic rather than democratic or secular terms.

Ahmed Al-Chalabi, a leading secularist who supported US efforts to topple the regime – whom some have even attributed the US involvement in Iraq and dubbed him as the man 'who literally changed the world'[9] – complained to the British that the Americans had too many Islamist candidates for the Governing Council.[10] This long-time ally of America was forced to move into open opposition to them in 2003.[11] In fact, he was accused in April 2004 of forging Iraqi money, even though he was the head of the Governing Council's Finance Committee. In August 2004, he was accused of passing US secrets to Iran and giving flawed information to Americans, and arrest warrants were issued against him and his assistant and nephew, Salem Chalabi.[12] They were later acquitted of all charges.

Chalabi was secular and 'better known for love of all things Western', in Bremer's description, yet the US failed to keep him as an ally.[13] Their other important ally, Ayad Allawi, who was chosen as interim PM, also complains with scorn at Americans' lack of support for democracy. He blamed the US occupation of Iraq and the decisions made by the Americans, such as 'de-Ba'athification, disbanding the state (army and police)', for the failure of democracy in Iraq.[14] His party even accused Americans of supporting Islamist parties, rather than democratic ones as its spokeswoman, Maysoon Aldamluji clearly told me. She was convinced that Islamist parties 'enjoyed Western and regional support'.[15] She avers

> The Bush administration gave weight to Islamic parties in forming the Governing Council, and abided by the views of the Shia religious leadership (Marjiiya) in drafting the constitution. Even the timing of the first elections was obviously in favour of Islamic parties.[16]

The choice of Paul Bremer to lead Iraq was clearly a mistake, since he was not an expert on Iraq, as he publicly acknowledged. He had no prior involvement in the Iraqi crisis, and this was apparently one of the reasons why he was appointed.[17] He even regarded his experience as Ambassador to Malawi and Afghanistan as relevant to Iraq.[18] Other CPA senior staff were no better in their understanding of Iraq.

CPA advisor for 'religious affairs', Hume Horan, was criticized for his impractical ideas about Iraq's future role. Horan 'mused about the possibility, and desirability, of an Iraq, Israel, democratised Iran and Turkey axis at play in the Middle East, a vision fully endorsed by the neoconservatives in Washington'. 'Such an axis would act as an exemplar to the rest of the Arab world'.[19] Ali Allawi called it 'jaundiced reasoning, based on ideology-driven motives and a selective reading of history [which] was very prevalent in Baghdad in the early days of CPA'. 'It conveniently underplayed the significance of tendencies and actual events that fell outside the framework of analysis'.[20] The huge US military power and influence were not used effectively to support democracy.

Larry Diamond, who was advisor for democracy to CPA, reported that many Iraqis were worried that the US would walk away after the transfer of power on 30 June 2004 and he assured them 'from my deepest conviction, this won't happen'.[21] He reported that one enlightened cleric in Babylon, Farqad Al-Qizwini, implored him as he was leaving the province; 'Remember, you said you would be with us until the end'.[22]

This shows that people were worried that the US would abandon the democracy project. They didn't really believe the US was serious about democracy in Iraq and were worried it would walk away. Qizwini was part of an American intellectual, theological and political effort to reconcile Islam and democracy which Diamond describes as 'bold'.[23] He is known for his liberal Islamic views and he was a natural ally for the US and democratic forces. Yet, the Americans yielded to pressure from SCIRI and didn't include Qizwini in the Governing Council because 'he was too liberal for their tastes'.[24] SCIRI had vetoed the inclusion of other Shia liberals according to Diamond. Despite their military might, the Americans showed weakness before Islamist parties to the detriment of democratic forces.

Sami Al-Askari argues that the US 'had unlimited possibilities to interfere since it had over 100,000 soldiers on the ground'.[25] Even in 2010, Al-Askari says that the US 'secretly supported and encouraged the secular "Iraqia List" to form a government and take away the leadership of the government from Islamist "SoL"'.[26] However, this didn't happen and the US in the end backed a second term for Maliki.

Shorouq Al-Abayachi, charges 'the Americans weren't really serious about establishing democracy in the whole area'.[27] She catalogues her evidence on why she believes in this scenario. 'The Americans declared Iraq as the first front for fighting terrorism in order to protect America'. She contends this has helped to spread the phenomenon of 'militarism and weapons and led to the weakness of the law and state control and spread of militias and armed groups outside the control of the state'. She goes on:

Iraq was turned into an arena for regional and international conflicts which contributed to most of the country's current ills: the failure of building the Iraqi state according to a specific national identity; the control of the state by Islamist parties which govern on the basis of sectarianism; the disappearance of the middle class and the advent of a class of warlords steeped in militarism and corruption; the spread of illiteracy, ignorance and poverty in a big way among Iraqis; and the spread of corruption.[28]

Al-Abayachi blames Americans for all that and she explains why:

They could have protected Iraqi borders instead of opening Iraq as a basic front for fighting terrorism, inviting all terrorists of the world to Iraq in order to fight them. They shouldn't have put Iraq under occupation, instead, they should have formed a national transitional government that introduces a transitional programme for three years at least based on the removal of the effects of the Saddam totalitarian regime and preparing the way for real democratic elections under full international supervision. They should have achieved the project of Iraqi reconstruction without corruption and disputes between the State Department and the Pentagon. They should have respected the dignity of the Iraqi people before anything else.[29]

These are the possible options Al-Abayachi believes the Americans could have done to save democracy. Some points, such as not backing democratic forces and forming a transitional government for a longer period of time, are shared by others.

Ali Allawi stated that 'the inability of the coalition to impose law and order created another set of problems that gave rise to wide-scale human rights abuses'. There were reports of politically motivated killings which targeted the known members of the former security apparatus.[30] Allawi reveals that the politically motivated killings in Baghdad alone reached several hundred in May 2003. What is shocking is that 'religious leaders appeared to sanction the killings'.[31]

The campaign of killings got wider and wider: 'By June 2003, the killings began to include academics, artists, bureaucrats, teachers, journalists, and professionals who were not seen to be part of the regime's control and repression'.[32] This chaotic situation that followed the fall of the regime was acknowledged by Paul Bremer himself.[33] He even asked for extra US military police to patrol Iraqi streets.[34]

Adnan Al-Janabi, blames the US for dismantling the Iraqi state 'with disastrous consequences'. 'The Americans didn't come to build, instead they demolished an existing state', he charges.[35] Akeel Abbas lists American failure as one of the reasons for the failure of democracy in Iraq: 'The initial US failure in keeping the peace and restoring basic services has given a strong and lasting impression that democracy does not work, giving rise again to the familiar anti-democratic desire/theme of the strong man as the saviour'.[36]

Hussein Al-Hindawi argues that the American call for democracy in 2003 was false. He repeats 'there was no truth in their call for democracy. Building a democracy doesn't depend on Ahmed Al-Chalabi, for example'.[37] He blames the Americans for a number of mistakes. First, they were 'listening to what Najaf was saying' when writing the Iraqi provisional constitution in 2004. This view is shared by Maysoon Aldamluji. He also blames the Americans for handing power over to a group of Iraqis who 'were totally ignorant in law, even in Sharia law'. He argues that 'none of them was like (Ayatullah) Hussein Na'eeni who proposed a constitution to limit the authority of the ruler' in the early twentieth century.[38]

Maysoon Aldamluji also blames Americans for their lack of support for democracy.[39] Farid Ayar even accuses Americans of corruption and lack of support for democratic forces in the country.[40]

Samir Sumaidaie, however, contends Americans have made efforts in the direction of building a democracy, but he blames others for standing in the way of these efforts:

> The effort made by the Americans to help install democratic structures such as a constitution and elections etc. were hijacked, sabotaged, and used as a stepping stone to jump to a position of power. Once that was achieved, power was consolidated using non-democratic means.[41]

The question is how can this be hijacked from a superpower that everyone fears and reveres, especially when it had an advanced army of 130,000 soldiers on the ground?[42] Although it's true the Americans have made efforts to create a democracy in Iraq, these efforts were not enough to establish a strong democracy. This shows that the US commitment to democracy in Iraq was not solid, which is why they abandoned their efforts at the first juncture.

Kanan Makiya admits the US role was diminishing gradually in Iraq but he blames Iraqi politicians. 'The US departed because the Iraqi political parties and the political class turned their back to it. It could have contributed to the development of Iraq economically, culturally and scientifically', but it had to leave because most politicians were reluctant to support its presence in Iraq.[43] Most of those who blame the Americans are secular and closer to the democratic project than Islamists who blame the Americans for everything else except building a democracy.

Ali Allawi blames the confusion over plans for the governance of Iraq on the US administration's 'lack of clarity about its intentions in post-Saddam Iraq'. He notes that 'by the time the military option appeared to have been definitely selected, it was too late to start seriously thinking about the administration of a post-war Iraq'.[44]

Larry Diamond also acknowledges that the US invaded Iraq without a 'coherent, viable plan to win the peace', although he contends there was preparation and the State Department planned for the Iraqi transition in October 2001 in what was called then 'the Future of Iraq Project' which produced the 'The Transition to Democracy in Iraq' report.[45] But the report, according to Diamond, didn't offer a 'coherent or finished blueprint for the post-war political order', although he believes it produced a 'viable strategy for filling the vacuum of authority'.[46]

But the US administration was not the only one at fault, according to Ali Allawi, who also apportions blame to the Iraqi opposition for not having formulated a unified vision for post-Saddam Iraq. Allawi refers to the 'Transition to Democracy' report, compiled by the Democratic Principles Working Group (DPWG) and edited by the lawyer, Salem Chalabi, Ahmed Chalabi's nephew, and the academic and author, Kanan Makiya, both of whom were close to INC. He argues this report, which is close to the thinking of the Pentagon, was 'the most complete statement of what the liberals and westernised groups within the Iraqi opposition sought for Iraq's political future'.[47]

Allawi mentions that some voices within DPWG criticized Makiya's attempt to 'present the report as a collective effort and refused to acknowledge it as more than the work of fringe elements'. He quotes Ghassan Al-Attiyya, whom he described as an 'important political thinker', as saying that

> the transitional authority would depend on the way the regime was overthrown. If it were under some UN approval, the UN would have the final say on the nature of Iraq's transitional authority. If it was the result of a unilateral action by the Anglo-American coalition, the coalition would be the arbiters of the transitional authority.[48]

Since the removal of the regime was done without UN approval, it means that Al-Attiyya puts the responsibility of what happened next in Iraq squarely on the US and UK.

Allawi classifies Iraqi opposition members participating in the London Conference in 2002 into three groups. The first are 'idealists' who congregate around Ahmed Chalabi. Their chosen vision for post-Saddam Iraq was the 'Transition to Democracy Report' and their tactic was to have the conference adopt it. The second group comprised the 'realists' who represented the views of the US administration, which needed an Iraqi cover for the evolving plan to attack Saddam. No commitment would be made at the conference beyond general statements of encouragement for democratic rule and respect for civil and human rights. It was clear at that point, in Allawi's view, that Washington was not going to hand power over to the Iraqi opposition since it was divided and didn't merit US support.[49]

The third trend at the conference was the leaders of the opposition parties who had diverse expectations as to what they wanted to achieve as far as their own narrow interests are concerned. Washington held little expectation for the conference but this didn't stop the main opposition groups from using it as a platform to cement their control over the political process and forming a mechanism for coordinating with the US in the run-up to the war.[50] Some groups, such as SCIRI, had feared it would lose out under an American military government, but it ended up the party that benefitted most from the American invasion.

The US administration was against the idea of forming a provisional Iraqi government, which was favourable to opposition groups such as the INC. The

INA, according to Allawi, did not have a public stance on the issue, although it worked against it because it wouldn't take into account 'internal opposition' to Saddam. The CIA was opposed to such a government because it thought it would alienate internal opposition and dissuade it from any attempt to change the regime.[51]

In the end, the opposition conference in London succeeded in extracting a role for the opposition in the future administration of Iraq. It formed a 65-person committee from exiled opposition groups, the 'Coordination and Follow up Committee' (CFC). Some independent Islamists protested that SCIRI had appropriated the role of other Shia Islamists. Ultimately, the London conference did avoid the discussion of what Allawi called 'serious issues' such as the role of religion in public life.[52] The 65-member committee met in the resort of Salahuddeen in northern Iraq in January 2003 and selected a 6-member leadership council made up of: Jalal Talabni (PUK), Masaud Barzani (KDP), Abdul-Azeez Al-Hakim (SCIRI), Ahmad Al-Chalabi (INC), Ayad Allawi (INA) and Adnan Al-Pachachi.[53]

As the US forces entered Iraq and the regime fell, Islamist forces and their allies who laid a claim to the loyalty of the population filled the power vacuum and parallel power structures evolved in almost every town and city of Iraq, although they remained undetected by officials appointed by the occupying authorities.[54] This happened despite US warnings to SCIRI that, if it tried to get organized forces from its Badr Brigade into Iraq, they would be treated as enemy combatants.[55] But this threat was not carried out as there was no exchange of fire between US troops and Badr.

The Sadrist movement, which was not known in the West prior to the war, sprang to life and was able to secure Sadr City – east of Baghdad – within days of regime fall. As Ali Allawi points out, 'the movement had not been quashed by the Saddam regime, as many had thought, because it went underground'.[56] One of the incidents that may have weakened the trust in the American effort was their lack of support for those Iraqis who supported them and believed in their cause.

One such Iraqi ally was Abdul-Majeed Al-Khoei, the son of the late grand Ayatullah Abul-Qassim Al-Khoei, who was the Shia's world-wide leader until his death in 1992. Al-Khoei was approached by the CIA to help in the effort of controlling the Shia city of Najaf. He was flown into Najaf by a US military helicopter on 3 April, but was murdered by the supporters of Muqtada As-Sadr on the 10th of the month.[57]

Al-Khoei would have played an important role in the post-Saddam Iraq due to his family's position and the respect he enjoyed with most Iraqis. He was seen as a 'moderating force in Shia Islam and useful counterweight to the Iranian regime'.[58] He had been trying to reduce tensions between Sunni and Shia and find common grounds between the two sects for many years prior to his involvement with the Americans in Iraq in 2003.[59]

He was killed because there was not enough US protection for him. American troops stationed nearby didn't interfere, as commanders were instructed 'not to

174 of city be interpreted

approach the heart of the city lest it be interpreted as infringement of the sanctity of the city'.[60] This must have sent a signal to all those who supported the US project in Iraq that they were not protected. If Mr Al-Khoei was left to die, they would be in a worse position.

The Bush administration's position on Iraq in the aftermath of the Iraq war was 'riddled with expedient decision-making, departmental infighting, conflicting strategies, and policy incoherence'. This undermined the credibility of the parties with whom the US had been engaged with varying degrees of enthusiasm, even though the 'CPA had to deal with the same cast of characters'.[61] It's surprising that Ayatullah Sistani was more concerned with democracy than the Americans. On 8 March 2004, Sistani issued a statement criticizing article 61C of the TAL considering it as 'usurping the democratic rights of Iraqis to choose their own constitution'.[62] The article was demanded by the Kurds and accepted by the CPA which presented it to the drafting committee very late in the process.[63]

According to Adam Przeworski, outcomes under democracy 'hold only if they are mutually enforced in self-interest or enforced externally by some third party'.[64] This third party, the US in Iraq's case, was not willing to stand behind democratic outcomes.

In conclusion, the Americans did not do enough to support democratic secular forces; instead, they left the door open for Islamist parties and their armed groups to control Iraq. They knew, as acknowledged by Bremer, that Islamists were the 'best organized' and they would win early elections, while others lacked organization and support.[65] Islamist militias were operating uninterrupted and undetected.

At the same time, the Iraqi expert exiles who returned to Iraq under the Iraqi Reconstruction and Development Council (IRDC) were side-lined and never consulted by the CPA.[66] IRDC was dissolved in June 2003 when the CPA handed power to Iraqi interim government. Although the makeup of IRDC was completely Iraqi, it's not regarded as such by Americans, who dissolved it when they dissolved the CPA. Instead of having a leading role as an Iraqi democratic entity, it was treated as a temporary US organization and it reported to Paul Bremer instead of the Governing Council.[67] Most IRDC members returned to their countries of exile after the organization was dissolved, depriving Iraq of an educated and experienced class of people who could have served the country and consolidated democracy.

Americans never really considered Iraqi expatriates as full Iraqis and have always had a temporary role for them, even though most of them, if not all, were enthusiastic to serve their country and resettle in Iraq if the conditions were right. Many of them rebuilt their old homes or built new ones to start a new life in the new Iraq but were never encouraged to do so by the Americans who started dealing with Islamist parties, treating them as the real Iraqis. It seems that being secular and Westernized was a disqualification of being Iraqi as far as the Americans were concerned.

Hostile environment

Iraqi democracy has faced difficulties from hostile neighbouring countries that are not democratic. Almost all of the surrounding countries are not democracies, and they never welcomed the change in Iraq, despite the fact they were all, except perhaps Jordan, either hostile or not on friendly terms with the Saddam regime. Turkey, for example, refused to grant the US a passage to Iraq in 2003, even though it was a member of the US-led NATO Alliance.[68]

Haggard and Kaufman (1995) state that 'successful democratic opposition in one country has an impact on the perceptions and behaviour of actors in neighbouring countries or those with strong cultural links'.[69] The democratic change in Spain, for example, resonated throughout Latin America, while the 'People's power' revolution in the Philippines challenged other Asian dictatorships. Events in Poland and East Germany had influenced other Eastern European countries.[70]

Larry Diamond acknowledges that 'the efforts to bring democracy to Iraq were unfolding in a hostile regional environment' and this has hindered the progress of democracy.[71] He contrasts it with the advent of democracy to Eastern Europe where there was a 'welcoming supportive group of democratic neighbours in the West' as well as the desire of Eastern European nations to join EU.

In Asia, when democracy spread to the Philippines, Taiwan and Korea, there was the example of consolidated democracy in rich and successful Japan. In Latin America, democracy spread in the 1980s because of the influence of the democratic change in Spain, which has strong cultural links to the continent, in addition to the full-scale support of the US and Western European countries. In addition, democracy had existed in some Latin American countries before the reversals to dictatorship, so people were familiar with it.

Diamond reports that Iraqis were worried about the US not taking into consideration the fact that 'all neighbouring states are undemocratic'. One of his Iraqi interlocutors told him that 'there will be a campaign against democracy' in Iraq.[72] Not only was the regional environment hostile, but even the Iraqi internal environment was hostile. Kamal Field listed this as a major impediment. Field argues that democracy 'didn't come as a result of mass desire'. 'It's actually like a plant that was growing in a hostile environment'.[73] The regional environment was hostile to democracy and this was a major reason why it has not succeeded in Iraq. As we will see in the next section, not only is the regional environment hostile, but there were also active interferences from regional countries to disrupt the course of democracy in Iraq and stop its fusion outside it. The US never put enough pressure on some of these countries to support the new Iraq. Many of them have been US allies for decades and could have yielded to US pressure.

Outside interference

This relates to regional countries, in particular Iran, Turkey, Syria, Qatar and Saudi Arabia. Since democracy is alien to Arab culture, and most Arab countries, with the exception of Lebanon and partially Kuwait and recently Morocco, have never had any form of a representative government, its introduction in Iraq alarmed states that fear most this new phenomenon.

The five states above are believed to have interfered directly or indirectly to impede the progress of Iraqi democracy. Every one of them has its own reasons, but the main reason for the majority, except Turkey perhaps, is the 'fear of the domino effect' that democracy might have in their own countries, in addition to fear of, or animosity to, Shia rule in Iraq, except for Iran which welcomed it, although it has not welcomed democracy.

The spread of democracy geographically has been due in a big way to international pressure. As mentioned in the previous chapter, successful democratic opposition in one country has an impact in neighbouring countries or those with which it has strong cultural links. The democratic change in Spain had an impact on Latin America. The 'People's power' revolution in the Philippines impacted on Asian dictatorships. Events in Poland and East Germany influenced other Eastern European countries.[74] Iraq has many cultural and religious links to countries in the region, and the regimes ruling there became alarmed at the prospects of democracy in Iraq.

The fear of democracy was fuelled largely by American talk of bringing democracy to the Middle East and how Iraq would be an exemplar for the whole region. This was laid out in President Bush's speech on 6 November 2003 on his vision for the Middle East.[75] There is also the Eastern European example where all communist regimes fell one after the other.

Adam Przeworski regarded the change there as one event or 'one and a half' since what happened in Romania was caused by what had occurred in Czechoslovakia, and that resulted from the breakdown in East Germany, and that followed the political changes in Hungary, and what showed the Hungarians a way out was the success of negotiations in Poland.[76]

The Syrian regime played a very negative role and most foreign fighters were believed to have come through Syria.[77] There have also been reports that the Syrians had training camps for foreign fighters. In 2009, the Iraqi PM, Noori Al-Maliki filed a complaint against Syria with the UN for playing a destabilizing role in Iraq.[78] Because ISIS, and Al-Qaeda before it, embraces a doctrine similar to the Wahabi doctrine prevailing in Saudi Arabia, many observers, as well as Iraqi and Syrian officials, blame Saudi Arabia either for supporting terrorists or for not doing enough to fight terrorism.[79] Saudi fighters within ISIS form the second largest group among Arab fighters after Tunisians.[80]

Qatar is also frequently accused by Iraqi officials of supporting insurgents and fighters in Iraq.[81] Turkey has been accused by the Iraqi government and several factions of supporting militias and providing logistical support for foreign fighters in Iraq. An Iraqi MP, Mr Shakhawan Abdullah, accused it of paying the salaries of members of an Iraqi Sunni militia.[82] Iran's influence in Iraq is acknowledged by friends and foes alike. Most Iraqi Islamist opposition groups were based in Iran and supported by it in varying degrees.

Sami Al-Askari has given a catalogue of interferences by other countries. 'Since the fall of Saddam, the Iraqi political scene has been subjected to foreign interferences and influences', he says. He goes on:

> The military invasion and the fears it raised in the region, and the opportunities created by the collapse of the Iraqi state ... have offered huge opportunities for regional and international parties to interfere in Iraq so as to serve their interest.

He also blames Iraqi politicians 'who were ready to deal with this interference and welcome it so as to serve their interests and their aims as they compete among themselves'. Al-Askari asserts

> the presence of Iran is most visible in the Iraqi political scene among the regional powers. Iran was able to build bridges with its old allies and make new allies and this has offered it the opportunity of influence in the Iraqi scene.[83]

But the Iranian role in Iraq was not necessarily to destabilize the new regime entirely but to support its Islamist allies within it at the expense of others, and this has given them an edge over others. Because Iraqi Islamists do not believe in liberal democracy, as I have established, the Iranian role has become an impediment to democracy since it supports factions that are not committed to it.

Al-Askari points to the Turkish role as 'the defender of Iraqi Sunnis'. He charges that Turkey formed an axis with Saudi Arabia and Qatar to compete with the growing Iranian role. He contends the Iranian and Turkish roles were 'exposed' during the elections of 2010:

> Iran managed to group all Shia groups, except SoL, in a bloc (NIC). After the results were announced, Iran was active in putting pressure on all the players to make compromises which led to the formation of the second Al-Maliki government.[84]

He argues Turkey managed, with a mandate from the official Arab establishment, to group all the Sunnis in one list (Iraqia) and install the Shia Ayad Allawi as its leader in a bid to claw back the leadership of the government from the Shia Alliance:

> This Turkish endeavour was about to succeed if it wasn't for the Federal Court with regards to the formation of parliamentary lists, and the success of Iran in bringing both Shia blocs, SoL and NIC, in a parliamentary list that was able to achieve quorum to form the government.

He even accused the UN mission (UNAMI) of bias and trying to influence election results in favour of Iraqia.[85]

Ayad Allawi also blames foreign influence, colonialism, occupation, lack of self-determination and domestic reasons for 'severely impairing the evolution of democracy in Islamic countries'.[86] Kanan Makiya maintains that Iran is responsible for whatever is happening to Iraq now. 'It's Iran who supported the religious parties. Without Iran they would have had no influence'.[87] But, Iran is a theocracy, not a democracy, and it wouldn't be expected to support a true democracy. On the contrary, it has no interest in having a true democracy on its borders.

Samir Sumaidaie contends what happens in Iran or Saudi Arabia has an influence on democracy in Iraq:[88]

> If the Iranian theocratic regime suffers an internal crisis and collapses, it would have an impact. If the situation in the Gulf and in particular Saudi Arabia is dramatically changes, it would have a profound influence on the whole region.

He also asserts that 'regional powers see democracy building in Iraq as a threat to their survival'. He regards the 'malign influence' of Iran, Turkey and Israel, as an impediment to democracy.[89]

Abdul-Khaliq Hussein regards relations with Iran, Turkey, the Arab world, USA, EU and the rest of the world as a challenge to democracy in Iraq. He adds, 'a few old-fashioned regional governments do not want Iraqi democracy to succeed, because they fear it will inspire their own peoples, and that's why they support sectarianism and terrorism in Iraq'.[90] Whada Al-Jumaili regards Iraqi political leaders as 'weak' due to the 'influence of foreign diktats' on them.[91]

Foreign interference in Iraq has impeded democracy in a big way. This was done through support for armed groups to destabilize the country and also financial support for Iraqi political parties in return for taking expedient positions. Armed groups and militias are supported, financially and logistically by regional powers and they constitute a major obstacle to democracy. Only the state should have exclusive coercive powers over its citizens.

Insurgency

Many observers regard the insurgency as the most serious impediment to building a new political system in Iraq because it's a serious threat to its stability and prosperity. It was neither expected nor acknowledged by the Americans at the beginning.[92] The first detailed study on insurgency was conducted by Professor Ahmed Hashim which came three years after it began.[93] Larry Diamond reckons the resistance began in July 2003 when the Americans faced 'a guerrilla war in Iraq against a much more entrenched enemy than it anticipated'.[94]

In August 2003, alone, there were two major attacks by the insurgency – one on the UN headquarters in Baghdad, killing the UN envoy, Sergio De Mello, and forcing the UN to withdraw from Iraq. The second was in Najaf, killing the Islamist Shia leader, Baqir Al-Hakim, together with around a hundred of his companions.[95] The insurgency is associated with extremist Sunni Islamists who are violent and have a disdain for anything Western. But Bremer regarded every surge in violence as a sign that 'the resistance was getting more desperate'.[96] Instead of acknowledging it and providing remedies for its motives and alleviating the suffering of the Iraqi people, Bremer ignored it and thought Iraq 'was not a country in chaos'.[97]

As we saw in Chapter 10, the security vacuum left by disbanding the Iraqi army and the unemployment and discord created by the de-Ba'athification law pushed many Iraqis to become enemies of the new order. Since there was an occupation by a foreign power, it attracted jihadists from across the world to come to Iraq and join the insurgency. According to the Telegraph, fighters came to Iraq and Syria from Tunisia, Saudi Arabia, Russia, Jordan, Turkey, France, Morocco, Lebanon, Egypt and Germany.[98]

Ahmed Hashim is highly critical of the US counter-insurgency campaign, and he blames it for playing 'a key role in the outbreak and perpetuation of the insurgency'.[99] He accuses US decision-makers of a 'rigid and inflexible ideological approach' which undermined the chances of implementing policies vital in any successful counterinsurgency strategy. Policies such as measured reactions and minimal use of force, political responses, integrated civil–military operations and rectitude towards civilians and prisoners have been largely absent from the US efforts to suppress the insurgency.

Instead, US forces focused on killing the insurgents while turning a blind eye to cultural sensitivities and showing callousness towards civilian casualties. Hashim attributes the US military's failure to have an effectively prepared counterinsurgency strategy to the 'organizational or military culture, defined here as those values or beliefs that promote a conventional-warfare mindset to such an extent that little or no consideration is given to the study and effective preparation for the prosecution of small wars'.[100]

Paul Bremer warned the US Congress in 2003, 'If we fail to recreate Iraq with a sovereign democracy sustained by a solid economy, we will have provided the terrorists with an incredible advantage in their war against us'.[101] In the end, the terrorists did have that advantage with the failure of the Americans to recreate Iraq. Bremer didn't practice what he preached. He created millions of unemployed people and was insensitive to the sufferings of Iraqis.

Maysoon Aldamluji blames the US for the breakout of the insurgency. 'The army and security forces were dismantled, leaving a massive vacuum that gave way to insurgency and militias to compromise Iraq's security and sovereignty'.[102] Wahda Al-Jumaili asserts 'the security challenge is serious and it has affected democratic transition in a big way'.[103] Ibrahim Al-Haidari blames 'irresponsible' American conduct which 'helped deepen chaos and produced a political and administrative vacuum which resulted in fragile security and the spread of violence, terrorism and social fragmentation'. He contends that they have failed in providing an 'atmosphere conducive for a margin of real freedom and democracy'.[104]

Security deteriorated mainly due to the resistance to occupation by various groups, internal and external. Shorouq Al-Abayachi contends that Iraq was turned into a 'basic front for fighting terrorism' by Americans, who 'invited all terrorists of the world to Iraq in order to fight them'.[105] Walid Al-Hilli contends that 'the political process must be conducted in a proper security environment with the existence of free competition and equal opportunities for all'.[106]

Abdul-Khaliq Hussein regards 'Sunni terrorism' as an impediment to democracy. 'Iraqi democracy was born at the time when Sunni Islamic terrorism was at its high'. He blames the 'religious leaders of the Wahabi sect' and BP remnants for that. He blames the Sunnis for 'exacerbating sectarian conflict because they have lost their power and found themselves at a disadvantage because of democracy. They have even collaborated with the terrorists like al-Qaeda and ISIS' he exclaims.[107]

Although the insurgency is entirely Sunni, not all Sunnis cooperated with al-Qaeda or ISIS. On the contrary, Iraqi Sunnis had the most to lose from the activities of terrorist groups such as ISIS. Sunni imams were beheaded for refusing to pledge allegiance to ISIS.[108] On the other hand, it was Sunnis who drove out Al-Qaeda from Iraq during the US surge campaign in 2006–2008 in what was called the 'Awakening Councils'.[109] Democracy must not disadvantage anyone in a country if they act peacefully and abide by the law of the land.

The insurgency has impeded democracy in a big way since it targeted election rallies and IHEC officials, candidates, civic centres, mosques, markets, schools, universities, state institutions, civil society organizations, academics, doctors, professionals and journalists. It has driven millions of Iraqis to flee the country, especially the educated and experienced.

Democracy requires law and order, state bureaucracy, stability and more importantly, peace. The insurgency has turned Iraq into a battleground, far away from the environment conducive to democracy. It has weakened all state institutions which are needed for democracy to take root. I have classified insurgency as exogenous because many of its fighters were foreigners and it was supported by foreign countries. Although there were many Iraqis among the insurgents, it was an international jihadist campaign against the change that the US effected in Iraq which removed Sunni rulers and replaced them with Shia ones. Whatever the classification, it's a serious impediment to democracy.

Armed groups and militias

All armed groups constitute a threat to the state. ISIS took control of three provinces in 2014, 2015 and 2016, but government forces managed to free them all, although terrorism is still a serious threat to the stability of the country. ISIS is recognized internationally as a terrorist group and Iraq is getting help from the US, Iran and other countries to fight it back. It has caused havoc all over Iraq, but it will be defeated sooner or later since it has no practical political programme. It belongs to ancient history. But the main challenge to democracy will be militias linked to Islamist political parties which proliferated over the last two years after ISIS took control of Musil in June 2014. Militias have been a military/political factor in Iraq since 2003.

When the US military entered Iraq in early 2003, it warned Islamic militias not to enter Iraq and get organized forces and if they did they would be treated as enemy combatant.[110] But that warning was not heeded; they did get organized forces, although 'they remained undetected by officials appointed by the occupying authorities'.[111] Some of them entered into battles with the US and Iraqi armies.

Sami Al-Askari identifies Sunni and Shia armed groups and militias as being a serious problem. He stated that these groups 'imposed their understanding of religious and moral values and practices on others'. This was extended to even killing those who didn't apply 'their understanding of religion and morals'. He argues this was made possible by the almost complete absence of the state during the period after the fall of the regime.[112]

But, as the state got stronger, the main militias which are Badr and the Mahdi Army, integrated with Iraqi forces or demobilized after the threat of Sunni jihadi terrorism diminished after 2008.[113]

Militias resurged after the breakout of the war in Syria where some 5000 Iraqis went to fight in Syria against Al-Qaeda and ISIS, not necessarily supporting the Assad regime.[114] PM Al-Maliki had to deploy two combat-hardened militia units which returned from Syria in June 2014 to Iraq to fight ISIS after the collapse of the Iraqi army in Musil.[115] The turning point for the resurgence of Shia militias was when ISIS took control of Musil and Ayatullah Sistani issued a jihad fatwa to fight ISIS which 'provided the mechanism for the enormous and rapid expansion of militias'.[116] The fatwa was expedient for political groups to form their own militias, which are loosely gathered under the banner of Popular Mobilization Unit (PMU) or Hashd.

It is difficult to know how many militias there are in Iraq now or how many have been formed after 10 June 2014, or the number of men who joined them as tallies differ from one group to another. The US War College estimates the number of Shia militias in Iraq to be over 50.[117] These militias, with tens of thousands of trained armed men, are not going to disappear after the removal of ISIS. Their presence will constitute a threat to democracy and to the state itself, which is already weak. This has pushed people to depend on militias for protection as Akeel Abbas explained: 'Sect-based militias are more trusted and effective than the state itself'.[118]

In 2007 the two main militias, Badr and Mahdi Army, clashed. As a result, several officials, including the governors of two provinces (Muthanna and Diwaniyya), were killed.[119] The UN warned that the existence of militias will pose a problem for Iraq in the long term.[120]

The US Controller General, David Walker, said in 2007 testimony before the Sub-committee on Defence, in the US House Committee on Appropriations that militias have penetrated Iraqi ministries.[121] Maysoon Aldamluji believes militias have compromised Iraq's security and sovereignty.[122]

It's now established there are several armed militias operating in Iraq, in addition to terrorist groups such as ISIS. The Shia militias, at least the new ones, were formed after the jihad fatwa of Ayatullah Sistani and he may be the only one who has the moral authority to call upon them to demobilize. It's doubtful that he would while ISIS's threat is hanging over Iraq. Sistani is now 86. If he dies before the stabilization of the country, the legitimacy that armed groups got from his fatwa will be difficult to challenge.

Armed groups do not respect the law or people's choices and most of them are sect-based religious organizations, which impose their understandings of religion on those under their control. This has happened in Iraq and it's bound to happen in the future. Unless militias are pacified or dissolved, democracy will be in name only.

Notes

1 Diamond (2005) op. cit. p. 32
2 Ibid., p. 51
3 Hamid Alkifaey, Al-Hayat newspaper, 22/6/2003
4 Diamond (2005) op. cit. pp. 55–57
5 Ibid., p. 46
6 Ibid., p. 58
7 Ibid., p. 123. For the Iraqi 1991 intifada, see *Routledge Handbook of the Arab Spring* (2014) (ed. Larbi Sadiki, chapter 35)
8 Allawi (2007) op. cit. p. 111
9 Aram Reston, *The Man Who Pushed America to War*, Nations Books (2008) p. xi
10 Bremer (2006) op. cit. p. 89
11 Ibid., p. 88
12 David Holly, 'Arrest warrant issued for Chalabi', *LA Times*, 9/8/2004: http://articles. latimes.com/2004/aug/09/world/fg-warrants9
13 Bremer (2006) op. cit. p. 90
14 Interview with Ayad Allawi
15 Interview with Maysoon Aldamluji
16 Ibid.
17 Allawi (2007) p. 106
18 Bremer (2006) op. cit. p. 90
19 Allawi (2007) p. 109
20 Ibid.
21 Diamond (2005) op. cit. p. 123
22 Ibid., p. 125
23 Ibid., p. 117
24 Ibid., p. 42
25 Interview with Sami Al-Askari
26 Ibid.
27 Interview with Shorouq Al-Abayachi
28 Ibid.
29 Ibid., p. 107
30 Allawi (2007) p. 144
31 Ibid., p. 145
32 Ibid.
33 Bremer (2007) pp. 18–19
34 Ibid., p. 32
35 Interview with Adnan Al-Janabi
36 Interview with Akeel Abbas
37 Interview with Hussein Al-Hindawi
38 Ibid.

39 Interview with Maysoon Aldamluji
40 Interview with Farid Ayar
41 Interview with Samir Sumaidaie
42 Total number of coalition troops was 170,000 (Bremer (2006) op. cit. p. 4); the number of American troops was 130,000 of that total (CNN, 28/3/2003): http://edition.cnn.com/2003/WORLD/meast/03/27/sprj.irq.war.main/
43 Interview with Kanan Makiya
44 Allawi (2007) op. cit. p. 84
45 Diamond (2005) op. cit. p. 27
46 Ibid.
47 Allawi (2007) p. 84
48 Ibid.
49 Ibid., p. 85
50 Ibid.
51 Ibid., p. 86
52 Ibid.
53 Ibid., p. 88
54 Ibid., p. 91
55 Ibid., p. 90
56 Ibid.
57 Ibid., pp. 92–93
58 Ibid., p. 92
59 Hamid Alkifaey, *Sky News*, 10/4/2003: www.cbsnews.com/news/reports-two-clerics-hacked-to-death/
60 Allawi (2007) op. cit. p. 93
61 Ibid., p. 110
62 Ibid., p. 223
63 Ibid., p. 221
64 Przeworski (1996)
65 Bremer (2006) op. cit. p. 242
66 Feisal Istrabadi, Farouk Darweesh and Isam Khafaji, Dawn, 12/8/2003: www.dawn.com/news/134650/iraqi-exiles-feel-excluded-reconstruction
67 Bremer (2006) op. cit. p. 32
68 Karen Kaya, 'The Turkish American crisis of March 1 military review', July/August 2011, p. 74: http://fmso.leavenworth.army.mil/documents/The-Turkish-American-Crisis.pdf
69 Haggard and Kaufman (1995) op. cit. p. 25
70 Ibid.
71 Diamond (2005) op. cit. p. 21
72 Ibid., p. 107
73 Interview with Kamal Field
74 Haggard and Kaufman (1995) op. cit. p. 25
75 *The Economist*, 'Bold vision for the Middle East', 7/11/2003: https://goo.gl/ovCuGZ
76 Przeworski (1991) op. cit. p. 3
77 Noori Al-Maliki, AFP France, 4/9/2009: https://goo.gl/d9h8rz. Also, Mamoon Al-Abasi quoting Mowffak Al-Rubaie, Middle East Eye, 20/10/2015: https://goo.gl/iv2Igi
78 Trend News Agency, 3/9/2009: http://en.trend.az/azerbaijan/society/1534046.html Also, *The Jerusalem Post*, 3/9/2003: https://goo.gl/vj9tGt
79 Sky, 5/7/2016: https://goo.gl/x2xBGv
80 Ashley Kirk, *Telegraph*, 24/3/2016: https://goo.gl/5vmYkk
81 Aljazeera, 'Maliki: Saudi and Qatar at war against Iraq', 9/3/2014: https://goo.gl/3TjCci
82 Shirwan Abbas, Rudaw, 30/12/2015: www.rudaw.net/english/middleeast/291220151
83 Interview with Sami Al-Askari

84 Ibid.
85 Ibid.
86 Interview with Ayad Allawi
87 Interview with Kanan Makiya
88 Interview with Samir Sumaidaie
89 Ibid.
90 Interview with Abdulkhaliq Hussein
91 Interview with Wahda Al-Jumaili
92 Allawi (2007) op. cit. p. 170
93 Hashim (2006) op. cit.
94 Diamond (2005) op. cit. p. 42
95 Allawi (2007) op. cit. p. 172
96 Diamond (2005) op. cit. p. 42
97 Ibid.
98 Ashley Kirk, *Telegraph*, 24/3/2016: https://goo.gl/8hTUKQ
99 Hashim (2006) op. cit. p. 275
100 Ibid.
101 Allawi (2007) p. 197
102 Interview with Maysoon Aldamluji
103 Interview with Wahda Al-Jumaili
104 Interview with Ibrahim Al-Haidari
105 Interview with Shorouq Al-Abayachi
106 Interview with Walid Al-Hilli
107 Interview with Abdulkhaliq Hussein
108 Dean Obeidallah, 'ISIS's gruesome Muslim death toll', *The Daily Beast*, 10/7/2014: www.thedailybeast.com/articles/2014/10/07/isis-s-gruesome-muslim-death-toll.html
109 Global Security, The Sahwa/Awakening Councils/Sons of Iraq, https://goo.gl/vYZIFI
110 Allawi (2007) op. cit. pp. 89–90
111 Ibid., p. 91
112 Interview with Sami Al-Askari
113 Cigar, February 2015, op. cit. p. 3
114 Ibid., p. 4
115 Ibid., p. 5
116 Ibid.
117 Ibid., p. 14
118 Interview with Akeel Abbas
119 BBC report, 20/8/2007: http://news.bbc.co.uk/1/hi/world/middle_east/6954467.stm
120 House of Commons Defence Committee 6th report on Iraq, op. cit. p. 64: https://goo.gl/lL4U6b
121 David Walker, 'US Government Accountability Office', 23/4/2007: https://goo.gl/ccSM2j
122 Interview with Maysoon Aldamluji

12 Structural factors

Stateness

Since democracy is a system of governance, it requires a state; without a state, there is no democracy.[1] Charles Tilly defines the state as follows:

> an organization which controls the population occupying a definite territory is a state in so far as: 1 – It's differentiated from other organizations operating in the same territory, 2 – it's autonomous and 3 – its divisions are formally coordinated with one another.[2]

The legitimacy of the state must not be questioned by any substantial group within it. If there is a 'nationality group that claims the right of self-determination' as is the case with the Kurds in Iraq, then the state legitimacy is questioned and this complicates matters for democracy or even for inter-state peace.[3] 'When a large minority in a country is considered by another country as irredenta and where titular nationality and its leaders pursue an aggressive nation-building policy that alienates minorities, who then turn to neighbouring countries for support' then there is a reason to question the state.[4]

In northern Iraq, there is a substantial Kurdish minority that has been pursuing a policy of 'self-determination' since the creation of the Iraqi state. This has weakened Iraq as a state and created a stateness problem. The Kurdish minority has never settled in Iraq since the creation of the Iraqi state in 1921. According to Michael Eisenstadt, there were Kurdish rebellions against central government as early as 1919–1920, as well as in later years (1923–1924, 1931–1932 and 1935–1936).[5] In 1927 there were disturbances in northern Kurdish areas led by the two prominent leaders, Sheikh Ahmed of Barzan and Sheikh Mahmud.[6] The two leaders have also demanded independence, although their aim was parochial, depending on tribal support.[7] Prior to Iraq's full independence and proposed membership of the League of Nations, Sheikh Mahmud led an armed revolt demanding the separation of Kurdistan and turning it into a British protectorate.[8] The revolt was suppressed with the help of RAF and Sheikh Mahmud was sent into exile in Nassiria, southern Iraq. Later, the Kurdish leaders' demands were modified and petitioned the League of Nations for cultural autonomy and self-rule.[9]

Iraq followed an Arabization programme in education and text books which emphasized secular and progressive themes, Arab nationalism and patriotism rather than ethnic separatism favoured by the Kurds.[10] This policy has further alienated the Kurds, especially during the Ba'ath regime when the state adopted a pan-Arab ideology. The Kurdish separatist movement sought military support from Iran, exploiting the latter's dispute with Iraq over sovereignty over the Shat Al-Arab waterway, especially after Iran abrogated the 1937 treaty.[11] The Kurdish insurgency became a serious threat to the Iraqi state after many factions joined Barzani, and with the assistance of Iran, the insurgency developed into a full-scale war in 1974.[12] The threat of the insurgency to Iraq forced the Ba'ath regime to enter into humiliating negotiations with the Shah of Iran which culminated in the signing of the 1975 treaty of Algiers in which Saddam Hussein accepted Iran's claim that the Thalweg line should form the border between the two countries in Shat Al-Arab, and in return, Iran would cease all support for Barzani and the Kurdish separatists. The Kurdish revolt collapsed within days and 150,000 peshmerga with Kurdish leaders crossed the border to Iran, while thousands others accepted the offered amnesty from the government.[13]

But demands for Kurdish independence continued even after the setback of 1975. The Kurdish armed movement resurged in later years. It remained at war with the central government almost continuously, except in periods where there was some temporary understanding. In 1991, following the failure of the intifada, the UN created a safe haven for the Kurds in the three provinces where most of the Kurdish population resides. Ever since, the Kurds had enjoyed quasi-independent status. Perhaps this is one of the reasons why irredentist feelings among Kurds have been enhanced, because the sequence of elections didn't serve the consolidation of the state since it started within their region. In Spain, for example, national elections were held before regional elections and this had helped to constitute 'the supportive legal and effective membership of the national (Catalan), state (Spanish) and super-state (European Community)'.[14]

Iraqi Kurdish writer, Kamran Qaradaghi, says the Kurds have made a 'resolution' regarding the establishment of a Kurdish state and it's now a matter of time.[15] Qaradaghi says the Iraqi democracy has not been successful and the Kurdish sense of belonging to Iraq was weak and has become even weaker after the crackdown on them during the previous regime. He specifically mentioned 'the Anfal operations, ethnic cleansing, the use of chemical weapons and mass graves' during the seventies and eighties of the last century. 'These events have deepened the Kurdish feeling of not belonging to the Iraqi state, especially after the declaration of republican Iraq as an integral part of the Arab nation'. The Kurds insisted on removing the reference to the Arab identity of Iraq from the interim, then permanent constitution in 2004 and 2005 respectively. In a recent survey, 82 per cent of Kurds want independence.[16] As Peter Galbraith put it 'for the older generation, Iraq was a bad memory ... the new generation has no feeling of being Iraqi'.[17]

Sunnis have also been talking of a federal region of Iraq, as mentioned earlier. The Sunni leader, Usamah An-Nujaifi said they were 'unhappy' with the current arrangement. This current 'unhappiness' could develop into something more serious and perhaps a separate Sunni entity might develop. Some 25 per cent of Sunni Arabs support ISIS according to Carnegie Endowment.[18] Only 13 per cent of Sunni Arabs believe things in Iraq are heading in the right direction, 58 per cent feel unfairly represented and 50 per cent feel Iraq is a divided country.[19]

As for the Shia Arabs majority, most of them have deep pride in being Arabs, sharing tradition, customs and sense of Arab identity with the great clans and confederations of Arabia, despite the doctrinal differences.[20] But the fact that they are Shia in a largely Sunni Arab world, which by and large discriminates against them, especially in Saudi Arabia and some Gulf states, makes them feel they need Iran to turn to for support.[21] If the Kurds choose independence, which looks likely, although it will face huge practical difficulties, and if the Sunnis follow suit or go for a federal entity, the Shia may feel compelled to forge closer relations with Iran. Maysoon Aldamluji, a secular Sunni, argues that 'the indifference of some Arab countries to the Shia cause, compared with the ease in relations with the Iranian leadership, has pushed Shia leaders towards Iran'.[22] Iran in this case becomes more influential in Iraq and this is not a good outcome for democracy as long as Iran remains a theocracy.

Some prominent personalities, such as Samir Sumaidaie, say it's unwise for the Shia to turn to Iran, as this will increase the likelihood of confrontation with Arab countries, and he may be right in theory, but politics do not always work according to theory.[23] Akeel Abbas blames discrimination on the assertion of sectarian identity, be it Shia or Wahabi. The Shia, he asserts, never complained before from discrimination by other Arabs against them.[24]

Maysoon Aldamluji contends that Iraq isn't going for division; 'it's hard pill to swallow', she avers. She also rejects the discrimination concept and her evidence is the Lebanese Hizbulla leader, Hassan Nasrullah, was 'idolized by Arabs until he sided with Bashar Al-Assad'. She adds 'the Shia are proud Arabs who refuse to be subordinated to Iran'.[25] Faleh Abdul-Jabbar contends the Iraqi national identity has collapsed and it has been replaced by sect, class or race. 'This collapse of the idea of national identity … limits democracy and weakens it', he asserts.[26]

Civic nationalism is shaped by the presence of strong administrative institutions and flexible elite interests that can adapt to democratization. For civic nationalism to emerge, 'liberal institutions [should] precede mass politics'. Under such conditions, elites do not feel threatened by the changes brought about by the democratic transition and 'nationalism is likely to be inclusive and will probably take a civic form'.[27] Civic nationalism is nurtured by attachment to an assemblage of political ideas and institutions rather than to an ascriptive loyalty, such as ethnic identity. Snyder argues that belligerent nationalism can thrive even in cases with strong liberal press and lively civil society, such as Weimar Germany. 'Racist, authoritarian nationalism', he notes, 'triumphed at the end of the Weimar Republic, not despite the democratization of political life, but because of it'.[28]

As we saw earlier, democratization could lead to weakening of the state and perhaps division. Khalil Osman argues that 'democratization intensified the process of the hardening of ethnic and sectarian identities in post-2003 Iraq ... democratization undermined the prospects of coexistence among various communities and fomented inter-communal conflict'.[29]

Ali Allawi detected a key shift in Shia thinking 'from the politics of victimization to an insistence on their right as a majority'. As such, a mere 'acknowledgement of democracy and democratic rules of practice would no longer be sufficient to assuage the majority of the Shia'.[30] While, he admits, not all the Shia subscribed to this new thinking, a very large majority did so, 'moving the fulcrum of political identity and loyalty away from secular groups to and towards Islamists and sectarian figures. The pattern of Iraqi political life had decisively altered'.[31]

As Allawi has noticed, there were three contrasting currents flowing together in the drive to establish Iraq's sovereignty. The first comprised the CPA, the liberals and the Kurdish camp. They were trying to 'fashion the outlines of a federal and secular state in the broadly familiar terms of a modern pro western democracy'. The second comprised UN envoy Brahimi, the UN and Arab countries who sought to maintain 'some vestige of the old united Iraq with a clear Arab identity and re-empower Sunni Arabs'.

The third was represented by 'Sistani who articulated the demands of the Shia and ... insisted on a role for Islam and its teachings in the new order'.[32] Sistani dominated the proceedings 'not by his detailed interventions in the political process, but by setting markers that he considered sacrosanct such as the broad acknowledgement of Islam'.[33] Sistani, according to Allawi, achieved his objectives, not just through reference to Islam, but by inference to democratic theory'.[34]

Dia Shakarchi regards the feeling of belonging to a sect (rather than a state) as 'the biggest impediment to the process of democratic transition' followed by belonging to religion, ethnicity and region. He also senses a weak sense of belonging to the motherland in Iraq.[35] Wahda Al-Jumaili regards the 'ambition of the Kurds and their attempts to impose their will on the central government and their exploitation of Sunnis-Shia differences as a problem for democracy'.[36] Abdul-Khaliq Hussein regards the Kurdish issue as one of the challenges to democracy. He argues the Kurds are 'suspicious of any regime in Baghdad even the one that is elected democratically. That's why they are always in conflict with the federal government, and this poses a threat to democracy'.[37] The presence of diverse cultures and more than one nation makes pursuing democratization difficult. 'Congruence between polity and demos would facilitate the creation of democratic nation-state'.[38] Conversely, polis/demos incongruence creates problems for democratic consolidation unless carefully addressed.[39]

In sum, Iraq has a stateness problem, and this is not conducive to democratic consolidation. The state in all democracies acts as the 'specialised agency for enforcing compliance' and, as time goes by, the state becomes independent of political forces in doing this task.[40] The state's autonomy of intervention by political forces, that is controlled by institutional framework, is 'of fundamental importance in any democracy'.[41]

But what happened in Iraq, in the words of Ali Allawi, was 'the corroded and corrupt state of Saddam was replaced by the corroded, inefficient, incompetent and corrupt state of the new order'.[42] The state institutions are partisan, and since parties are exclusively sectarian or ethnic, the institutions are similarly fashioned. Ministers brought their party followers and relatives to their ministries with no fear of breaking the law.[43] This trend has weakened the state and national identity further.

Rentier state

Iraq depends almost completely on its oil revenue. According to David Nummy, US advisor to the Iraqi finance ministry in 2003, oil revenue constitutes 98 per cent of the Iraqi budget.[44] Luay Al-Khateeb, non-resident fellow at Brookings Institute in Doha, says oil revenues constitute 43 per cent of GDP, 99 per cent of exports and 90 per cent of all federal revenues. Thus, to increase overall revenues, the government is always under pressure to increase oil production capacity regardless of market volatility.[45]

In 1990, Samuel Huntington listed Iraq, together with Iran and others, in the upper-middle-income zone, which is above where transition to democracy might be expected. He said the economic preconditions for democratization were present, but democratization has not occurred.[46] But Huntington had one qualification regarding democratization in these countries. 'The economic well-being of these countries was dependent on oil exports, a situation that enhanced the control of the state bureaucracy and hence provided a less favourable climate for democratization'.[47]

Samir Sumaidaie contends that since Iraq is a rentier state, whoever controls the oil, gains immense political advantage by building a structure of patronage.[48] He contends that oil prolongs undemocratic systems and if it wasn't for the oil, the Iranian regime 'would have gone under long time ago'. Maysoon Aldamluji regards the 'rentier economy' as one of the impediments to democracy.[49]

Farid Ayar explains that the rentier state

> makes people dependent on the state because all resources are in the hands of the government and citizens become dependent on the person who has the money and that is the Prime Minister. He distributes the money as he sees fit and this is one of the biggest obstacles to democracy.

He argues if a private sector exists, 'taxpayers and people in general can hold government officials to account'.[50] Adnan Al-Janabi, a specialist in oil, affirms the 'rentier state' is the most difficult problem to surmount and it's a serious impediment to democracy.[51]

Bassim Anton, an economist, argues that Iraq's dependence on oil revenues

> has weakened democratic transformation because it has led to the stoppage of other productive sectors, especially industry, which are considered the magnet for attracting businesses to productive factories which act to create cultures and facilitate the exchange of information and interests.

He states that selecting workers on the basis of economic interests achieves 'part of democracy'.[52]

Another economist, Kadom Shubber, contends that economic diversification should be part of any sound economic strategy of every nation. 'A well-balanced economy assists in building a mature and healthy democratic system' and this 'requires people to be able to think freely, independently, and confidently'. 'When individuals view their livelihood to be dependent on a linkage with a political party or an organ of the State, their judgment can be impaired, even paralysed, and hence might follow diktats handed down to them', he explains. 'Even a "socialist" system can be anti-democratic', because the state employs most workers and they can be 'strongly impacted by the political party that happens to be in power'.

Shubber contends that Iraq 'had a better-functioning democracy in the 1920's, 30's and 40's than in subsequent decades when substantial increases in oil revenues were forthcoming'. 'As oil income began to flow in increasing amounts, other economic sectors were neglected, while the ruling class saw no pressing need to take heed of people's views or to subject themselves to national scrutiny'.[53]

Oil prices have collapsed since 2015 and this has eliminated 60 per cent of oil's previous market value.[54] Everyone now recognizes that dependence on oil has many drawbacks. Thus, falling oil prices 'may present a real opportunity for reform in Iraq'.[55] When Iraq moves away from the rentier state, people will have more say in their own affairs since they will be paying through taxes to finance state activities. Economic restructuring takes a long time to have an effect. With other problems facing the country, this may even take longer.

Experts say high oil prices have intensified corruption and widened bureaucracy. Tim Arango explains,

> When oil was selling at $90 to $100 a barrel ... the cash fed a corrupt political system based on patronage. Instead of investments in public services, the money fed an unsustainable expansion of government payrolls and with it a rise in consumer spending.[56]

Rentier state is clearly a problem for democracy and unless Iraq moves away from it, democracy will remain weak.

Reforms of the economy are urgently needed to reduce reliance on oil revenue. But can the current government or even system undertake such necessary reforms with all the party rivalries and infighting? 'Fragmented and polarized party systems heighten partisan rivalries, magnify conflicts among organised interests and weaken the capacity of the executive to initiate reform'.[57] Political factors can lead politicians to discount future gains because of impending elections or to avoid protests or riots.[58] This has happened several times in Iraq, once when the government decided to abolish the ration card and again when it wanted to increase the prices of electricity.[59]

Level of economic prosperity

I have established that democracy requires a state to consolidate, but this state must be strong and economically prosperous for democracy to be stable. In addition, there is a need for a strong middle class, high levels of literacy and education, limited inequality, a productive market economy and a vigorous civil society.[60] This has been proven, although democracy has expanded to poor countries such as Mali, which didn't meet the classic conditions since it has high level of illiteracy, dire poverty and life expectancy of 44 years.[61]

Iraq had suffered in its recent history from two devastating wars, 12-year sanctions, a brutal dictatorship which led to a steady economic decline and destruction of the middle class. Per capita income had fallen by over a half to $1000. Education and health levels had declined sharply, child mortality rates had increased several times, and infrastructure had deteriorated while foreign debt had piled up to a staggering $200 billion. Over 40 per cent of Iraqi adults are illiterate.[62]

Iraq was in the upper-middle-income zone in 1990, which is above where transition to democracy might be expected.[63] But with the deterioration and destruction listed above, most of which had taken place after 1990, Iraq was well below the economic level required for democratization. In addition, Iraq was wholly dependent on oil exports as we saw in the last section, which enhanced the control of the state bureaucracy and provided a less favourable climate for democratization.[64]

One of the five conditions that must exist for democracy to be consolidated is institutionalized economic society.[65] This didn't exist in Iraq then, nor does it exist now. The other four are: lively civil society, autonomous political society, rule of law and independent associational life and usable state bureaucracy.

Democratization in Iraq coincided with economic, infrastructure, social and educational devastation and that was not conducive to successful democratization since people lacked the basic necessities required for a normal modern life. Iraq has faced dire economic difficulties over the last two years due to falling oil prices. It's struggling to meet its obligations to state employees and is unable to maintain basic services such as education and health care. In sum, the low level of economic development doesn't help push democratization forward.

Weak institutions

It was established earlier that democracy needs civil society, political society, economic society, rule of law, and a functioning state bureaucracy. Under the dictatorship of Saddam Hussein, there were neither political nor civil societies. Since the state controlled everything and depended on oil revenue, there was hardly any economic society that is not related to the state in which abound the practices of coercion, nepotism and whim.

The state under dictatorship was

> an engine of power, accumulating resources, deploying patronage and maintaining control over its inhabitants ... centered on the restrictive circles of

Saddam Hussein's associates, linked to him either through bonds of kinship and regional background or through history of personal trust.[66]

Samuel Huntington called the regime type in Iraq, alongside the one in Cuba, a 'personal dictatorship'.[67] According to Ali Allawi, when the Americans entered Iraq in April 2003, they found the institutions of the state 'moribund and the state exhausted', while 'the ideology that had held Ba'athist rule together had decayed beyond repair'.[68]

For Saddam, and Al-Bakir before him, even the Ba'ath Party 'was an extension of their personal power through a system of patronage which they alone would control'.[69] Despite the socialist rhetoric of the regime, all economic directives were geared to enhancing the control of the regime and its associates.[70]

Kadom Shubber contends by 2003 Iraq had

> antiquated bureaucracy, without any internationally acceptable legal system or transparent or just enforcement framework. The State apparatuses became by far the most violent, savage and erratic part of Iraqi society, thereby convincing ordinary people the only effective deterrent to malpractice, crime, corruption and other wrongdoings was harsh punishment or the prospect of it.[71]

Samir Sumaidaie charges that 'although the new system has some of the trappings of democracy, it remains without some of the important institutions to make it work'.[72]

Faleh Abdul-Jabbar contends the independent institutions are now undermined. They have been added to executive institutions, such as the Sunni and Shia endowments which manage mosques, and the two must be separated in a democracy. 'There is ambiguity regarding them, and now the council of ministers wants to take charge of them. These must be independent of the executive authority and supervised by parliament, not the government'.[73]

Ayad Allawi lists the 'absence of law and order, lack of institutions, failure of the judiciary and its control by the executive and the dismantling of the state', as reasons for the failure of democracy. He explains that 'the starting point for the democratic process is the presence of the rule of law, basic rights of citizens and citizenship, and the presence of institutions that can defend democracy' and these are non-existent.[74]

Akeel Abbas asserts that state machinery performance is 'abysmally poor, particularly in its upper echelons and decision-making bodies'.[75] He blames this on religious and sectarian slogans which 'helped bring unqualified officials who may have hidden their inabilities behind their religious rhetoric'.

Maysoon Aldamluji charges that one of the impediments to democracy is 'the absence of democratic institutions and the weakness of the judicial system'.[76]

Shorouq Al-Abayachi blames a weak social fabric and state institutions for the failure of democracy. She states:

> in the light of the rupture in the social fabric of Iraqi society, which is based on sectarian and ethnic basis, and the absence of the force of law and

security, as well as the absence of real developmental programmes and a vision for social and institutional reforms, all these have weakened, in a big way, the prospects of an entrenched democratic experiments over the next ten years.[77]

Wahda Al-Jumaili contends the state is generally weak and blames other social ills such as sectarianism on state weakness.[78] Ibrahim Al-Haidari blames the rise of undemocratic forces on the 'weakness of the state and the spirit of citizenship, the split identity and the non-development of real and effective democratic forces in society'.[79]

It is now established that Iraqi state institutions were weak under Saddam and became weaker and corrupt under the new order and this is an impediment to democracy.

Corruption

Democracy is consolidated

> when a particular system of institutions becomes 'the only game in town',[80] when no one can imagine acting outside the democratic institutions, when all losers want to do is to try again within the same institutions under which they have lost.[81]

When democracy becomes 'self-enforcing' we can think of it as established and entrenched within a society. This means when all the participants feel they find it best for their interests to use the existing system and have hope to get improvement sometime in the future. In other words, when democracy becomes a benefit to all and it's harmful for any political force to try and subvert it.

But is this enough to protect democracy? No, says Adam Przeworski. He suggests some 'rules of punishment, a bureaucracy to detect noncompliance and a set of incentives for the bureaucracy to detect it and apply the rules'.[82]

But punishment cannot be effective if detection techniques are not working, especially when officials are easily bribed.[83] Corruption is widespread in Iraq and all the efforts to limit it have failed. Not a single person in Iraq today disagrees with this fact. One 'courageous' MP admitted that 'everyone is corrupt including me. I was offered $5m by someone to stop investigating him. I took it, and continued prosecuting him anyway!', Mishaan Al-Jabouri was quoted as saying.[84] Sami Al-Askari explains that corruption is widespread and 'the prevailing social culture doesn't condemn it to the point that some people envy corrupt officials and wish they had the opportunity to practice financial corruption themselves and make illegal material gains'.[85]

Ayad Allawi regarded corruption as one of the impediments to democracy.[86] So did Samir Sumaidaie, Waleed Al-Hilli, Kadom Shubber, Kanan Makiya, Dia Shakarchi, Ali Allawi, Sharwan Al-Wa'eli, Farid Ayar, Abdul-Khaliq Hussein, Shorouq Al-Abayachi and Kamran Qaradaghi, among others.[87] Shakarchi charges that 'Corruption was strengthened through hiding behind religious and sectarian slogans'. He senses a 'mutual cover up of corruption among the same political foes'. Corruption cases are brought against individuals from rival parties but a deal is always reached to drop cases against each other.

Judiciary is perceived to be biased as the Federal Court has passed many rulings that were thought to be in favour of the government, especially under the premiership of Noori Al-Maliki, when the court allowed the formation of election lists after the announcement of election results.[88] This could create a potential for 'endless negotiations after every election'.[89]

There were also many verdicts passed against individuals accused of corruption or terrorism but were overturned after 'deals' were struck or after the new PM, Haider Al-Abadi, took over from the previous PM.[90]

Sharwan Al-Wa'eli points to politicians 'who can be bought with an armoured car or half a million dollars'. He reveals that he referred more than 500 corruption cases to the Commission of Public Integrity (CPI) but the judiciary didn't act because there was no oversight. 'Even MPs who signed the referral of cases are now outside parliament', he reveals. 'This is a message to anyone who speaks out against corruption; it will backfire on you' he exclaims.

He claims there are judges who occupy important positions but have 'weak points'. 'He who has a weak point is led easily', Al-Wa'eli declares. In other words, they can be easily blackmailed. He is referring to judges who cooperated with the Saddam regime. Those judges are weak because if they do not cooperate with the new rulers, they will be dismissed as 'Ba'athists or remnants of the previous regime'.

Kamal Field emphasizes the need for 'good governance' which he believes is still lacking in Iraq. 'According to international experience, democracy requires the strict application of law and this is proportionately linked to the educational and cultural state of society', he asserts. Bassim Anton regards corruption as an impediment to democracy.

Farid Ayar sees corruption as the biggest problem in Iraq today. He also blames the US for corruption, and says, 'Some Americans who came to Iraq were corrupt. There was corruption in many of the contracts that they brought to us including contracts for the IHEC'.[91] Adil Abdur-Raheem warns that 'an environment conducive to corruption' has been created by the 'politicians' double standard' and this can render the democratic political process devoid of its content.[92]

CPI director, Hassan Al-Yassiri, announced early in March 2016 that he had asked the central government to issue arrest warrants for 2165 officials charged with embezzlement of public funds, and the list includes six ministers.[93]

Ali Allawi describes current politicians as 'utterly unprincipled and corrupt' who seek to 'enhance their individual and family claims on power'.[94]

Corruption exists in all ministries. An entire battalion of the Iraqi police was found to be non-existent, while corruption is widespread in the army with ghost employees and shortage of supplies.[95] PM Al-Abadi announced that he has identified 50,000 'ghost soldiers' who didn't exist and he scraped their positions.[96]

The US embassy accused the Maliki government of being 'incapable of even rudimentary enforcement of anticorruption laws'.[97]

James Mattil, the US senior consultant to CPI, told the Senate 'Iraq's endemic corruption is an integral element of the insurgency, providing money, personnel and motivation to insurgents and terrorists'.[98] Terrorist groups, such as ISIS, have funded their activities through corruption before they seized territories in Iraq.[99]

Corruption is a serious impediment to democracy in Iraq because it weakens state institutions which are responsible for enforcing the system and render them ineffective. The judiciary, election commission, parliament, police, army and even the integrity commission, are all accused of corruption and very few people trust them. Corruption is responsible for funding insurgents and terrorists. Those who are hostile to democracy try to link democracy to economic success 'because they expect economic crises to turn some civilians against democracy which will increase the probability of a successful subversion to which they would respond ... by overthrowing democracy'.[100] Unless corruption is brought under control, democracy in Iraq will remain vulnerable.

Weak and divided secular movement

I have explained the strengths and weaknesses of Islamist parties throughout the study, and how they managed to get into power through fair means and foul. But one of the important factors that helped Islamists seize and maintain power is the weakness and division among secular parties, right from the outset. The two main secular parties, INA and INC, which are led by two formidable and resourceful leaders, Ayad Allawi and Ahmed Al-Chalabi, were so hostile to each other that they preferred to form alliances with Islamists rather than with each other.

Ahmed Al-Chalabi joined the main Shia list, UIA, and became deputy PM in 2005. When UIA splintered into two lists, SoL and NIC, he joined SIIC within NIC. Ayad Allawi had a unique opportunity when he was chosen to be the interim PM in 2004, but he was unable to unite secular groups under his leadership. When he lost the premiership in 2005, he remained at the political periphery until 2010 when he formed an alliance with Sunni Islamists such as Tarik Al-Hashimi and Mahmoud Al-Mash-hadani and others, but couldn't make rapprochement with Ahmed Al-Chalabi or other secular groups and personalities. Although he managed to maintain his nationalist line, the group he was leading looked more Sunni than pan-Iraqi.

Allawi admits that secular parties have failed. 'National and socialist parties have failed after decades of being in power'.[101] He attributes the failure to external factors such as the Cold War, although he admits they are also due to intrinsic factors.

The third secular force was the Dialogue Front led by Salih Al-Mutleg. Although Al-Mutleg was able to join with Ayad Allawi in 2010 to form the Iraqia List, it was a temporary and fragile alliance that disintegrated immediately after the elections when Mutleg abandoned Iraqia and joined the Maliki government, becoming deputy PM. Ahmed Al-Chalabi died in November 2015, and his INC party has no prospect of remaining in politics, since it was almost a 'one man show' right from the beginning. His companion and head of security, Aras Habib, a Shia Kurd, has succeeded him. Allawi has maintained his pan-Iraqi secular nationalist stance, but he failed to form a true democratic party with obvious successors should he decide to retire, considering he is in mid-seventies. Al-Mutleg has apparently given up on pan-Iraqi nationalist politics. After the 2014 elections,[102] in which he lost half of his parliamentary seats, he joined the Sunni alliance of UIF.

For democracy to succeed, there must exist a united, dynamic and really democratic national force with clear policies and charismatic leaders. This has continued to elude Iraq. Ayad Allawi acknowledges secular parties have failed. Farid Ayar charges 'secular parties in third world countries are too negligent'.[103] Wahda Al-Jumaili hopes to see a civil state that believes in human beings and asserts this can only develop if 'civic parties that believe in humanity before anything else develop'. She blames secular parties for lacking serious propositions for a national inclusive plan.[104]

Dia Shakarchi blames secular parties for being hesitant in declaring their secular views while Hani Fahs says 'secularism has a bad connotation in our culture' although it's associated with democracy.[105] Kamal Field asserts that people are influenced by the views of clergymen or tribesmen because 'the options available ... are a few'.[106] This shows if there was a solid secular movement, the electorate would have more choices. Akeel Abbas argues 'without secular parties that transcend sects and ethnicities, Iraq will continue to be prey to sectarian and ethnic strife'.[107]

As we saw earlier, Islamist parties have united at crucial times to defeat their opponents, and this has happened in 2005, 2010 and 2014, while secular parties have failed to do so. In 2010, there was one strong list (Iraqia) but it was made up of disparate Islamist and nationalist parties which were not able to last long. Unless there is a solid secular and democratic movement that has a long-term political aim (as opposed to personal ambitions of individual party leaders), Islamist parties would continue to dominate the political scene in Iraq. Since Islamists, by their own admission, are not committed to liberal democracy, this will continue to be an impediment to democracy.

Absence of capable national leaders

The Iraqi democratic process has failed to produce national leaders and statesmen who command national respectability and approval. In the words of Ali Allawi 'there were only Shia, Sunni and Kurdish politicians, a smattering of self-styled liberals and secularists, each determined to push their particular agenda forward'.[108] Kanan Makiya describes the political class as 'small men with no vision. They treated Iraq as booty'.[109] Samir Sumaidaie calls the whole process 'kleptocracy'.[110] Maysoon Aldamluji lists the lack of vision among the ruling elite as one of the obstacles to democracy.[111] Wahda Al-Jumaili, too, blames the 'discord, division and weakness of social peace and favouring sub-identities over national identity' on the failing of politicians who are decision makers.[112]

When the people are divided ethnically and religiously, political leaders cannot win without using sectarian rhetoric. Islamists are divided even within the same sect. Secularists are always divided. This problem will continue until leaders with national, cross-sectarian and cross-ethnic discourse are found. One of the main reasons for the success of the Spanish democratization was the 'innovative leadership of Prime Minister Adolfo Suarez'.[113] He managed to stir the democratization process delicately but steadily, including all political forces but insisting on the application of basic democratic principles such as holding national elections and articulating key issues of democracy. One of the factors contributing to the first and second reverses according to Samuel Huntington was the weakness of democratic values among key elite groups and the general public.[114]

Iraq has no capable leaders who can rise to the status of nation builders. The absence of national leaders can be blamed on the sectarian and ethnic divisions and the instability of the country since independence in 1921. Without principled and inspiring leaders, with a clear vision for the future, democracy cannot be consolidated and reversal could take place, or worse, disintegration of the country.

Divided polities

Iraqis are divided on sectarian, religious and ethnic grounds. This can be seen in their political discourse as one can clearly detect the ethnicity, sect or religion of an Iraqi from the direction of their political discourse. Divided polities make matters difficult for democracy since they reflect the conflicting identities and mutual suspicion among citizens. Political differences are normal in a democratic country, but deep divisions among the people on constitutional essentials always impede national reconciliation and encourage politicians to exploit them. The more linguistic, cultural and national diversity there is, the more difficult politics becomes, because it would be difficult to reach an agreement on the fundamentals of a democracy.

There are many states that are multi-national, multi-cultural and multi-lingual, and it is difficult to make them homogeneous; perhaps the only democratic way to make them homogeneous is through voluntary assimilation.[115] Some political elites, especially among minorities, emphasize primordial values and characteristics for emotional and self-interest reasons. This is a new phenomenon; it didn't exist in preindustrial societies, but now exists even in agrarian societies.[116]

The problem of divided polities can be overcome by state policies that grant inclusive and equal citizenship that give all citizens a common 'roof' of state-mandated and enforced individual rights. There is also a need to explore a variety of non-majoritarian and non-plebiscitarian formulas.[111] Federalism is an option but only if there are spatial differences between the different groups. In Iraq, the spatial differences between groups are not always well defined. But most important is for the state to adopt a policy of enhancing public reason and at the same time discouraging, maybe barring, divisive discourse.

Notes

1 Linz and Stepan (1996) op. cit. p. 17. Also Diamond (2005) op. cit. p. 23
2 Linz and Stepan (1996) op. cit. p. 17
3 Ibid., p. 26
4 Ibid.
5 Eisenstadt and Mathewson (2003) op. cit. p. 68
6 Tripp (2007) op. cit. p. 62
7 Ibid.
8 Ibid., p. 66
9 Ibid.
10 Judith Yaphe (Eisenstadt and Mathewson, 2003) op. cit. p. 48
11 Tripp (2007) op. cit. p. 194
12 Ibid., p. 2004
13 Ibid., pp. 2004–2005
14 Linz and Stepan (1996) op. cit. p. 102
15 Interview with Kamran Qaradaghi
16 Greenberg Quinlan Rosner Research, August–September 2015, NDI, 23/11/2015: https://goo.gl/Hp72pk
17 Diamond (2005) op. cit. p. 22
18 Renad Mansour Carnegie Endowment, 3/3/2016: https://goo.gl/v2qFIH
19 Greenberg Quinlan Rosner Research, August–September 2015, NDI (footnote 730)
20 Judith Yaphe, *US Policy in Post-Saddam Iraq* (2003) op. cit. p. 39
21 Interviews with Kadom Shubber, Samir Sumaidaie, Kamran Qaradaghi respectively
22 Interview with Maysoon Aldamluji
23 Interview with Samir Sumaidaie
24 Interview with Akeel Abbas
25 Interview with Maysoon Aldamluji
26 Interview with Faleh Abdul Jabbar
27 Snyder (2000) pp. 76–77
28 Ibid., p. 118
29 Interview with Khalil Osman
30 Allawi (2007) p. 137
31 Ibid., p. 138
32 Ibid., p. 231
33 Ibid.
34 Ibid., pp. 231–232
35 Interview with Dia Shakarchi
36 Interview with Wahda Al-Jumaili
37 Interview with Abdulkhaliq Hussein
38 Linz and Stepan (1996) op. cit. p. 25
39 Ibid., p. 26
40 Przeworski (1991) op. cit. p. 25
41 Ibid.
42 Ibid., p. 460
43 Musings on Iraq, 'How the US ran into party politics', 9/1/2013: https://goo.gl/zcWgXk
44 Bremer (2007) op. cit. p. 28
45 Brookings, 13/12/2015: www.brookings.edu/opinions/iraqs-economic-reform-for-2016/
46 Huntington (1991) op. cit. p. 312

47 Ibid., p. 313
48 Interview with Samir Sumaidaie
49 Ibid.
50 Interview with Farid Ayar
51 Interview with Adnan Al-Janabi
52 Interview with Bassim Anton
53 Interview with Kadom Shubber
54 Luay Al-Khateeb-Brookings, 13/12/2015, op. cit.
55 Ibid.
56 Tim Arango, *India Times*, 1/2/2016: https://goo.gl/GlFq8k
57 Haggard and Kaufman (1995) op. cit. p. 14
58 Ibid., p. 157
59 Rami Ruhayem, 'Iraq struggles to reform "inefficient" ration system', BBC, 21/7/2012: www.bbc.co.uk/news/world-middle-east-18916653
60 Diamond (2005) op. cit. p. 19
61 Ibid., p. 20
62 Ibid., pp. 20–21
63 Huntington (1991) op. cit. p. 312
64 Ibid., p. 313
65 Linz and Stepan (1996) op. cit. pp. 7–15
66 Tripp (2007) op. cit. p. 216
67 Huntington (1991) op. cit. p. 41
68 Allawi (2007) op. cit. p. 16
69 Tripp (2007) op. cit. p. 191
70 Ibid., p. 197
71 Interview with Kadom Shubber
72 Interview with Samir Sumaidaie
73 Interview with Faleh Abdul-Jabbar
74 Interview with Ayad Allawi
75 Interview with Akeel Abbas
76 Interview with Maysoon Aldamluji
77 Interview with Shorouq Al-Abayachi
78 Interview with Wahda Al-Jumaili
79 Interview with Ibrahim Al-Haidari
80 Linz and Stepan (1996) p. 5
81 Przeworski (1991) p. 26
82 Ibid., p. 27
83 Ibid.
84 Martin Chulov, *Guardian*, 19/2/2016: https://goo.gl/B4vfem
85 Interview with Sami Al-Askari
86 Interview with Ayad Allawi
87 Interviews with all the names mentioned above
88 David Ghanim, *Iraq's Dysfunctional Democracy*, Praeger (2011) op. cit. p. 122
89 Kenneth Pollack, 'A government for Baghdad', Brookings Institute, 27/7/2010: https://goo.gl/HtjqZw
90 Going Global East Meet West website, 22/12/2014: https://goo.gl/V4Xnn2
91 Interview with Sharwan Al-Waeli
92 Interview with Adil Abdur-Raheem
93 Rudaw report, 3/7/2016: https://goo.gl/g9L9ws
94 Interview with Ali Allawi
95 Arab Anti-corruption Organization, 2016: https://goo.gl/kLhRY2
96 Ned Parker, 'Power failure in Iraq as militias outgun state', Reuters 21/10/2015: https://goo.gl/CShh3e
97 The Nation, 30/8/2007: https://goo.gl/39YaSv

98 James F. Mattil, Senate Democratic Policy Committee, no specific date (2007): https://goo.gl/fc4ADC
99 Brooke Satti Charles, Security Intelligence, 10/10/2104: https://goo.gl/l9pmOh
100 Przeworski (1991) op. cit. p. 33
101 Interview with Ayad Allawi
102 Election Guide, Iraq, 2014: www.electionguide.org/elections/id/2425/
103 Interview with Farid Ayar
104 Interview with Wahda Al-Jumaili
105 Interviews with Dia Shakarchi and Hani Fahs
106 Interview with Kamal Field
107 Interview with Akeel Abbas
108 Allawi (2007) op. cit. p. 460
109 Interview with Kanan Makiya
110 Interview with Samir Sumaidaie
111 Interview with Maysoon Aldamluji
112 Interview with Wahda Al-Jumaili
113 Linz and Stepan (1996) op. cit. p. 93
114 Huntington (1991) op. cit. p. 290
115 Linz and Stepan (1996) op. cit. p. 30
116 Ibid., p. 31
117 Ibid., p. 33

13 Conclusion

The original contribution of this book to the body of knowledge is that it has identified the main impediments to democracy in Iraq and provided insight, through its recommendations, into finding ways to overcome those impediments and consolidate democracy. The book has explored the democratization process in Iraq thoroughly, examined it from within, taken the opinions of different participants, experts and observers, compared it, in certain relevant aspects, to the experiences of other countries in southern Europe, eastern Europe and Latin America, which have democratized in the last few decades, and finally weighed up the progress made so far and the challenges ahead, in an academic and impartial way.

Although the book pertains to Iraq, many of its findings can be generalized to other Arab and Muslim countries because Iraq shares, in varying degrees, many cultural and religious characteristics with Arab and Muslim countries. Since democracy is a new phenomenon in the Arab world, this study sheds some light on impediments facing democracy in Arab and Muslim societies, and therefore, it has enhanced the theory of Arab democracy and raised awareness about impediments which are likely to be encountered in other countries if they decide to democratize.

One of the basic pillars of democracy is liberalism, and this has been explored in detail, taking the thoughts of one of the leading scholars of liberalism, John Stuart Mill, into account. It has also examined the role of religion in politics and examined in detail the ideas of one of the most important political thinkers in this field, John Rawls, who has studied this phenomenon in depth and provided some important insights that can be useful to the Iraqi experience.

Rawls' ideal of a political conception of justice that is 'free-standing' in order to appeal to all citizens is what is needed in Iraq. Our modern society, as described by Rawls, is characterized by pluralism, objection to oppression, quest for justice, debate and dissensus. Therefore, no single religion or philosophical doctrine can be affirmed by all free people. Thus, in order to enable all citizens to feel equal, it's important that the democratic state doesn't adopt any religious or philosophical doctrine.

The book also explored democracy as a concept and how it developed over the years and what are its main institutions and benefits through the ideas of

Robert Dahl, Joseph Schumpeter, John Dunn, Samuel Huntington, Juan Linz, Alfred Stepan, Adam Przeworski, John Keane, Barrington Moore and Larry Diamond. Their ideas were not accepted entirely but compared and discussed in connection with realities in Iraq.

Since democracy cannot just happen without a preliminary process of liberalization and democratization, there was a need to examine the experiences of other countries such as Spain, Portugal, Greece, and Latin American and Eastern European countries. Each country has a different process depending on the type of the non-democratic regime it was governed by.

In Eastern Europe, the Polish experience was totally different to the Romanian one because the non-democratic regimes in both countries were different. Similarly, the Spanish experience, which was considered most successful, was different to the Greek's or even to neighbouring Portugal's. Democratization becomes a lot easier if the non-democratic regime was authoritarian as was the case in Spain and Poland. But it becomes a lot more complicated if the previous regime was totalitarian, post-totalitarian, or worse, a sultanistic or personal dictatorship such as Romania and Iraq.[1]

In addition to the complication left by the previous regime, which could be formidable, especially if it's totalitarian or sultanistic, under which democracy crafters have to start from scratch by establishing political, civil and economic societies, as well as the rule of law and functioning bureaucracy, there are other problems to be considered, such as stateness, economic development and educational standard.

Spain was considered a classic example of success since, like Iraq, it had irredentist tendencies in the Basque and Catalan regions but it managed to overcome them. It surpassed all the problems due to the exceptional qualities of Prime Minister Adolfo Suarez, the support it received from European countries and the US, the sequence of elections (national then regional) and the inclusive policies that were pursued, allowing all political parties to participate in elections, even those connected to irredentist tendencies and terrorism. This success may not have been possible if it wasn't for the liberalization policies and openness of the authoritarian regime of Gen. Franco. Iraq could have benefited, and perhaps it could still do so, from the Spanish experience of inclusiveness and dealing with irredentist tendencies, notwithstanding the difference between the Franco and Saddam regimes.

The type of democratic system is also important for any democracy. A presidential system gives more powers to the president who owes his powers directly to the people who elected him or her, and therefore, doesn't always conform to the parliament's wishes, while a prime minister has to always satisfy parliament which has the power to withdraw confidence from his or her government. The book didn't elaborate on this issue because Iraq has already adopted a parliamentary system which is regarded as better for countries which are ethnically and religiously diverse.

In order to be relevant to Islam, which matters a lot in the Iraqi recent experience, the study explored the thoughts of Sheikh Ali Abdu-Razik on the issue of caliphate/imamate, or Islamic government, which he proved was not necessary in Islam, if not harmful to it. The book also examined, as time and space allowed, the thoughts of other important scholars such as Hani Fahs, who was interviewed exclusively for this study, Muhammed Mahdi Shamsuddeen, Muhammed Hussein Fadhlalla and Abdulla Nuri among others, who believed (respectively) in secular democracy, people's right to decide for themselves on how they live or be governed, establishing a state for human beings and nothing is absolute except God.

There is no role more relevant to democratization in Iraq than the one played by the Shia spiritual leader, Ayatullah Ali Sistani, which was largely positive but controversial due the exploitation of Islamist parties of his name and position. Sistani insisted on holding elections for the national assembly, not favoured by the Americans and secular Iraqi parties, and also encouraged the people to vote and limited the role of Islamist parties in connection with the permanent consti- tution. Holding elections before drafting the constitution had negative implica- tions since the winners imposed their wishes on the losers and enshrined them in the constitution. Balanced constitutions are the ones written before parties knew their political weights.

I examined the two trends in Shia Islam, the quietist tradition of Ayatullah Khoei and interventionist trend of Ayatullah Khomeini. Ayatullah Sistani is believed to stand in between, but closer to quietist than interventionist, support- ing no unnecessary intervention but no complete abdication of politics.

I have clearly identified what I regard as impediments to democracy after studying the process from different angles. I identified 26 impediments to demo- cratization in Iraq, some of which can be overcome easier than others since they are not on the same level. Most of them could be overcome if the political will existed and the right leaders were found but only with the support of the inter- national community. Other impediments such as stateness, the role of religion, sectarianism, divided polities and the absence of innovative leaders would require exceptional efforts on the part of Iraqis first, but the international com- munity can still back real democrats in Iraq when and if the will to promote democracy exists.

Democracy in Iraq has faltered but it has not failed completely, since it's still going, although with difficulty, but perhaps not for long. There are many chal- lenges ahead, some of which may be insurmountable without support from a strong sponsor. Only the US can deliver such support, but the US seems to have given up on democracy in Iraq. The Obama administration left Iraq to its fate. Trump's administration cannot be relied upon to support democracy. It seems more concerned with Iran than Iraq.

Democracy has many enemies, internal and external, and may not survive without international support and protection.

Some of the ingredients for democracy, such as freedom of expression, access to communication and pluralism, are present and may be permanent. Others, such as personal freedoms, human rights and legal rights are not always avail- able and could be taken away if Islamist parties consolidate their control over the country. On 22 October 2016, Islamists passed a law banning the production, importation and distribution of alcohol in Iraq. More strict applications of Sharia might be on the way if this law is not reversed. It is in the interests of all parties concerned to make the system work, since the alternatives are harmful to everyone for the time being, but some groups believe they have more rights, or power, than others and hence conduct their affairs accordingly.

Adam Przeworski states that because 'any order is better than a disorder, any order is established'.[2] I believe this is what has prevailed so far in Iraq – 'any order'. But the battle between different forces is still flaring. However, according to Hardin (1987), democracy has never been internally subverted in any country in which it lasted for 20 years with the exception of Uruguay.[3] Democracy in Iraq is still under 20 years old. Akeel Abbas contends, 'without secular parties that transcend sects and ethnicities, Iraq will continue to be prey to sectarian and ethnic strife'.[4]

Even secular parties find themselves 'forced' to adopt religious rhetoric which gives the entire political and electoral process a false religious character that is not truly representative. This false spirit of political religiosity will deepen sectarian identities and undermine Iraq's national identity. I argue that as long as the electoral system allows parties based on religion, sect and ethnicity, to operate, it will be difficult to achieve fully consolidated democracy.

Democracy could progress if Western countries have wider engagement with Iraqis, and if they really help the forces of modernity, moderation and reason, which are formidable if they can organize and coordinate their efforts. As Larry Diamond acknowledged, 'it requires a prolonged international engagement with Iraq costing billions of dollars and lasting for a number of years'.[5] It looks that the Islamic Republic of Iran has the upper hand, currently and in the foreseeable future, because it has worked hard to build good relations with most political groups, some of which are directly linked to it.

The US has increased its involvement in Iraq after the ISIS takeover of Musil and other areas in 2014 in an effort to help the country rid itself of the terrorist challenges. But so has Iran. If the US involvement is consolidated, it will strengthen the hands of the democrats and forces of moderation and reason, even among current Islamists. However, the rise of the American right is not conducive to enhancing democracy and moderation across the world. On the contrary, extremism in the West feeds, and provides justification, for extremism in Arab countries, especially when its leaders and promoters hold power. It makes matters worse for democracy if those right-wingers are allies of Israel as is the case with the administration of Donald Trump.

Iraq, even under Islamist rule, will need the help and support of the international community, given its current economic difficulties. This is a window the international democratic forces could use to support democracy. Economic help should be conditional on achieving progress on democracy and respect for civil liberties. If the Western democracies do not engage with Iraq, Islamists, and their Iranian backers, will have the upper hand for a long time to come. It's a continuous battle between forces of modernity and conservatism, secularism and religiosity.

There is no single route to the consolidation of democracy. It's a 'process through which acceptance of a given set of constitutional rules becomes less directly contingent on immediate rewards and sanctions and increasingly widespread and routinized'.[6] According to Haggard and Kaufman,

> the transformation of the institutional arrangements and understandings that emerged at the time of transition into relations of cooperation and competition that are reliably known, regularly practiced and voluntarily accepted by those persons or collectives that participate in democratic governance.[7]

Democratization in Iraq is a flaring battle between the modernists and the traditionalists, federalists and centrists, separatists and unionist, Arabists and Iraqists, and more importantly, between Islamists and secularists. It's going to be a long battle, but democracy will eventually triumph, as it has done elsewhere in the world, when a compromise is reached. Democracy has arrived in Iraq through an arduous and unorthodox route. It has given people freedom and dignity after long years of fear, oppression and humiliation. Islam and democracy must be reconciled in order for them to live side by side, supporting and protecting each other. They share the values of peace, equality, prosperity, human development and justice for all.

Democracy can and will support peaceful and humane Islam, but what needs to be established is whether Islam can also reciprocate and support democracy. The enemies of democracy, with their foreign backers, are trying to set it against Islam for short-term political gains for them and strategic gains for their backers. They have succeeded but only partially so far. The challenge ahead is how can democracy survive in this hostile environment with so many formidable enemies? The tie and turban will continue to interact and the battle will continue for generations to come. Instead of defeating each other, they can live alongside each other since both are there to serve humanity.

Recommendations for reform and further research

Finally, the study finds that for democracy to consolidate in Iraq the following points need to be explored further and addressed:

1 The clear evidence from the research carried out for this study strongly suggests there is a stateness problem in Iraq, which means there is a need for a radical redrawing of institutions and perhaps also of the map of the nation. There cannot be consolidated democracy and freedom in Iraq until the issue of the Kurds is properly addressed. As long as they aspire to join a state other than Iraq, their commitment to the state will be questionable and compromised. Democracy requires all the citizens of the state to feel part of it, obey its laws and work towards strengthening the economic and political system. This is not happening now because of the ambiguity of the Kurdish issue. The Kurds want to establish their own state, but they are unable to,

because neighbouring countries do not accept it. This is likely to continue in the foreseeable future and it means continued instability for Iraq.

2   The Iraqi Constitution is ambiguous and contradictory at certain points. It must be amended in order to remove all ambiguous articles and restrictions on democratic activity and amendment. In particular, articles 2 and 142–4th must be repealed. Research must continue to find the most suitable constitution for a democratic Iraq. It must serve all Iraqis, and no Iraqi should find it in conflict with his or her basic beliefs and convictions. At the same time, it must conform to international law and international human rights conventions.

3   Iraq needs to adopt a totally secular modern system that rejects all types of discrimination between citizens. A total separation between religion and politics is needed to preserve national unity and social harmony and enhance national identity. Civil society is the right place for all religious and philosophical debates.

4   Most political parties are currently based on religion, sect or race. For a stable country, political parties need be formed on a national political and economic basis and no national party should be established on the basis of ethnicity, religion or sect.

5   Iraq has suffered from outside interference in the past. Therefore, and in line with international norms, all political parties, groups, unions, syndicates and organizations must not have secret dealings or relationships with foreign countries or organizations. All their dealings must be declared. This should be enshrined into law. A national independent observatory must be set up to monitor all aspects related to this issue.

6   Iraq needs a proportional representation electoral system, with the whole country as one constituency. This will ensure a wider representation for all groups, especially minorities and those with spatial differences. This system will reduce tension since it guarantees representation for all groups with substantial followings. It also promotes national agendas and discourages regional, ethnic or sectarian tendencies.

7   Iraq has been depleted of its educated and skilled people who have immigrated to other countries. This phenomenon needs to be halted through giving incentives for people to stay and for those abroad to return. For democracy to be consolidated, the country needs to retain its young, capable and professional workforce. All rights acquired by Iraqis in other countries, such as citizenship or residence permits, must never be used as a basis for discrimination. Further research into the problem could provide further evidence of the magnitude of this serious brain drain.

8   De-Ba'athification, or Accountability and Justice Law, has hindered Iraq's progress since it has deprived it from experienced managers and professionals. This law needs to be abolished and all cases of abuse during the previous regime must be dealt with by ordinary courts. Further research into the damage this law has caused to Iraq as well as the perceived benefits could provide more insight into the problem and possible solutions. Those wronged by the law must be compensated appropriately.

9 No Iraqi citizen, except those convicted of crimes, should be barred from participation in the democratic process or holding any public office at any level. Currently, there are legal and practical impediments to people's participation such as the Accountability and Justice Law.

10 All armed groups outside the army and police must be banned. Ways need to be found to incorporate current militias within the state, giving them specific national tasks to implement, as happened in the US after independence. This area is very ambiguous at the moment due to the secret nature of militias and their incorporation into the Popular Mobilization Unit (PMU) or Hashd. Further research could uncover more evidence as to the scale of the threat militias pose to democratization and the stability of the country.

11 The electoral commission must be totally independent of political parties, and nominations and appointments to its managerial board must be done through professional measures. They should be administered through the judiciary with international monitoring. The commission should have its own independent regulatory body that is open to regular monitoring by international bodies and civil society organizations. The UN should be involved in the selection of IHEC's management board as was the case with the first one in 2004, which is regarded as efficient and impartial. Commissioners must be truly independent and apolitical.

12 Independent commissions must be fully independent and each of them must have its own independent regulatory body to oversee its performance and make its findings available to the public. No partisan nominations to the executives of these commissions should be allowed.

13 Since democracy is linked to the free market, Iraq needs a diversified market economy and the government must encourage, enhance and support the private sector and allow and encourage the development of the middle class. This must not be done at the expense of a comprehensive welfare system that ensures basic support for the poor, needy and sick.

14 Revenue from natural resources, such as oil and gas, must be paid into a fund, which can only be used to support the Iraqi state infrastructure. Iraq must cease dependence on oil revenue so that its government would be more accountable to taxpayers. Further research into this phenomenon will be helpful to disclose how damaging oil revenue has been to the democratization process and how it contributed to the creation of the Saddam dictatorship and enticed officials to be corrupt.

15 Employment in state institutions should be done through a central system which operates on the basis of merit. No political, familial, racial or sectarian consideration should be given to any appointment.

16 Government activities should be open and transparent, and all transactions and procedures should be simplified and done electronically in order to prevent corruption. The principle of good governance and e-government should be applied to reduce corruption and speed up procedures.

17 Sectarian and racial discourse inflames hatred and tension between different people and must be eliminated from public debate; this should be done by

the legislation and regulation of the media and the establishment of an independent monitoring body. The whole area of political discourse vis-à-vis religious discourse needs thorough and detailed research as to which religious discourse is less harmful to democratization and which one isn't.

18   All Iraqi media outlets must be independently funded and administered, and no partisan or sectarian channels should be allowed. The state broadcaster, Al-Iraqia (IMN), needs to be independent and run by non-partisan professionals in order to deliver impartial and accurate information to the Iraqi public at large. Media outlets must disseminate impartial and accurate information. Their output must always be in line with the ideal of public reason, enhancing it and strengthening Iraqi national identity.

19   Educational institutions should be run by an independent and apolitical body which must ensure that all Iraqis are entitled to free elementary and secondary education which must be compulsory to guarantee a minimum standard of education. University education should be regulated according to the needs of the country and means available to the state. Incentives should be available for students to enter certain fields that are currently less popular but are vital for the economy. The area of elementary, secondary and university education needs to be explored further in line with the needs of the economy and the financial abilities of the state. Syllabi must enhance the national identity, public reason and Iraqi polity; therefore, they must not include any sectarian, ethnic or any divisive material.

20   The independence of the judiciary should be treated as sacrosanct and an independent regulatory body should be established to monitor the activities of judges, lawyers and the courts to ensure a high level of propriety and conformity with the law and professional conduct code. Judges should also be guaranteed protection for life in order to give them the self-confidence needed to administer justice fairly and without fear. This is important in a tribal society where revenge is commonplace.

21   Police must be trained and educated to the level required by a democratic modern state. They must particularly be exposed to international human rights conventions and laws. There should also be an independent body to monitor their performance.

22   International conventions on human rights, trade, economic development and labour must be respected and Iraq should sign and abide by all international conventions and norms, which are vital for the consolidation of democracy. This will enhance Iraq's integration in the democratic international community and protect Iraq's democratic institutions.

23   With all due respect to cultural, religious and tribal values that people observe, the ultimate arbiter in the country should be the law of the land. No Iraqi should be exempt from the law and no arrangement should be allowed to subvert the law under any circumstances. However, tribal and religious values that accord with international law and democratic principles can be tolerated. Further research is needed find out the extent to which these values can be tolerated, which ones support public reason and which ones

are entrenched and need some time to disappear. Different parts of Iraq vary in the strength and type of tribal values people observe and any research should take this into consideration.

24 The ministry of culture should play a pivotal role in enhancing public belief in democracy, human rights, respect for diversity, personal freedoms and the peaceful resolution of disputes within society. Ever since democratization began, the ministry of culture has been neglected wittingly or unwittingly with disastrous consequences. Iraq is new to democracy and lacks democratic culture, and finding remedies should be the realm of the ministry of culture or functionally similar institution. Research into the type of activities the ministry of culture should engage in is needed.

25 There is a need to nurture and sponsor reforms in religion so that it can conform to democracy, international law and modernity. Moderate forces need to be supported so that they become effective in persuading people that social, political and economic progress can only be made via moderate and peaceful endeavours. The educational and cultural establishments should sponsor debate on the role of religion in a modern society in order to educate people that there should be no conflict between religious ideals and modern democratic principles and civil liberties which form the basis for democracy.

26 Since the Iraqi nation is deeply divided with many polities, it's important to establish an independent institution whose purpose is to explore ways to cement the Iraqi identity, bring the different polities closer, identify reasons that cause divisions and find remedies for them. Such an institution must continue to monitor political and religious discourse and make recommendations to the government on ways to enhance the public reason.

These reforms will consolidate democracy, enhance fairness and strengthen national identity, increase social harmony and stabilize the country politically and economically.

Notes

1 Samuel Huntington regarded Saddam's regime as 'personal dictatorship'; Huntington (1991) op. cit. p. 41
2 Przeworski (1991) p. 86
3 Ibid.
4 Interview with Akeel Abbas
5 Diamond (2005) op. cit. p. 19
6 Haggard and Kaufman (1995) op. cit. p. 15
7 Ibid.

Appendix

Translation of sermon given by Sheikh Jaafar Al-Ibrahimi

This well-known Iraqi preacher said the following in a sermon held in Samawa (undated) broadcast by the Anwar TV Channel. YouTube link, Al-Anwar TV, undated (www.youtube.com/watch?v=eDSDc_L8ZF8). Accessed on 4 May 2016.

> Our problem as a country is not ISIS, not Al Qaeda, not the Kurds or the other components. The problem is the so called United Iraqi Alliance (UIA). This is the reality, leave politics and media talk aside. If you review these people in your mind now, they were 'no bodies' (not known). Has any one of you known them before the establishment of the 169 or so called 'The Candle'? No one knew them. I didn't know them.
>
> But I came to Samawa, Khidhir, Warkaa, Majid and other places in order to promote the list of 169 on behalf of the 'marji'aya' (religious authority) and the 'fudhala' (senior clerics). I, and other clerics, representing the religious establishment, have introduced those people (members of 169 list) to the people (of Iraq). We have got them into power. Before the establishment of list 169, no one has heard of them. Najaf has helped them gain power, but when they got into power, they did not respect Najaf. They didn't listen to Najaf's directions. In fact they now fight Najaf and do not miss an opportunity to marginalize Najaf and its role and weaken its voice, just like the Abbasids.

Bibliography

Abbas, Mouchreq. (2013) 'Iraqi Shiite leaders adapt to changing times', Al-Monitor: www.al-monitor.com/pulse/politics/2012/05/al-sadr-and-al-hakim-the-descend.html

Abbas, Mushreq. (3/3/2014) 'Iraqi justice minister presses Shiite personal status law', Al-Monitor: www.al-monitor.com/pulse/originals/2014/03/iraq-justice-minister-push-shiite-personal-status-law.html

Abbas, Sirwan. (30/12/2015) 'Turkey funds Sunni militia in Iraq, lawmaker says', Rudaw: http://rudaw.net/english/middleeast/291220151

Abuzeed, Adnan. (5/5/2014) 'Iraq State Education increasingly religious', Al-Monitor: https://goo.gl/M661aD

Acikyildiz, B. (2014) *The Yezidis: The History of a Community, Culture and Religion* I.B. Tauris

Ahmad, Malak. (2014) *The Iraqi Literary Syndicate Commemorates the Anniversary of the 14th July Revolution*, Baghdad

Al-Abasi, Mamoon. (20/10/2015) 'Iraq asked Syria's Assad to stop aiding "jihadists"', Middle East Eye: https://goo.gl/iv2Igi

Al-Alawi, Hassan. (1983) *Abdul Kareem Qassim, a Vision after the Twenty*, London, Az-Zawraa House

Al-Alawi, Hassan. (1986) *Al-Jawahiri, the Compendium of the Time*, publications of the Syrian Ministry of Culture

Al-Alousi, Muhammed. (1992) *Shia and Sunna*, London, Darul Hikma

Al-Ani, Tahir Tawfeeq. (24/7/2016) Russia Today (Arabic): https://goo.gl/py0FqT

Al-Ansary, Khalid. (2010) 'Iraq's Sadr calls for ban on bars, nightclubs', Reuters

Al-Azzawi, Abbas. (1935) *The History of Yazidis and the Origins of their Beliefs*, Baghdad, Baghdad Printing House

Al-Bukhari, Muhammad. (1987) *Sahih al-Bukhari*, Hamdaan

Al-Chaderchi, Kamil. (1971) *From the Papers of Kamil Al-Chadirchi*, Beirut, Dar Al-Talieeah,

Al-Dabbagh, Iman Abd al-Hamid. (2011) *The Muslim Brotherhood in Iraq (1959–1971)* Amman, Al-Ma'mun

Al-Dulaymi, Adnan Muhammad Salman. (2012) *The End of the Journey: A Biography and Memoirs*, Amman, Al-Ma'mun

Al-Ghabra, Shafiq Nadhim. (Summer 2001) 'Iraq's culture of violence', Middle East Quarterly: www.meforum.org/101/iraqs-culture-of-violence

Al-Hafidh, Mahdi. (22/8/2015) 'MP Al-Hafidh calls for new technocratic government', New Sabah newspaper (Arabic): www.newsabah.com/wp/newspaper/58576

Al-Haidari, Faraj. (22/1/2009) 'Iraq religious parties may face election backlash', Missy Ryan, Reuters: http://uk.reuters.com/article/us-iraq-election-religion-sb-idUKTRE50L07120090122

Al-Haidari, Muhammed. (18/2/2004) 'Sistani representative: Islam is the basis of legislation', Al-Wasat Magazine: www.alwasatnews.com/530/news/read/370641/1.html

Al-Haj, Azeez. 'Democracy masks': www.aswat.com/en/node/4734

Al-Jaffal, Omar. (30/4/2104) 'Iraqi elections marred by hit squads targeting candidates', Al-Monitor: https://goo.gl/wKGe1S

Al-Hamdani, Hamid. (No Date) 'From the memory of history', www.ahewar.org/debat/show.art.asp?aid=269154

Al-Hassani, Abdulrazzak. (No Date) *The Great Iraqi Revolution*, Al-Muhibbeen Establishment-Qum-Iran

Alghad Press: http://alghadpress.com/

Aljazeera. (9/3/2014) 'Maliki: Saudi and Qatar at war against Iraq': https://goo.gl/3TjCci

Al-Juboori, Shatha. (14/12/2009) 'Head of the Liberal List (Ahrar): Iran manages ruling parties in Iraq with remote control', Alsharq Alawsat: https://goo.gl/R1APkF

Al-Khatteeb, Luay. (13/12/2015) Iraq's Economic Reform for 2016, Brookings: www.brookings.edu/opinions/iraqs-economic-reform-for-2016/

Al-Khayyoon, Rasheed. (30/5/2012) 'Basra: prohibition of music', Al-Ittihad: www.alittihad.ae/wajhatdetails.php?id=66094

Al-Ibrahimi, Sheikh Ja'afar. Video: www.youtube.com/watch?v=eDSDc_L8ZF8

Al-Kubaisi, Sheikh Ahmed. www.youtube.com/watch?v=U2E8M81ntnw

Al-Kubaisi, Sheikh Ahmed. www.youtube.com/watch?v=2u0ABgtC3RA

Al-Maliki, Noori. (24/4/2009) 'Maliki blames Syria for attacks, Assad denies claim', AFP www.france24.com/en/20090901-maliki-blames-syria-attacks-assad-denies-claim

Al-Nafisi, Abdallah Fahad. (1973) *The Role of the Shia in the Political Development of Modern Iraq*, Beirut, Al-Nahar Publishing

Al-Najafi, Ayatullah Basheer. (2014), video: www.youtube.com/watch?v=hAjA-5oump8

Al-Rasheed, Muntadhar and Al-Shibeeb, Dina. (22/9/2012) 'Iraqi night clubs under attack by mysterious agents': http://english.alarabiya.net/articles/2012/09/22/239550.html

Al-Rihani, Ameen. (1959) *Kings of Arabia*, Beirut, Al-Rayhani

Al-Sadr, Muhammed Baqir. Last recorded call, video: www.youtube.com/watch?v=wQqnzWZ2jOk

Al-Sa'edi, Ibrahim. (no date) 'The origin of Turkmen in Iraq', Turkmen Tribune: http://turkmentribune.com/IT/12.html

Al-Salhy, Suadad. (20/4/2006) 'Alfadila Party replaces its leader, Nadim Al-Jabiri, after accusing him of working to split in the coalition', Al-Hayat Newspaper https://goo.gl/pmIKqy

Al-Salhy, Suadad. (19/6/2013) 'Iraqi Shi'ites flock to Assad's side as sectarian split widens', Reuters: https://goo.gl/EwgmZG

Al-Salhy, Suadad. (20/2/2016) 'Unity through division: The Sunni plan to save themselves and Iraq', Middle East Eye: https://goo.gl/VKxs4z

Al-Tabari, Imaduldeen. 'The tools of the Shia in reaching the issues of the Sharia', http://alkafeel.net/islamiclibrary/hadith/

al-Uzri, Abd al-Karim. (1982) 'History of Iraq in Memoirs', Al-Abjadiyya Centre, Beirut

Al-Uzri, Abdul Kareem. (1991) *The Problem of Governance in Iraq*, self-published, London

Al-Wardi, Ali. (2005) *Glimpses of Iraq's Modern History*, Volumes 1–6, Darul Kitab Al-Islami

Alkifaey, Hamid. (19/9/2002) 'Throw out Saddam, free my nation', *Independent*: https://goo.gl/W7yI1f

Alkifaey, Hamid. (17/7/2003) 'Breaking the silence', *Guardian*: https://goo.gl/qZG3Rh

Alkifaey, Hamid. (22/11/2013) 'When the State remains silent over the violation of the law', Al-Hayat: http://alhayat.com/Details/575020

Alkifaey, Hamid. (18/3/2014) 'What interest would the Ja'afari personal status law serve for Iraq', Al-Hayat: https://goo.gl/GHV3eF

Alkifaey, Hamid. (20/6/2014), 'Impartiality of the Iraqi state is necessary for its remaining coherent', Al-Hayat: http://alhayat.com/Opinion/Writers/3074554

Alkifaey, Hamid. (2014) *Routledge Handbook of the Arab Spring*, Routledge, London

Allawi, A.A. (2007) *The Occupation of Iraq*, New Haven and London, Yale University Press

Allawi, A.A. (2014) *Faisal I of Iraq*, New Haven, Yale University Press

Almada Press. (2014) 'Convert Ul-Sadr City to a Governorate' Baghdad

Alsdr, Mohammed Baqr. Video on the last recorded Voice of Mohammed Baqr Al-sdr: www.youtube.com/watch?v=wQqnzWZ2jOk

Altoma, Salih J. (1997) 'In Memoriam: Muhammad Mahdi al-Jawahiri (1900–1997)', *Arab Studies Quarterly*, 19 (4) (Fall 1997), pp. v–viii

Amin, Imam Hassan A. (11/12/2015) 'What is this thing called jihad or Islamic Holy War?', *The Huffington Post*: https://goo.gl/nwbt5Q

Arab Anti-Corruption Organization. (2016) 'Iraq's "untouchable" corruption in Iraqi ministries': https://goo.gl/KJ6XZ9

Arango, Tim. (2015) 'Iraq's premier narrows divide, but challenges loom', *NY Times*: https://goo.gl/ACXeyc

Arango, Tim. (1/2/2016) 'Iraq's new threat: Calamity from falling oil prices', *Economics Times*: https://goo.gl/GOXzVL

Bakri, Nada. (18/1/2010) 'The rise and fall of a Sunni in Baghdad', *NY Times*: https://goo.gl/t5yH4x

Batatu, Hanna. (2004) *The Old Social Classes and the Revolutionary Movements of Iraq*, London, Saqi Books

Bayat, Asef. (2007) *Making Islam Democratic*, Palo Alto, CA, Stanford University Press

Bayless, Leslie. (2012) 'Who is Muqtada al-Sadr?', *Studies in Conflict & Terrorism* 35 (2) 135–55

BBC. (16/3/1988) 'Thousands die in Halabja gas attack': https://goo.gl/Qhec4y

BBC. (1989) 'Massacre in Tiananmen Square': https://goo.gl/u48xuv

BBC. 'Who's who in Iraq: Vice-presidents'. (6/4/2005): http://news.bbc.co.uk/1/hi/world/middle_east/4416873.stm

BBC. (20/8/2007) 'Roadside bomb kills Iraq governor': http://news.bbc.co.uk/1/hi/world/middle_east/6954467.stm

BBC. (23/1/2008) 'Iraq parliament approves new flag': http://news.bbc.co.uk/1/hi/world/middle_east/7203222.stm

BBC. (27/3/2010) 'Iraq PM Malki Vowed to challenge election results': http://news.bbc.co.uk/1/hi/world/middle_east/8590417.stm

BBC. (25/1/2010) Profile: 'Chemical Ali' http://news.bbc.co.uk/1/hi/2855349.stm

Bernhardsson, M.T. (2013) *Reclaiming a Plundered Past: Archaeology and Nation Building in Modern Iraq*, University of Texas Press

Blair, David. (2003) 'The bloodstained past of Saddam's sons', *Telegraph*

Blaydes, Lisa. (2013) 'Compliance and resistance in Iraq under Saddam Hussein: Evidence from the files of the Ba'ath Party': http://cpd.berkeley.edu/wp-content/uploads/2015/03/ComplianceResistanceFeb2015.pdf

Borger, Jonathan and Steele, Julian (2006), ' "He's the right guy": Bush defends embattled Maliki', *Guardian*

Bowen, G. (2009) 'Document analysis as a qualitative research method', *Qualitative Research Journal*, 9 (2) 27–40

Bremer, Paul. (2006) *My Year in Iraq*, New York, Simon & Schuster

Brinkerhoff, Derick W. and Mayfield, James B. (2005) 'Democratic governance in Iraq? Progress and peril in reforming state-society relations', *Public Administration and Development* 25 (1) 59–73

Buckley, Jorunn Jacobsen. (2002) *The Mandaeans: Ancient Texts and Modern People*, Oxford University Press

Cervellati, Matteo, Fortunato, Piergiuseppe and Sunde, Uwe. (2009) 'Democratization and the rule of law', Working Paper

Charles, Brooke Satti. (10/10/2014) 'Funding terrorists: The rise of ISIS', Security Intelligence: https://securityintelligence.com/funding-terrorists-the-rise-of-isis/

Cheek, Julianne. (2004) 'At the margins? Discourse analysis and qualitative research', *Qualitative Health Research* 14 (8) 1140–1150

Chilton, Paul and Schäffner, Christina. (2002) *Politics as Text and Talk: Analytic Approaches to Political Discourse* 4, John Benjamins

Chirri, Mohamad Jawad-Imamah-al-islam.org: https://goo.gl/sfm7Z0

Chulov, Martin. (19/2/2016) 'Post-war Iraq: "Everybody is corrupt, from top to bottom. Including me"', *Guardian*: www.theguardian.com/world/2016/feb/19/post-war-iraq-corruption-oil-prices-revenues

Cigar, Norman. (June 2015) 'Iraq's Shia warlords and their militias', US Army War College Press

Cockburn, Patrick. (2008) *Muqtada: Muqtada al-Sadr, the Shia Revival, and the Struggle for Iraq*, Simon & Schuster

Cockburn, Patrick. (17/2/2014) 'Withdrawal from politics of disillusioned Shia leader Muqtada al-Sadr will only add to Iraq's political turmoil – but he may not officially retire', https://goo.gl/JULc5J

Cockburn, Patrick and Sengupta, Kim. (25/10/2005) 'Sunni voters fail to block Iraq's new constitution', *Independent*: https://goo.gl/Vaj3hk

Cole, Juan (2003) 'The United States and Shi'ite religious factions in post-Ba'thist Iraq', *The Middle East Journal*, pp. 543–566

Committee to Protect Journalists. (8/9/2008) Hadi al-Mahdi: https://cpj.org/killed/2011/hadi-al-mahdi.php

Committee to Protect Journalists. (1992–2014) '166 journalists killed in Iraq since 1992/ Motive Confirmed', https://cpj.org/killed/mideast/iraq/

Corn, David. (30/8/2007) 'Corruption is "norm" within Iraqi government', The Nation: www.thenation.com/article/secret-report-corruption-norm-within-iraqi-government/

Counter Terrorism Project, Asaib Ahlul-haq: www.counterextremism.com/threat/asaib-ahl-al-haq

Coughlin, Con. (2007) *Saddam: The Secret Life*, Pan Books

CPA: www.iraqcoalition.org/regulations/

Dahl, Robert Alan. (1973) *Polyarchy: Participation and Opposition*, Yale University Press

Dahl, Robert Alan. (1991) *Democracy and its Critics*, Yale University Press

Dahl, Robert Alan. (1998) *On Democracy*, Yale University Press

Dann, Uriel. (1969) *Iraq under Qassem: A Political History 1958–1963*, New York, Praeger

Davis, Eric. (2005) *Memories of State: Politics, History and Collective Identity in Modern Iraq*, University of California Press

Davis, Eric. (3/9/2011) Foreign Policy Research Institute, U.S. Foreign Policy in Post-SOFA Iraq: www.fpri.org/article/2011/09/u-s-foreign-policy-in-post-sofa-iraq/

Dawson, Catherine. (2009) *Introduction to Research Methods: A Practical Guide for Anyone Undertaking a Research Project*, How To Books

Deghash, Saleem.)9/10/2015) 'Fadhlalla's theory on state for human being', Bayanat. org: http://arabic.bayynat.org/ArticlePage.aspx?id=19169

Diamond, Larry. (2005) *Squandared Victory*, New York, Henry Holt

Dodge, Toby. (2012) *Iraq: From War to a New Authoritarianism*, Routledge

Donaghy, Rory. (19/6/2014) 'Rouhani vows to protect Iraqi Shia shrines', Middle East Eye: https://goo.gl/eDZ4At

Dunn, John. (2005) *Setting the People Free: The Story of Democracy*, Atlantic Books

Economist, The. (7/11/2003) 'Bold vision for the Middle East': www.economist.com/node/2202949

Eisenstadt, Michael and Mathewson, Eric. (2003) *US Policiy in Iraq: Lessons from the British Experience*, Washington Institute for Near East Policy

Election Guide: www.electionguide.org/elections/id/2425/

Elias, Afzal Hoosen. 'Taqleed', Zam Zam Publishers-online version: https://goo.gl/QChvkL

Eliash, Joseph. (1979) 'Misconceptions regarding the juridical status of the Iranian "Ulamā"', International journal of Middle East studies-10. (01) pp. 9–25

Fakhir, Adel. (1/3/2014) Rudaw: http://rudaw.net/english/middleeast/iraq/01032014

Flick, U., Von Kardorff, E. and Steinke, I.. (2004) *A Companion to Qualitative Research*, Sage

Fontan, Victoria. (2009) *Voices from Post Saddam Iraq*, Greenwood

Foreign Affairs. (September/October 2016): www.foreignaffairs.com/articles/tunisia/political-islam-muslim-democracy

Foreign Policy Research Institute. (September 2011) 'U.S. foreign policy in post-SOFA Iraq': www.fpri.org/article/2011/09/u-s-foreign-policy-in-post-sofa-iraq/

Freeman, Colin. (8/6/2013) 'Iran's "democratic elections" only missing one thing – choice', *Telegraph*: www.telegraph.co.uk/news/worldnews/middleeast/iran/10108015/Irans-democratic-elections-only-missing-one-thing-choice.html

Fung, Katherine. (19/3/2013) 'Record number of journalists killed during Iraq War', Committee To Protect Journalists: https://goo.gl/jRwgzv

Gabbay, Rony E. (1978) *Communism and Agrarian Reform in Iraq*, Croom Helm

Gee, James Paul. (2014) *An Introduction to Discourse Analysis: Theory and Method*, Routledge

Ghabra, Shafeeq N. (Summer 2001) 'Iraq's culture of violence', *Middle East Quarterly* pp. 39–49: www.meforum.org/101/iraqs-culture-of-violence

Ghanim, David. (2011) *Iraq's Dysfunctional Democracy*, Oxford, Praeger

Gilgum, F. (1994) 'A case for case studies in social work research', Social Work 39

Going Global East Meet West. (22/12/2014) 'Former CBI Governor, Sinan al-Shabibi and former Minister of Communications Mohammed Allawi acquitted and released': https://goo.gl/ajK3cv

Global Security. Iraqi National Alliance. (INA): www.globalsecurity.org/military/world/iraq/ina-2009.htm

Goldenberg, Suzanne. (2003) 'Uday: career of rape, torture and murder', *Guardian*.

Gowen, Annie and Alwan, Aziz. (9/9/2008) Washington Post: https://goo.gl/LK0CFL

Gray, Matthew. (2011) 'A theory of "late rentierism" in the Arab States of the Gulf', Center for International and Regional Studies, Georgetown University

Greenberg Quinlan Rosner Research. (August–September 2015) NDI: www.ndi.org/files/ August%202015%20Survey_NDI%20Website.pdf

Guest, John S. (1993) *Survival among the Kurds: A History of the Yezidis*, Routledge

Haddad, Fanar. (2011) *Sectarianism in Iraq: Antagonistic Visions of Unity*, Oxford University Press

Hajjar, Nijmeh Salim. (1991) *Political and Social Thought of Ameen Rihani*, dissertation, University of Sydney

Hall, Stuart. (1992) *The West and the Rest: Discourse and Power*, Polity

Hall, Stuart. (1997) *Representation: Cultural Representations and Signifying Practices*, Sage

Hamid, Shadi. (May/June 2011) 'The rise of the Islamists', Foreign Affairs: www. foreignaffairs.com/articles/67696/shadi-hamid/the-rise-of-the-islamists

Hashim, Ahmed. (2005) *Insurgency and Counter-insurgency in Iraq*, Cornell University Press

Hashim, Wa'el. (18/8/2014) 'Why and how Mr Noori Al-Maliki resigned', Sistani.org: www.sistani.org/arabic/in-news/24950/

Hastings, Michael. (2015) 'A quiet Christmas for Christians in Iraq', Middle East https:// goo.gl/VlsOin

Heffernan, Michael. 'What's the difference between Shia and Sunni Muslims?': http:// islam.about.com/cs/divisions/f/shia_sunni.htm.

Held, David. (2006) *Models of Democracy*, Stanford University Press

Hobsbawm, Eric. (2008) *Globalization, Democracy and Terrorism*, Abacus

Holly, David. (9/8/2004) 'Arrest warrant issued for Chalabi', *LA Times*: http://articles. latimes.com/2004/aug/09/world/fg-warrants9

House of Commons Defence Committee sixth report. (2004/5) *Iraq: An Initial Assessment of Post Conflict Operations*: https://books.google.co.uk/books?isbn=0215023196

Howard, Michael. (2005) 'Iraqi minister incensed by airport display bans alcohol', *Guardian*

Huggard, Stephen and Kaufman, Robert. (1995) *The Political Economy of Democratic Transitions*, Princeton University Press

Human Rights and Democracy Report. (21/4/2016(Foreign and Commonwealth Office: https://goo.gl/8aSpj6

Huntington, Samuel P. (1991) *The Third Wave: Democratization in the Late Twentieth Century*, University of Oklahoma Press

Hussain, Jassim M. (1982) *The Occultation of the Twelfth Imam: A Historical Background*, Muhammadi Trust

Ibrahim, Yousif. (10/5/1996) *NY Times*: https://goo.gl/RYZfXu

Independent High Election Commission: www.ihec.iq/en/

Institute for the Study of War. Fact Sheet on Iraq's major Shia Political Parties and Militia Groups: https://goo.gl/bXlZrn

Inter Parliamentary Union: www.ipu.org/parline-e/reports/arc/2151_10.htm

Interview, Researcher, 'Akeel Abbas'

Interview, Researcher, 'Kamal Field'

Interview, Researcher, 'Adnan Al-Janabi'

Interview, Researcher, 'Abdulkhaliq Hussein'

Interview, Researcher, 'Basim Jameel Anton'

Interview, Researcher, 'Shorouq Al-Abayachi'

Interview, Researcher, 'Farid Ayar'

Interview, Researcher, 'Hani Fahs'

Interview, Researcher, 'Samir Sumaidaie'

Interview, Researcher, 'Sami Al-Askari'

Interview, Researcher, 'Faleh Abdul-Jabbar'

Interview, Researcher, 'Ayad Allawi',

Interview, Researcher, 'Waleed Al-Hilli',

Interview, Researcher, 'Kadom Jawad Shubber'

Interview, Researcher, 'Kanan Makiya'

Interview, Researcher, 'Hussain Al-Hindawi'

Interview, Researcher, 'Dia Shakarchi'

Interview, Researcher, 'Adil Abdur-Raheem Muhammed'

Interview, Researcher, 'Ali Allawi'

Interview, Researcher, 'Sharwan Al-Waeil'

Interview, Researcher, 'Maysoon Aldamluji'

Interview, Researcher, 'Ibrahim Al-Haidari'

Interview, Researcher, 'Kamran Qaradaghi'

Interview, Researcher, 'Hashim Ghanim'

Interview, Researcher, 'Adnan Sayegh'

Interview, Researcher, 'Khalil Osman'

Interview, Researcher, 'Habib Al-Shammery'

Iraq Country Study Guide (2013) *International Business Publication*, Vol. 1, p. 159: https://goo.gl/32Iy5n

Iraqi, Ministry of Interior. 'Iraq's Constitution': www.iraqinationality.gov.iq/attach/iraqi_constitution.pdf

Iraq News (27/6/2014): '30,000 Indians volunteer to fight in Iraq to defend Shia shrines': https://goo.gl/UVox59

Istrabadi, Feisal, Darweesh, Farouk, Isam Khafaji. (12/8/2003) 'Iraqi exiles feel excluded: reconstruction', Dawn: www.dawn.com/news/134650/iraqi-exiles-feel-excluded-reconstruction

Jafri, Syed Husain M. (1979) *Origins and Early Development of Shi'a Islam*, London, Longman

Janssen, Johannes. (1997) *The Dual Nature of Islamic Fundamentalism*, Cornell University Press

Jerusalem Post. (3/9/2009) 'Maliki appeals to UN to help stop what he terms a hostile act': https://goo.gl/vNgFdT

Joffe, Lawrence. 'Ayatollah Mohammad Baqir al-Hakim', *Guardian*: www.theguardian.com/news/2003/aug/30/guardianobituaries.iraq

Joseph, John. (2000) *The Modern Assyrians of the Middle East: A History of Their Encounter with Western Christian Missions, Archaeologists, and Colonial Power*, Brill

Kafala, Tarik. (25/3/2003) 'The Iraqi Baath party', BBC News-Online: http://news.bbc.co.uk/1/hi/world/middle_east/2886733.stm

Kaplan, Fred. (15/12/2005) Slate: https://goo.gl/3zQqHu

Kazimi, Nibras. (9/5/2008) 'What happened in Basra?', NY Sun: www.nysun.com/opinion/what-happened-in-basra/76187/

Kaya, Karen. (July/August 2011) 'The Turkish American crisis of March 1', *Military Review*: http://fmso.leavenworth.army.mil/documents/The-Turkish-American-Crisis.pdf

Kedouri, Elie. (2014) *In the Anglo-Arab Labyrinth: The McMahon-Husayn Correspondence and Its Interpretations, 1914–1939*, Routledge

Kerry, Mark. (2008) *Tigers of the Tigress*, Dog Ear

Khayyoon, Ali. (1988) *The Tanks of Ramadhan: The Story of the 14th Ramadhan 1963 Revolution in Iraq*, Baghdad, Cultural Affairs Publishing House

Khomeini, Ruhollah. (1979) *Islamic Government*, Manor Books

Khomeini, Ruhollah. (1985) *Islam and Revolution: Writings and Declarations of Imam Khomeini*, translated and annotated by Hamid Algar, KPI

King, Charles. (2000) 'Electoral systems', Georgetown University: http://faculty.georgetown.edu/kingch/Electoral_Systems.htm

Kirk, Ashley. (24/3/2016) 'Iraq and Syria: How many foreign fighters are fighting for Isil?', Telegraph: www.telegraph.co.uk/news/2016/03/29/iraq-and-syria-how-many-foreign-fighters-are-fighting-for-isil/

Langworth, Richard. M Churchill's historian: https://richardlangworth.com/worst-form-of-government

Le Billon, Philippe. (2005) 'Corruption, reconstruction and oil governance in Iraq', *Third World Quarterly* 26 (4–5) pp. 685–703

Liamputtong, Pranee and Ezzy, Douglas. (2005) *Qualitative Research Methods*, Oxford University Press

Lijphart, Arend. (Jan 1969) *World Politics*, volume 21, issue 2

Linz, Juan. (1978) *The Breakdown of Democratic Regimes*, Johns Hopkins University Press

Linz, Juan and Stepan, Alfred. (1996) *Problems of Democratic Transition and Consolidation*, Johns Hopkins University Press

Lipka, Michael and Ghani, Fatima. (14/11/2013) 'Muslim holiday of Ashura brings into focus Shia-Sunni differences', Pew Research Centre: https://goo.gl/uuZbCs

Luciani, Giacomo. (1994) 'The oil rent, the fiscal crisis of the state and democratization', in *Democracy without Democrats*, I.B.Tauris, pp. 130–155

Makiya, Kanan. (1994) *Cruelty and Silence: War, Tyranny, Uprising, and the Arab World*, W.W. Norton

Mallat, Chibli. (1993) *The Renewal of Islamic Law*, University of Cambridge Press Syndicate

Mamouri, Ali. (14/11/2013) 'Iraq's religious minorities and Shiite mourning holidays', Al-Monitor: https://goo.gl/SieY5S

Mamouri, Ali. (2/5/2016) 'Will secular parties gain upper hand in Iraq?', Al-Monitor : https://goo.gl/I4bJIy

Mansour, Renad. (3/3/2016) Carnegie Endowment: http://carnegieendowment.org/2016/03/03/sunni-predicament-in-iraq-pub-62924

Marr, Phebe. (1985) *The Modern History of Iraq*, Boulder, CO, Westview

Mattil, James F. (2007) 'Have Bush administration reconstruction and anti-corruption failures undermined the U.S. mission in Iraq?', Senate Democratic Policy Committee: www.dpc.senate.gov/hearings/hearing43/mattil.pdf

Martin, Paul. (18/3/2013), 'Interview with Paul Bremer', The Independent: https://goo.gl/vQ1IB8

Mason, Jennifer (1996), *Qualitative Researching*, London, Sage

McGeough, Paul. (17/7/2004) 'Allawi shot prisoners in cold blood: witnesses', Sunday Morning Herald: www.smh.com.au/articles/2004/07/16/1089694568757.html

McKeon, Richard, ed. (1951) *Democracy in a World of Tensions*, UNESCO: http://unesdoc.unesco.org/images/0013/001335/133513eo.pdf

Mears, Carolyn Lunsford. (2009) *Interviewing for Education and Social Science Research*, Palgrave Macmillan

Mill, John Stuart. (2002) *On Liberty*, Dover

Moghadam, Assaf. (2003) 'The Shi'i perception of Jihad', Alnakhla: https://goo.gl/1OY4Ra

Mohammed, Abeer and Al-Sharaa, Hazim. (17/3/2011) 'Minority businesses fear alcohol ban', IWPR: https://iwpr.net/global-voices/minority-businesses-fear-alcohol-bans

Momen, Moojan. (1985) *An Introduction to Shi'i Islam: The History and Doctrines of Twelver Shi'ism*, Yale University Press

Moore, Barrington Jr. (1967, 1993) *Social Origins of Dictatorship and Democracy*, Beacon Books

Moukalled, Diana. (11/4/2014) 'An eye for an eye will make Iraq blind', Al-Arabia: https://english.alarabiya.net/en/views/news/middle-east/2014/04/11/An-eye-for-an-eye-will-make-Iraq-blind.html

Mouline, Nabil. (2014) *The Clerics of Islam*, Yale University Press

Muhammed, Muhanned. (17/1/2011) 'Club, shops attacked in Iraq alcohol clampdown', Reuters: http://uk.reuters.com/article/us-iraq-alcohol-idUSTRE70G45320110117

Mundi Index. (2014) 'Iraq Demographics Profile 2014' www.indexmundi.com/iraq/demographics_profile.html

Musings on Iraq. (2013) 'How US ran into party politics': http://musingsoniraq.blogspot.co.uk/2013/01/how-united-states-ran-into-party.html

Nader, Rabih. (12/6/2014) 'Iraqi women make gains in parliamentary elections', Al Monitor: www.al-monitor.com/pulse/originals/2014/05/iraq-parliamentary-elections-women-gains.html

Nakash, Yitzhak. (1994) *The Shi'is of Iraq*, Princeton University Press

Neuman, Jeffrey and White, Brooke. (13/12/3005) 'Iraq's Sunnis play the election card', Washington Instiute, www.washingtoninstitute.org/policy-analysis/view/iraqs-sunnis-play-the-election-card

Neuman, W.L. (2011) *Basics of Social Research: Qualitative and Quantitative Approaches*, Pearson

Obeidallah, Dean. (10/7/2014) 'ISIS's gruesome Muslim death toll', *The Daily Beast*: www.thedailybeast.com/articles/2014/10/07/isis-s-gruesome-muslim-death-toll.html

O'Neil, Patrick H. (2007) *Essentials of Comparative Politics*, W.W. Norton

Odisho, Edward Y. (2001) 'The ethnic, linguistic and cultural identity of modern Assyrians', The Melammu Project: www.aakkl.helsinki.fi/melammu/pdf/odisho2004.pdf

Osman, Khalil. (2014) *Sectarianism in Iraq: The Making of State and Nation Since 1920*, Routledge

Parenti, Michael. (2010) *Democracy for the Few*, Cengage Learning

Pollack, Kenneth. (27/7/2010) 'A government for Baghdad', Brookings Institute: www.brookings.edu/research/opinions/2010/07/27-iraq-government-pollack

People Representation Act. (1918): www.historylearningsite.co.uk

Powell, Colin L. (2004) 'A strategy of partnerships', Foreign Affairs, 22–34

Przeworski, Adam. (1991) *Democracy and the Market*, University of Cambridge Press Syndicate

Quran, Holy. (1981) Arabic text and English translation, Elmhurst, NY, Islamic Seminary-Sarwar

Ra'uf, Adel. (2000) 'Islamic activism in Iraq between the Marja'iyah and Party Affiliation', Damascus, Iraqi Center for Media and Studies

Rahimi, Babak. (June 2007) 'Ayatollah Sistani and the Democratization of Post-Ba'athist Iraq', USIP: www.usip.org/sites/default/files/sr187.pdf

Ramzi, Khuloud. (21/7/2011) 'A family tie too tight: Nepotism runs deep in Iraqi politics', Niqash

Raphaeli, Nimrod. (2004) 'Understanding Muqtada al-Sadr', *Middle East Quarterly*, pp. 33–42: www.meforum.org/655/understanding-muqtada-al-sadr

Rawls, John. (1985) 'Justice as fairness: political not metaphysical', *Philosophy & Public Affairs*, pp. 223–251

Rawls, John. (1993, 1996, 2005) *Political Liberalism*, Columbia University Press

Razik, Ali Abdur. (1925) *Islam and the Fundamentals of Governance*, Lebanese Book House

Refworld: www.refworld.org

Reston, Aram. (2008) *The Man Who Pushed America to War*, Nations Books

Rice, Pranee and Ezzy, Douglas. (2007) 'Qualitative research methods: A health focus', Epidemiology: http://ije.oxfordjournals.org/content/30/1/185.full

Ritchie, J. and Lewis, J. (2003) *Qualitative Research Practice: A Guide for Social Science Students and Researchers*, Sage

Ruhayem, Rami. (21/7/2012) 'Iraq struggles to reform "inefficient" ration system', BBC: www.bbc.co.uk/news/world-middle-east-18916653

Rush, James. (7/7/2014) 'Ancient shrines become latest casualties of ISIS rampage', Daily Mail: https://goo.gl/d8HX5F

Russell, J. and Cohn, R. (2012) *Prince Faisal Bin Al Hussein*, Book on Demand

Russett, Bruce. (1994) *Grasping the Democratic Peace: Principles for a Post-Cold War World*, Princeton University Press

Ryan, Missy. (22/1/2009) 'Iraq religious parties may face election backlash', Reuters: http://uk.reuters.com/article/us-iraq-election-religion-sb-idUKTRE50L07120090122

Sadiki, L. (2014) *Routledge Handbook of the Arab Spring: Rethinking Democratization*, Routledge

Sadiki, Larbi. (2004) *The Search for Arab Democracy: Discourses and Counter-Discourses*, Columbia University Press

Saeed, Ali Kareem. (1999) *The Iraq of 8th February – From the Dialogue of Concepts to the Dialogue of Blood*, Beirut, Alkunooz Printing House

Salame, Ghassan. (2001) *Democracy Without Democrats*, I.B.Tauris

Salamey, Imad and Pearson, Frederic. (2005) 'The crisis of federalism and electoral strategies in Iraq', *International Studies Perspectives*, 6 (2) pp. 190–207.

Sapsford, Roger and Jupp, Victor. (2006) *Data Collection and Analysis*, Sage

Sasson, Jean. (2004) *Mayyada the Daughter of Iraq*, Bantam Books https://books.google.com/books?isbn=1448126398

Sattar, Omar. (10/10/2016) 'Sadrist call to change electoral law could push local elections to 2018', Al-Monitor: https://goo.gl/X0ZO7G

Schumpeter, Joseph A. (1943, 2010) *Capitalism, Socialism and Democracy*, Routledge

Shahroudi, Mahmoud Hashemi. Profile': www.hashemishahroudi.org/en/page-31

Shahroudi, Mahmoud Hashemi. 'The Next Ayatollah? 'profile': www.majalla.com/eng/2009/12/article5511928

Shbaro, Muhammed Isam. (1995) *The First Arab Islamic State*, Beirut, Nahdha Publishing House

Shanahan, Roger. (2/6/2004) 'The Islamic Da'awa Party: past development and future prospects', Rubin Centre: www.rubincenter.org/2004/06/shanahan-2004-06-02/

Simon, Bob. (28/5/2004) 'Muqtada Sadr's battle against US', CBS News: www.cbsnews.com/news/muqtada-sadrs-battle-against-us/

Sistani, Ayatullah Ali-Website: www.sistani.org/english/book/48/2286/

Sky. (17/6/2014) 'Iraq accuses Saudi Arabia of promoting "genocide"' http://news.sky.com/story/iraq-accuses-saudi-arabia-of-promoting-genocide-10400485

Slavin, Barbara. (June 2008) 'Mullahs, Money, and Militias', USIP: www.usip.org/sites/default/files/sr206.pdf

Sluglett, Peter. (2007) *Britain in Iraq: Contriving King and Country*, I.B. Tauris

Snyder, Jack. (2000) *From Voting to Violence*, W.W. Norton

Stockton, David L. (1990) *The Classical Athenian Democracy*, Oxford University Press

Transitional Administrative Law. (2004) Global Security: https://goo.gl/paiGTj

Tawfeeq, Jomana Karadsheh and Mohammed, Tawfeeq. (13/12/2013) 'British contractor beaten in Iraq over alleged insult to Islam', CNN: http://edition.cnn.com/2013/11/13/world/meast/iraq-uk-contractor-attacked/

Tawil, Camille, (2011) *Brothers in Arms*, Al-Saqi Books

Taylor, Guy. (6/5/2015) 'Kurdish leader says his people will one day declare independence', *Washington Times*: https://goo.gl/6IkO1n

Tibi, Bassam. (1997) *Arab Nationalism: Between Islam and the Nation-State*, Macmillan

Totten, Michael J. (16/2/2006) 'No, Iran is not a democracy', *World Affairs Journal*: www.worldaffairsjournal.org/blog/michael-j-totten/no-iran-not-democracy

Trend News Agency. (3/9/2009) 'Iraq PM challenges Syria to explain militant aid': http://en.trend.az/azerbaijan/society/1534046.html

Tripp, Charles. (2000, 2002, 2005) *A History of Iraq*, Cambridge University Press

UN Iraq Fact Sheet, Electoral Assistance Division www.un.org/News/dh/infocus/iraq/iraq-elect-fact-sht.pdf

UN Resolutions (2003) www.un.org/en/ga/search/view_doc.asp?symbol=S/RES/1483(2003)

UN Resolutions (2003) www.un.org/en/ga/search/view_doc.asp?symbol=S/RES/1500(2003)

UN Resolutions (2003) www.un.org/en/ga/search/view_doc.asp?symbol=S/RES/1511(2003)

Van Dijk, Teun Adrianus. (2008) *Discourse and Power*, Palgrave Macmillan

Voice of America. (27/10/2009): www.voanews.com/a/a-13-a-2003-05-06-31-an-66851487/375890.html

Walker, David. (23/4/2007) Stabilizing and Rebuilding Iraq, US Government Accountability Office: https://goo.gl/E7NmYe

Ward, Allen M. (2004) 'How democratic was the Roman Republic?', *New England Classical Journal* 31 (2) 101–119

Weisgerber, Marcus. (23/2/2016) 'Back to Iraq: US military contractors return in droves': https://goo.gl/PKKbyf

Williams Jr., Nick B. (14/11/1991) 'Hussein names half-brother to high Iraqi post', LA Times: http://articles.latimes.com/1991-11-14/news/mn-1894_1_security-forces

Winters, Jeffrey A. (2011) *Oligarchy*, Cambridge University Press

Wodak, Ruth (2009) *The Discourse of Politics in Action: Politics as Usual*, Palgrave Macmillan

Wodak, Ruth (2012) 'Language, power and identity', *Language Teaching* 45 (2) 215–233

Yentob, Alan and White, Canon Andrew. (28/11/2011) 'Iraq's Jews 'under threat', BBC Radio. http://news.bbc.co.uk/today/hi/today/newsid_9649000/9649767.stm

Yin, Robert. (2003) *Case Study Research. Design and Methods*, London, Sage

Young, Gavin and Wheeler, Nik. (1980) *Iraq, Land of Two Rivers*, Collins

Young, John Hardin. (2009) *International Election Principles*, American Bar Association

Zubaida, Sami. (18/11/2005) 'Democracy, Iraq and the middle east', Open Democracy: www.opendemocracy.net/democracy-opening/iraq_3042.jsp

Index

Al-Abadi, Haider 8–9, 90
Al-Abayachi, Shorouq 117, 132; on the middle class 146; on US failure in democratization 169–170; on weak social fabric 192–193
Abbas, Akeel 7, 100, 113–114; on contradictions in Iraqi constitution 162; on de-Ba'athification 151; on electoral systems 159; on impediments to democracy 144–145, 170; on sectarianism 131
Al-Abboodi, Sheikh Najih 4
Al-Abboudi, Qassim 161
Abdul-Jabbar, Faleh: on Ba'ath party 152; on freedom and democracy 138; on independent institutions 160–161, 192; on Iraqi constitution 6, 162; on religion and democracy 99–101, 107; on sectarianism 130
Abdur-Raheem, Adil 108–109, 132, 141
Absent Imam, the 83, 84
Abubakir 82, 83
Accordance Front (AF) 4, 5
Accountability and Justice Law see de-Ba'athification
accountability in democracy 87, 129, 157; absence of in Iraq 100, 130
alcohol, prohibition of 6, 22, 30, 91, 162, 204
Aldmaluji, Maysoon: blames US for insurgency 179; on de-Ba'athification 152; on failure of democratization 142; on Iraqi constitution 162; on Islamists 111–112, 131; on Shia Arabs 187; on US support for Islamic parties 168
Allawi, Ali: on Iraqi politics 188; on politically motivated killings 170; on prospects for democracy 60–61; on religion and democracy 109; on

sectarianism 131, 132; on the state of Iraq post invasion 52–53
Allawi, Ayad 3, 8, 62, 101, 195; on de-Ba'athification 151; on failure of Islamist parties 102–103; inaccurate reports on 18; on Iraqi constitution 162; on sectarianism 130; and US 168
Anton, Bassim Jamal: on the constitution 162–163; on oil revenues 189; on religion and democracy 116–117, 159; on weakness of democratic culture 146
Arab nationalism 50–51, 75–76, 186, 187; and democratic consolidation 62
Arab Spring 17, 136
Arab-Israeli War 1967 66
Argentina 59, 154
Arif, Colonel Abdu-Salam 124, 125
Aristotle 73
Armed Islamic Group (GIA) 89
army, Iraqi: corruption in 194; and democratization 144; disbanding of 155–156, 158, 179
Al-Askari, Sami: on corruption 193; on despotism 11; on foreign interference 177; on IHEC 161; on impediments to democracy 138; on Iraqi constitution 163; on militias 181; on sectarianism 132; on US failure in democratization 169
assassinations 96, 170
Athenian democracy 33, 34
Al-Attiyya, Ghassan 172
authoritarian regimes 32, 40, 54; transition to democracy 56, 59, 202
authority: in Iraqi government 58; of religious leaders 85, 88, 89, 94–95, 106–109; source of caliphs' 72
Ayar, Farid: on corruption 171, 194; on Islamist violation of electoral rules 95;